D1825094

Negotiating Spaces for Literacy Learning

ALSO AVAILABLE FROM BLOOMSBURY

Education and Technology, Neil Selwyn
Literacy on the Left, Andrew Lambirth
Mapping Multiple Literacies, Diana Masny and David R. Cole
Multimodal Semiotics, edited by Len Unsworth
New Technology and Education, Anthony Edwards
Transforming Literacies and Language, edited by Caroline M. L. Ho,
Kate T. Anderson and Alvin P. Leong

Negotiating Spaces for Literacy Learning

Multimodality and Governmentality

EDITED BY MARY HAMILTON, RACHEL HEYDON, KATHRYN HIBBERT AND ROZ STOOKE

Bloomsbury Academic
An imprint of Bloomsbury Publishing Plc

B L O O M S B U R Y
LONDON · NEW DELHI · NEW YORK · SYDNEY

Bloomsbury Academic
An imprint of Bloomsbury Publishing Plc

50 Bedford Square	1385 Broadway
London	New York
WC1B 3DP	NY 10018
UK	USA

www.bloomsbury.com

BLOOMSBURY and the Diana logo are trademarks of Bloomsbury Publishing Plc

First published 2015

© Mary Hamilton, Rachel Heydon, Kathryn Hibbert, Roz Stooke and Contributors, 2015

Mary Hamilton, Rachel Heydon, Kathryn Hibbert and Roz Stooke and Contributors have asserted their right under the Copyright, Designs and Patents Act, 1988, to be identified as authors of this work.

All rights reserved. No part of this publication may be reproduced or transmitted in any form or by any means, electronic or mechanical, including photocopying, recording or any information storage or retrieval system, without prior permission in writing from the publishers.

No responsibility for loss caused to any individual or organization acting on or refraining from action as a result of the material in this publication can be accepted by Bloomsbury or the authors.

British Library Cataloguing-in-Publication Data
A catalogue record for this book is available from the British Library.

ISBN: HB: 978-1-4725-8746-6
PB: 978-1-4725-8745-9
ePDF: 978-1-4725-8748-0
ePub: 978-1-4725-8747-3

Library of Congress Cataloging-in-Publication Data
A catalog record for this book is available from the Library of Congress.

Typeset by Integra Software Solutions Pvt. Ltd.
Printed and bound in Great Britain

Contents

About the Contributors

Peggy Albers is professor in the College of Education at the Georgia State University, USA. She teaches literacy courses at the graduate level and works with teacher preparation in literacy education. Peggy has published widely in literacy journals such as *Language Arts, English Education, Journal of Literacy Research* and *The Reading Teacher*. She has published four books: *New Methods in Literacy Research* (2014), *Literacies, the Arts and Multimodality (2010), Finding the Artist Within (2007)* and *Telling Pieces: Art as Literacy in Middle Grades Classes (2009). She* is also the founder of two online open-access web seminar series, Global Conversations in Literacy Research and Conversations in Doctoral Preparation. *Peggy's publications have* explored literacy practices in arts-integrated classes and visual discourse analysis. Her current interests are semiotics, children's literature, integration of multimedia into curriculum and doctoral preparation. When not teaching, she studies pottery at Callanwolde Fine Arts Center in Atlanta, GA, which has informed her research in arts-based literacy.

Richard Andrews is Deputy Vice-Chancellor (Research and Innovation) at Anglia Ruskin University in Cambridge, UK. Prior to this, he was a Professor in English and Dean at the Institute of Education, University of London, UK. He has published a number of books on poetry, argumentation and rhetoric, most recently *A Theory of Contemporary Rhetoric* (2013). He is a co-editor of *The Sage Handbook of E-learning Research* and *The Sage Handbook of Digital Dissertations and Theses* and co-series editor of *Cambridge School Shakespeare*, as well as chair of the series' international advisory board. He is on the editorial boards of a number of journals, including *Learning, Media and Technology, Informal Logic, Educational Research Review* and the *International Journal of Computer-Assisted Language Learning.* His current research interests include rhythms in free verse, argumentation in higher education and e-learning theory.

Lisa Björklund Boistrup is senior lecturer at Stockholm University, Sweden and Linköping University, Sweden. One of her research areas is classroom communication in mathematics classrooms. Here she specifically investigates assessments present in day-to-day classroom activities, often together with mathematics teachers in action research, where also the institutional framing is analysed. Another research area is to understand mathematics containing activities outside school such as workplaces. Lisa's most recent book is a Swedish book on classroom assessment in mathematics published in 2013.

Bill Cope is professor in the Department of Educational Policy Studies at the University of Illinois, USA. He is the principal investigator in a series of major projects funded by the Institute of Educational Sciences in the US Department of Education and the Bill and Melinda Gates Foundation, researching and developing multimodal writing and assessment spaces. From 2010 until 2013, he was Chair of the Journals Publication Committee of the American Educational Research Association. His recent books include the second edition of *The Future of the Academic Journal* (edited with Angus Phillips, 2014) and *Towards a Semantic Web: Connecting Knowledge in Academic Research* (with Mary Kalantzis and Liam Magee, 2010).

Rosie Flewitt is senior lecturer and researcher at University College London, Institute of Education, UK and in the London Knowledge Lab centre 'MODE', which specializes in multimodal methodologies for researching digital data and environments. Rosie's research interests include the complementary areas of young children's communication, language and literacy development in a multimedia age, inclusive practices in early education and early education research methods. She uses principally ethnographic and multimodal approaches to the study of early learning, particularly how children use combinations of modes, such as spoken and written language, gesture, images, sounds and layout, as they engage with written, oral, visual and digital texts as part of their everyday literacy practices. Her recent publications include *Understanding Research with Children and Young People* (with Alison Clark, Martyn Hammersley and Martin Robb, 2013).

Claire Fontaine is Ph.D. candidate in Urban Education at the Graduate Center of the City University of New York, USA. She works at the intersection of inequality and digital media with schools, communities and non-profit organizations. Using visual and narrative methods, her research examines young women's views of their own development in relation to participation in online networked spaces and contextualized by neoliberalism and a postfeminist media culture.

Mary Hamilton is Professor of Adult Learning and Literacy in the Department of Educational Research at Lancaster University, UK. She is associate director of the Lancaster Literacy Research Centre, and a founding member of the Research and Practice in Adult Literacy group. Her current research is in literacy policy and governance, socio-material theory, practitioner enquiry, academic literacies, digital technologies and change. Her most recent book is *Literacy and the Politics of Representation* (2012). Her co-authored publications include *Local Literacies* (with David Barton, 1998); *More Powerful Literacies* (with Lynn Tett and Jim Crowther, 2012) and *Changing Faces of Adult Literacy, Language and Numeracy: A Critical History of Policy and Practice* (with Yvonne Hillier, 2006).

Jerome C. Harste is Emeritus Professor of Literacy, Culture and Language Education at Indiana University, USA, where he was named the first Martha Lea and William Armstrong Chair in Teacher Education in IU's School of Education. Inducted into the Reading Hall of Fame in 1997, Jerome's early literacy research with Carolyn Burke and Virginia Woodward received the David H. Russell award for outstanding contributions to the teaching of English. Since then, he has received a number of prestigious awards including the Oscar Causey Award from the Literacy Research Association for lifetime contributions to research in reading (2013), National Council of Teachers of English (NCTE) Outstanding Language Arts Educator (2008) and NCTE's Distinguished Service Award (2013). Jerome has served as President of the NCTE, the National Reading Conference, the National Conference on Research in English and the Whole Language Umbrella. He is best known for his co-authored books on literacy learning in classrooms: *Language Stories & Literacy Lessons* (1984); *Creating Classrooms for Authors & Inquirers* (1995); *Creating Critical Classrooms* (2007); and *Teaching Children's Literature: It's Critical!* (2007). Jerry is a signature watercolourist, and his paintings have been featured on a number of literacy and language arts book covers and journals.

Rachel Heydon is professor and program chair, Curriculum Studies and Studies in Applied Linguistics, in the Faculty of Education, Western University. Her research interests coalesce around understanding how curricula might create expansive literacy and identity options for learners and the development of theories and methodologies to conceptualize and apprehend curricula. Current projects include studies of literacy curricula in full-day kindergartens and multimodal literacy curricula in intergenerational settings. Heydon's most recent book is *Learning at the Ends of Life: Children, Elders, and Literacies in Intergenerational Curricula* published in 2013.

Kathryn Hibbert is associate professor in the Faculty of Education and an Acting Associate Director of the Centre for Research Education and Innovation in the Schulich School of Medicine and Dentistry, Western University, Canada. She teaches pre-service courses in adolescent literacy and multiliteracies and graduate courses in multiliteracies, narrative methods and curriculum. Her current research projects include studies of multiliteracies within educational practice, clinical practice and the domain of mental health workers.

Mary Kalantzis is dean of the College of Education at the University of Illinois, Urbana-Champaign, USA. She was formerly dean of the Faculty of Education, Language and Community Services at RMIT University in Melbourne, Australia and President of the Australian Council of Deans of Education. With Bill Cope, she is co-author of *New Learning: Elements of a Science of Education* (2nd edition, 2012) and *Literacies* (2012) and co-editor of *Ubiquitous Learning* (2009).

Wendy Luttrell is Professor of Urban Education, Sociology and Critical Social Psychology at the Graduate Center, City University of New York, USA. Her research explores educational inequality, featuring how gender, race, class and sexuality systems of inequality take root in students' self-evaluations and actions. She is the editor of *Qualitative Educational Research: Readings on Reflexive Methodology and Transformative Practice (2010)* and the author of two award-winning books on this topic, *Schoolsmart and Motherwise: Working-Class Women's Identity and Schooling (1997)* and *Pregnant Bodies, Fertile Minds: Gender, Race and the Schooling of Pregnant Teens (2003)*. Her current longitudinal project, *Children Framing Childhoods* and *Looking Back*, examines the role that gender, race and immigrant status play in how diverse, young people growing up in working-class communities portray their social and emotional worlds. Throughout her career, Luttrell has directed community-based, university and teacher inquiry projects dedicated to advancing social justice in and around schools and that promote innovative research and teaching practices.

Sharon Murphy is professor at York University, Toronto, Canada. Sharon began her teaching career in Newfoundland and Labrador, where she taught special education for several years and worked as an educational consultant with the Newfoundland Department of Education. These early professional experiences taught her much about educational tests, their uses, misuses and limitations as tools for commenting on what children know. Since joining York University in 1988, Sharon has also served in administrative roles at the university (Director of the Graduate Program in Education, Associate Dean of Graduate Studies) and worked as a co-editor of *Language Arts*, a journal of the National Council of Teachers of English. Sharon teaches graduate and undergraduate students and writes about the dilemmas of educational assessment. Her most recent efforts are motivated by feeling the need to go beyond critique and move towards a set of principles for an ethically minded approach to educational assessment.

Guy Roberts-Holmes is senior lecturer at the Institute of Education, University of London, UK, where he leads the internationally acclaimed MA Early Years Education Programme. The main focus of his research is the relationship between early years policies, curriculum, assessment and pedagogy. Guy's recent publications in major journals include critical examinations of recent early years policy changes and their impact upon the 'datafication' of early years teachers professional roles, and pedagogy. Guy has also written a bestselling early years research methods book.

David Rose is Honorary Associate of the School of Letters Arts and Media at the University of Sydney, Australia and director of the *Reading to Learn* programme, an international literacy programme that trains teachers across school and university sectors, in Australia, Africa, Asia and western Europe. David's research is focused on providing teachers with the tools to enable all students to read and write successfully. His work has been particularly concerned with Indigenous Australian communities, languages and education programmes. His research interests also include language and cultural contexts, and language evolution. He is the author of *The Western Desert Code: An Australian Cryptogrammar* (2001), *Working with Discourse: Meaning Beyond the Clause* (with J. R. Martin, 2nd edition, 2007), *Genre Relations: Mapping Culture* (2008) and *Learning to Write, Reading to Learn: Genre, Knowledge and Pedagogy in the Sydney School* (2012).

Suzanne Smythe is assistant professor in Adult Literacy and Adult Education in the Faculty of Education at Simon Fraser University, Canada. Suzanne worked for many years as an adult literacy educator in Canada and South Africa. Her teaching and research interests address the working lives of community-based educators in the context of globalization, as well as processes of digital equity and inclusion. She is the principal investigator in the Adult Literacy and Digital Inequalities (ALDI) project, a multi-site ethnography that explores how adults access, learn and create with new technologies in contexts of inequality.

Roz Stooke is assistant professor in the Faculty of Education, Western University, Canada. Roz has worked as a primary teacher, public librarian and family literacy facilitator and now teaches courses in Curriculum Studies, Early Childhood Education and Literacy Education at the undergraduate and graduate levels. Her research explores the local and translocal organization of literacy curricula in formal and informal educational settings, including community settings such as libraries and playgroups. Her current research examines ways in which diversely situated educators of young children are integrating documentation practices in their curricula.

Vivian Maria Vasquez is Professor of Education at American University in Washington DC, USA, where she has worked in the School of Education, Teaching and Health for the past fifteen years. She was a pre-school and elementary school teacher for fourteen years in Ontario, Canada. Her research interests are in critical literacy, early literacy and information communication technology. Her publications include nine books and numerous book chapters and articles in refereed journals. She is also the host of the CLIP (critical literacy in practice) Podcast. Vivian has held offices in scholarly organizations including The National Council of Teachers of English, The American Educational Research Association, The International Reading Association and The Whole Language Umbrella. Her awards include the NCTE Advancement of People of Color Award (2013), the AERA Division B Outstanding Book of the Year Award (2006) and The James N. Britton Award (2005). She was also the first recipient of the AERA Teacher Research SIG Dissertation Award (2004). Most recently the NCTE Early Childhood Assembly honoured Vivian with a scholarship in her name – The Vivian Vasquez Teacher Scholarship.

Introduction

This book addresses two strong currents that are sweeping through the contemporary education field. The first is the opening up of possibilities for multimodal communication and representation as a result of developments in digital technologies and multimodal and multiliteracies theorizing. The second is the increasing weight of technologies of governance experienced by educators and learners in formal and informal education settings (Lindblad & Popkewitz, 2004; Comber & Nixon, 2009; Hamilton, 2009) and the numerous opportunities for surveillance and management of teaching and learning afforded by, in particular, digital data. In contrast to the possibilities for multimodal communication, these processes of governance, fuelled by the pressures of globalization, can be experienced by literacy educators and learners as narrowing the spaces for diverse expressions of literacy, pulling curricula and pedagogical practices towards forms that are increasingly out of alignment with the everyday informal practices, interests and funds of knowledge (González et al., 2005) of learners and educators.

Many scholars have identified the marginal positioning of multimodality within specific educational contexts (e.g. Peterson & McClay, 2010; Heydon, 2013). This book uniquely addresses the contradictory tensions experienced by educators by bringing together multimodality and issues of governance. It presents examples of creative and innovative theories and methodologies for understanding and promoting opportunities for multimodal literacy practices, curricula and pedagogy produced within an era of digital technologies and globalized educational policies. It explores theoretical as well as practical aspects of its topic. It illuminates examples of practices that expand communication and identity options, and explores tensions across a wide range of teaching and learning domains covering homes, early years' centres, primary and middle to secondary schools, universities and adult community-based programmes.

This book brings together contributions from scholars working in Canada and the United Kingdom, where the editors are based, as well as Australia, Sweden and the USA, where it is possible to examine the pressures and struggles that result from the current educational climate common to these countries. It opens a needed conversation across countries and contexts, addressing the intersection of technologies of literacies, education and self. It does so through diverse foci including philosophical, theoretical and methodological treatments of multimodality and governmentality; digital literacies, indigenous literacies, adult literacies and literacies of place. The breadth of these foci provides readers the opportunity to see a range of multimodal practices and the ways in which governmentality plays out (or not) across domains. Individual contributors elaborate on these foci by using a range of theoretical and methodological resources including socio-material theories such as actor network theory (Fenwick, 2010); situated literacies (Barton et al., 2000; Janks, 2009); Bernstein's (2000) sociolinguistics, systemic functional linguistics (Matthiessen et al., 2010) and critical childhood studies (James & James, 2012).

In writing this book we have in mind an audience of classroom teachers and curriculum managers who find themselves grappling with the contradictory trends we describe, and who are subject to managerial practices that further emphasize them. We also expect the book to be of interest to scholars, policy-makers and graduate students working in literacy studies, education studies, applied linguistics, social policy and communication studies, and anyone interested in innovative research methodologies and theories in these fields.

Multimodality

We draw on the work of Kress (2003) to define multimodality as the full range of social semiotic resources available within teaching and learning domains, including image, sound, number, the manipulation and choreography of physical materials and body movement. We are interested in multimodality less as a thing unto itself and more for what it might *do* or *produce*. Thus, our focus on multimodality is indeed a focus on multimodal *literacy*, and all of us involved in this book agree that

> the function of literacy is to enable one to do something (i.e., act and reflect). Literacy is in this sense a technology and like all technologies extends our human powers. However, this extension is never neutral given that literacy is never a universal 'Literacy' but is always a particular type of literacy that supports certain actions and reflections over others. (Arthur, 2012, p. xiii)

Consequently, the relationship(s) between literacy learning, literacy practices and power become elemental to our project. Each in their own way, the contributions to the book promote curricula and pedagogies that might give rise to expansive communication and identity options for learners and educators.

We nest multimodal literacy within a broader perspective of multiliteracies developed through the influential work of the New London Group (1996) and represented in this book in Chapter 1 by Kalantzis and Cope. The idea of multiliteracies has been taken up in various ways, and three key strands of this literature in particular are relevant to the contributions in this book. These strands are not mutually exclusive but emphasize different ways in which communication is constituted and changing in the contemporary world.

First, a strong strand in the multiliteracies literature highlights the linguistic diversity that underpins literacy learning and use: not just bilingual but also *multi*lingual learners using global languages with shifting usage as the world becomes ever more interdependent (Pennycook, 2006; Blommaert, 2010). Within sociolinguistics this complexity has been called *superdiversity* with cosmopolitan learners moving rapidly between local settings, which can no longer be treated as bounded communities (e.g. Blommaert, 2013).

The second strand extensively developed by scholars, such as Lankshear and Knobel (e.g. 2008), foregrounds the development of digital forms of communication, which have recast existing forms of written communication and – it can be argued – are creating new literacies specific to digital environments. There is considerable ambiguity around the term *digital literacies* (Gourlay et al., 2013), which are sometimes interpreted to mean general competence with digital devices. However, if we define the term as the way in which meaning-making resources are used and produced in online settings, then the relationship with print literacies becomes clearer and their implications for literacy learning and teaching are key.

The third strand of the multiliteracies literature foregrounds the diversity of cultures that learners and users bring to written communication and how these affect the resources, power relations and identities produced (e.g. Street, 2005). This strand has given rise to a large body of ethnographic work in particular, offering rich descriptions of situated literacy practices involving various print, digital and/or otherwise multimodal resources among different groups (e.g. Barton & Hamilton, 1998/2013; Gregory & Williams, 2000; Pahl and Rowsell, 2006; Street et al., 2009; Collier, 2013).

We hope that thinking about multimodal literacy through multiliteracies can harness multiliteracies' potentiality for providing suggestions for linking learners' (and educators') own semiotic resources and knowledge with educational experiences in the classroom. Moreover, we hope this can afford new avenues for educators and others to critique narrowly defined approaches to literacy so as to design and enact responsive and empowering curricula and assessment practices.

The contributors to this book each offer examples of the productivity of this approach and its creative potentials while also signalling potential constraints to communication and identity options that need to be negotiated. In conceptualizing these constraints, the book takes as its starting point the notion of governmentality.

Governmentality

Our exploration of governmentality begins as described by Foucault (1982, 1997) as the organized practices (discourses, rationalities and techniques) through which subjects are produced and controlled. Foucault crucially reframed the notion of power from a single node located in a political hierarchy to a dispersed and productive process that circulates through the everyday social practices of institutional life. Governmentality implicates all of us, therefore, as active participants, who express our agency through both complicity and resistance to the circuits and regimes of power within which we live our lives. Just as the idea of 'multiliteracies' has been taken up, critiqued and developed in the subsequent literature, so has the concept of governmentality taken on particular meanings. Rose (1999), for example, is interested in 'technologies of the self', and he describes governmentality as technologies and techniques that act 'on the choices and self-steering properties of individuals, families, communities, [and] organizations' (p. xxiii). He describes the ideal citizen in a liberal democracy as an individual who willingly (though perhaps unknowingly) engages in the 'games that govern' (p. xxiii).

Foucault's ideas have been productively taken up to analyse the development of social policy and its institutions in many different contexts, including education (e.g. Tamboukou & Ball, 2003; Rose et al., 2006). Meanwhile, the public bureaucratic forms of government that were dominant in education when Foucault first theorized the relationship between power and knowledge are vastly changed in terms of political processes and visions as well as in terms of the communication and knowledge creation processes outlined earlier. In other words, the technologies of governance are transformed. Scholars following contemporary developments in educational practices and policies have noted how the locus of power and governance is shifting away from the formal political processes in national states to policy networks, which are more complex, and in many cases are less visible, alliances of civil society, transnational bodies and corporate interests (Rhodes, 1996; Fitzsimons, 2002).

The causes and effects of these shifts are the focus of much contemporary research in the sociology of education from Ball's (2012) tracking of publically/privately financed policy networks in the United Kingdom, to Reckhow (2013) in the USA and Davidson-harden et al. (2009) in Canada, to analyses of regional governance within the European Union (Grek, 2010; Ozga et al., 2011; Lawn & Grek, 2012) and work on transnational policy borrowing and travelling (Steiner-Khamsi & Waldow, 2011). The rapid development of international assessments promoted by the OECD and UNESCO and explicitly designed to affect policy actors in national contexts is a growing focus for scholarship (Rizvi & Lingard, 2009, 2013; Meyer & Benavot, 2013). Less well-researched, but influential, are the corporate activities of businesses, such as Pearson publishers, and philanthropic initiatives, such as the Bill & Melinda Gates foundation (see Reckhow & Snyder, 2014).

The implications for research of these new conditions of governance are profound. Power/knowledge is dispersed in new ways and in locations that intersect and vary in how accessible they are to democratic control. Traditional educational institutions are repositioned along with the people and practices associated with them (Nespor, 2002). Problems and subjectivities are reframed, new choices emerge, new solutions are proposed for effective practice and perhaps most important for the topic of this book are the changes that have occurred in assessment and accountability practices. Such practices are a key vehicle through which policy framings and priorities link through into the everyday detail of classroom life, teacher education and curriculum design. They are embedded in institutional structures that can be slow to adapt to changing practices on the ground. Assessment is, unsurprisingly, then a pivotal focus for the discussions of multimodality in many of the contributions in this book.

Summary of individual chapters

The contributions in this book take up notions of multimodality and governmentality in diverse ways, but all contributions equally raise fundamental and timely questions about them. Chapter 1, through its confidence and hope in multimodality within a multiliteracies frame, raises the first question: How is power produced and exercised in and through literacies in this new era? Each question raises others such as: What is agency in communication? Who (or what) has it and how is it exercised or produced? What opportunities for literacy learning are produced across domains? What are the literacies and their functions that are practiced therein and whose interests do they serve? How are literacy curricula produced, configured and enacted and with what effects? How, for example, are learners and educators positioned within these literacies? How are the literacies implicated in the formation of subjectivities? What do people's bodies do in relation to these literacies? What are the implications for knowledge construction and the creation of identity and communication options? In what ways might multimodal literacies and their ensuing curricula and pedagogies extend and/or limit the powers of educators and learners? And why might these questions matter?

We invited contributors to each think through issues of multimodality and governmentality within the individual contexts they describe. Generally, we encouraged contributors to make explicit their investment in the core issues of the book and the conceptual framework(s) they draw on, and to provide a rich description of the multimodal curricular practices they feature. We asked contributors to provide an overview of the policies and practices in their region in order to orient the reader to the context of each chapter and to identify the tensions and interplay of different pressures experienced in this context. Finally, we asked contributors to consider the opportunities and challenges presented within this context and the implications for educators, learners and the greater community.

The first two chapters offer conceptual overviews of the terrain of literacies, multimodality and governance. Chapter 1, a provocative and optimistic contribution by Mary Kalantzis and Bill Cope (University of Illinois, USA), begins by describing the contemporary status of literacy in education and positioning multimodality squarely within the zeitgeist of multiliteracies. Kalantzis and Cope describe how the approach of multiliteracies, with its new affordances for meaning-making, is a vehicle for a radical departure from static and deterministic literacy regimes. The contribution provides detailed explications of concepts relevant to multimodality and goes on to argue for new ways of conceptualizing power and the exercise of power which reflect the massive changes that have swept historical structures of governance and communication. This first chapter boldly announces a new era, one which, as we argue earlier in this introduction, requires vigilance in order to promote expansive communication and identity options, but also one in which great possibilities may be afoot.

In Chapter 2, Sharon Murphy (York University, Canada) brings together issues of multimodality, education, ethics and assessment. The author raises and seeks to harmonize the tensions between authority and freedom and the practical and theoretical in conceptualizations of literacy. In conversation with Foucault's governmentality, the chapter begins by situating contemporary literacy assessment and proposes a theoretical complement to governmentality. Then, drawing on Arendt (1998/1958) as a frame for considering people's agency in a social world, the chapter forwards how agency can work within the ethos of 'big data' (Lohr, 2012).

More specifically, the chapter details how currently results of educational assessments are used to think about the qualities of societies, but multimodal conceptualizations of literacy are represented in a relatively narrow manner. From a Foucauldian perspective, this transformation of literacy practices into technical tools to delimit what is acceptable literacy practice represents a triumph of governmentality. The chapter argues for a shift in emphasis away from norms towards ideals as the driving force for literacy assessment and for education in general. The idea of *responsible principled action* is overlain across detailed schemes for its promotion in and through multimodal literacy assessment so as to illustrate its utility in finding *hope in dark times* and in observing that living a life of action is unpredictable and not without risks. The chapter concludes with a discussion of the need to move away from norms and towards ideals and foregrounds issues of agency and governmentality that thread throughout all subsequent chapters.

In Chapter 3, Wendy Luttrell and Claire Fontaine (CUNY, USA) describe a model of inquiry and analytic strategy called *collaborative seeing*, which draws on critical childhood studies and invokes an *ethics of care* to explore young people's emerging identities and multimodal literacies over time. In a climate of educational policies and practices that measure children's learning through an overly economically instrumentalist lens, the contribution argues that this makes it all the more urgent to develop alternative ways of seeing young people. Collaborative seeing is one such alternative approach. The chapter charts the evolution of the longitudinal research, *Children Framing Childhoods* and *Looking Back*, tracing the affordances and limitations – what was lost and what was gained – by each step of the emergent research design and analytic strategy (Luttrell, 2000). It also discusses how collaborative seeing sits in the middle of a continuum of participatory research, where at one end, youth and adults are positioned as co-researchers, and at the other end, youth participate in adult-led research and are guided or instructed in their visual media production towards a specific end with adult researchers doing the editing, coding, interpreting and analysis. At the heart of the project is a commitment to a *need to know more stance* about the complex layers of meanings and knowledge embedded in young people's representations, choices and intentions. Multimodality is explored through data drawn from digital narratives created by children using a range of visual sources including photos and video. The chapter discusses the potential of these activities for developing specific aspects of literacy and for different and productive understandings of children's literacy lives, and it includes an extended example of the social relations embedded in one child's gaming practices.

In Chapter 4, Rachel Heydon (Western University, Canada) critically examines findings from three case studies of early childhood literacy curricula. She draws readers' attention to the reciprocal relationship between young children's right to freedom of expression, including their right to expression in self-chosen media and modes, and their ability to participate in a curriculum as informants. Set against a background of reform in Ontario's early childhood education and care (ECEC) sector, her chapter employs actor-network theory (ANT) to map the literacy curricula in each classroom as a network and documents ways in which small differences between curriculum networks can produce radically different consequences for children's participation. Heydon argues that opportunities for multimodality were network effects. No one actor accounted for all the differences, though certain actors were imbued at times with more power than others. She also proposes that studies of governmentality are sometimes understood as overly predictive and deterministic. ANT studies provide fresh lenses for contemplating issues of governmentality and illustrate that power and agency are themselves network effects. The studies thus express a mobile and complex conception of power while identifying asymmetries in power in literacy curriculum production.

In Chapter 5, Roz Stooke (Western University, Canada) argues that critical scholars and leaders in the field of ECEC call for educators to create spaces for poetic ways of being with young children: that is, ways of being that are characterized by participation, love, eagerness and joy. ECEC has been a deeply fragmented field, but the critical scholars and leaders fear that as governments coordinate programs and services for young children, the prescriptive practices and standardized assessments associated with decades of neoliberal reforms in schooling will percolate into early childhood settings. Stooke's chapter considers ways in which pedagogical documentation, with its origins in ECEC and its deep connection to the emergent curriculum approach, might support educators in resisting the pull of instrumental discourses by disrupting time-honoured ways of looking at children's actions and interactions in educational settings. Central to pedagogical documentation's promise is its embrace of multimodal forms of expression for documenting moments of significance to children as well as educators, and Stooke notes that as documentation gains momentum in schools as well as ECEC, it can support children's and educators' access to multiliteracies. Through an examination of stories of practice provided by fourteen Ontario-based educators, she identifies ways in which the diversely situated educators were mobilizing pedagogical documentation for dialogue, reflection and planning, and proposes that documentation practices were mediating multidirectional flows of ideas and practices across the boundaries between settings, including ideas and practices associated with participation, love, eagerness and joy. Yet, she also discovered that time-honoured ways of looking and acting towards children are resilient. Her analysis brings into view several seemingly insignificant moments of translation that threaten to undermine educators' and children's efforts to look at learning in what one leader called 'useful ways'.

In Chapter 6, Rosie Flewitt and Guy Roberts-Holmes (University of London, UK) discuss The Phonics Screening Check, which was introduced in England for five- and six-year-old pupils in 2012 and involved the use of non-words and the promotion of synthetic phonics above other techniques of teaching reading. A year later, a revised EYFSP (Early Years Foundation Stage Profile) (2013) for five-year-olds brought an increased focus upon cognitive approaches to literacy learning, such as writing complete sentences with a pencil that can be read by an adult. This chapter argues that the power of these 'highly prescriptive systems of accountability' (Ball, 2013, p. 173) has had the effect of further drawing early years literacy into the state's regulatory and disciplinary gaze with a consequent narrowing of both the concept and practice of literacy pedagogy in these crucial stages of education. Through a Foucauldian analysis of data from nursery and early primary classrooms in England, the chapter critically examines the disciplinary effects of assessment technologies upon early literacy pedagogy and illustrates how some practitioners have *cynically complied* (Bradbury, 2013) with the new literacy regulations through a process of accommodation and resistance. The contribution illustrates how the phonics screening test itself misuses multimodal resources and overlooks the expansive possibilities of alternative pedagogies and assessment tools that are well known to teachers, such as the pedagogical documentation approach described by Stooke in Chapter 5.

In Chapter 7, Peggy Albers (Georgia State University, USA), Jerome C. Harste (Indiana University, USA) and Vivian M. Vasquez (American University, USA) take a close look at how critical multimodality has influenced the ways in which people communicate and how those changes in turn reposition both the producers and consumers of messages. The trio point out that even within spaces where educators are positioned as docile bodies, there is room to implement alternative ways to teach content. Drawing on rich examples of artists' work, they illustrate how multimodality can make visible the relations of power and how they operate. Importantly, they note that educators must participate in designing, producing and framing multimodal presentations to evoke social awareness alongside their students if they are to engage in critical multimodality.

In Chapter 8, Lisa Björklund Boistrup (Stockholm University, Sweden) focuses on a key notion in classroom communication: assessments taking place in day-to-day classroom-based communication between a teacher and students. In so doing, Boistrup underscores number in multimodality, provides empirically derived illustrations of some of the tensions described in Murphy's Chapter 2, and brings to light issues of multimodality and governmentality in Swedish classrooms. Assessment is here conceptualized broadly, referring to pedagogically oriented feedback as well as tests. Drawing on earlier studies (e.g. Torrance & Pryor, 1998), the chapter assumes that through assessments, students are invited, or not, into the domain of mathematics. Hence, there are power relations emerging, which are interrelated with institutional aspects (Foucault, 2003). Boistrup adopts a methodology where social-semiotics is coordinated with Foucault's (1993) concept of discourse in the analyses of data that originate from previous as well as current research in mathematics classrooms. A range of semiotic resources are taken into consideration, such as speech, symbols, body movements and images (Van Leeuwen, 2005). Multimodal excerpts in the chapter express how assessment acts are produced through various semiotic resources. The roles that these different resources play in assessment acts are also discussed as well as how the acts may acknowledge and introduce mathematical processes or procedures where the mathematical content is more absent. Construed assessment discourses (e.g. *Do it quick and do it right* and *Reasoning takes time*) are connected to traditions and decisions on different institutional levels. A concluding discussion addresses how it is essential for educators to understand what is taking place in mathematics classrooms as part of a broader institutional and governmental context where attention to the multimodal aspects of assessments is critical.

Chapter 9 by Kathryn Hibbert (Western University, Canada) builds on a belief that to exercise freedom, teachers need to become reacquainted with their own professional knowledge and power. Teachers largely enact the culture they live, and they have been living in a culture in which teacher proof materials proliferate and curricular prescription abounds. Hibbert argues that teachers have both the privilege and the responsibility to practice freedom. Living in an audit culture for so many years has placed the professional identities of teachers at risk. In *The Secret of Will*, she asks: How might educators break away from reductionist modes of assessment and capture learning in situ? How might changing the way teachers and students interact with one another translate teaching and learning? In response to these questions, she describes an exciting curriculum design project that leverages the affordances of cloud computing to breathe new life into the teaching of Shakespeare's plays to elementary school students. The cloud curriculum promises to reconnect students and teachers with opportunities to express their ideas in a variety of self-chosen ways, and Hibbert notes that documenting the learning process with students will make it visible to them so that they can build on strengths and add to their repertoires of strategies. By documenting the evolution of the project in this chapter, Hibbert seeks to demonstrate that multimodality, with its interdependence on a multiplicity of modes to make meaning, expands human capacity to create, represent and communicate knowledge and understanding in multiple ways.

In Chapter 10, David Rose (University of Sydney, Australia) draws together the two themes of this book, governmentality and multimodality, through the intersections between pedagogy, literacy and Aboriginal children. It begins by contextualizing issues in the education of Aboriginal students in the structures of contemporary education systems, drawing on Bernstein's (2000) theory of the *pedagogic device*, then follows this with detailed explications and illustrations of multimodal learning strategies that have been found successful for Aboriginal children's literacy acquisition. This chapter takes seriously its involvement with solution-based strategies, focusing on the structures and practices of schools that disadvantage many groups of learners, including Aboriginal children, and advocating for multimodal pedagogical strategies designed to provide Aboriginal children with opportunities for literacy success.

In Chapter 11, Richard Andrews (University of London, UK) considers the role of multimodality and governmentality as it plays out in the higher education context, with a specific focus on digital literacies. He argues that institutions of higher education remain mired in a more conservative approach with respect to regulation of assignments and capacities afforded to instructors. By taking this approach, universities often fail to embrace possibilities for composing in a variety of modes and media for academic purposes. In a globalized world calling for innovative responses to complex problems, he concludes that regulations ought to be adapted to allow for digital and multimodal assessment practices, which are likely to serve as artefacts that have value beyond the functional need to satisfy assessment criteria.

In Chapter 12, Mary Hamilton (Lancaster University, UK) reflects upon an alternative social imaginary embodied in a *user-run* programme, entitled *Pecket Well*, which emerged in the North of England in the early 1990s, but ended when changes to funding structures and assessment regimes made it impossible for them to continue. The story of Pecket Well has much to teach about what can happen when institutions are designed to serve people in the creation of a democratic and inclusive space for learning. Drawing on socio-material theory, Hamilton examines the links between governmentality and multiple forms of expression and studies the way the project formed and eventually unravelled. The language experiences, which Pecketwellians participated in through the collective, engaged them in literacy activities that were participatory and included the production of literacy artefacts, performances and importantly the development of their own governance. They were an example of how critical multimodality affords an opportunity for full civic participation, and their story points to the need for this to be enabled rather than constrained.

In the final chapter, Chapter 13, Suzanne Smythe (Simon Fraser University, Canada) examines ways in which the Canadian government defines and measures digital literacy. Smythe argues that representations of digital literacy in adult literacy policies overlay narrowly defined notions of literacy onto existing frameworks of essential skills training linked to entry-level jobs. Drawing on data from three provinces, she presents and discusses three stories, each of which illuminates how transnational projects such as the Organization for Economic Cooperation and Development's Program of International Assessment of Adult Competencies (PIAAC) find their way into community-based literacy programs and organize what happens in the programs from great distances. Smythe argues that large-scale assessments such as PIAAC restrict learners' access to digital technologies and multimodal forms of expression by privileging *minimal proficiency* reading skills required for entry-level jobs. The stories celebrate the creativity of educators and learners as they work around government policies to practice powerful literacies, but she argues nonetheless that access to digital technologies and multimodal modes of learning cannot on their own transform existing patterns of social inequality. She advocates for the cultivation of technoliteracies to promote powerful practices of critique, production, collaboration and extended practice through which people may *thrive*.

References

Arendt, H. (1998/1958). *The Human Condition* (2nd ed.). Chicago: University of Chicago Press.

Arthur, C. (2012). *Financial Literacy Education: Neoliberalism, the Consumer and the Citizen*. London: Springer.

Ball, S. (2012). *Global Education Inc.: New Policy Networks and the Neo-liberal Imaginary*. Abingdon: Routledge.

Ball, S. (2013). *The Education Debate: Politics and Policy in the 21st Century*. Bristol: Policy Press.

Barton, D., & Hamilton, M. (1998/2013). *Local Literacies: Reading and Writing in One Community*. London: Routledge.

Barton, D., Hamilton, M., & Ivanič, R. (Eds) (2000). *Situated Literacies: Reading and Writing in Context*. London: Routledge.

Bernstein, B. (2000). *Pedagogy, Symbolic Control and Identity: Theory, Research, Critique*. London: Taylor & Francis.

Blommaert, J. (2010). *The Sociolinguistics of Globalization*. Cambridge: Cambridge University Press.

———. (2013). *Ethnography, Superdiversity and Linguistic Landscapes: Chronicles of Complexity*. Bristol: Multilingual Matters.

Bradbury, A. (2013). *Understanding Early Years Inequality: Policy, Assessment and Young Children's Identities*. London: Routledge.

Collier, D. (2013). Relocalizing wrestler: Performing texts across time and space. *Language and Education, 27*(6), 481–497.

Comber, B., & Nixon, H. (2009). Teachers' work and pedagogy in an era of accountability. *Discourse: Studies in the Cultural Politics of Education, 30*(3), 333–345.

Davidson-Harden, A., Kuehn, L., Schugurensky, D., & Smaller, H. (2009). Neoliberalism and education in Canada. In D. Hill (Ed.) *The Rich World and the Impoverishment of Education: Diminishing Democracy, Equity and Workers' Rights* (pp. 51–73). Portland: Routledge.

Department for Education. (2013). Early years foundation stage profile 2013 return: Guide for the 2013 assessments – version 1.0. Retrieved from https://www.gov.uk/government/uploads/system/uploads/attachment_data/file/252766/eyfsp_2013_guide_v1_0.pdf (Accessed 5/1/2015).

Fenwick, T. J. (2010). (un) Doing standards in education with actor-network theory. *Journal of Education Policy, 25*(2), 117–133.

Fitzsimons, P. (2002). Neoliberalism and education: The autonomous chooser. *Radical Pedagogy, 4*(2), 3. (open access online journal).

Foucault, M. (1982). The subject and power. *Critical Inquiry, 9* (4), 777–795.

———. (1993). *Diskursen ordning* [The order of the discourse]. Stockholm: Brutus Östlings Bokförlag Symposium.

———. (1997). *Michel Foucault: 'Society Must Be Defended'*. New York: Picador.

———. (2003). *Övervakning och straff* [Discipline and Punish]. Lund, Sweden: Arkiv förlag.

González, N., Moll, L. C., & Amanti, C. (Eds.) (2005). *Funds of Knowledge: Theorizing Practices in Households, Communities, and Classrooms*. Mahwah: Routledge.

Gourlay, L., Hamilton, M., & Lea, M. R. (2013). Textual practices in the new media digital landscape: Messing with digital literacies. *Research in Learning Technology, 21*: 21438, 10.3402/rlt.v21.21438

Gregory, E., & Williams, A. (2000). *City Literacies: Learning to Read Across Generations and Cultures*. London: Routledge.

Grek, S. (2010). International organisations and the shared construction of policy 'problems': Problematisation and change in education governance in Europe. *European Educational Research Journal, 9*(3), 396–406.

Hamilton, M. (2009). Putting words in their mouths: The alignment of identities with system goals through the use of individual learning plans. *British Educational Research Journal, 35*(2), 221–242.

Heydon, R. (2013). Learning opportunities: A study of the production and practice of kindergarten literacy curricula. *Journal of Curriculum Studies, 45*(4), 481–510.

James, A., & James, A. (2012). *Key Concepts in Childhood Studies*. (2nd edn). London: Sage.

Janks, H. (2009). *Literacy and Power*. London: Routledge.

Kress, G. (2003). *Literacy in the New Media Age*. London: Routledge.

Lankshear, C., & Knobel, M. (Eds) (2008). *Digital Literacies: Concepts, Policies and Practices*. New York: Peter Lang.

Lawn, M., & Grek, S. (2012). *Europeanizing Education: Governing a New Policy Space*. Oxford: Symposium Books.

Lindblad, S., & Popkewitz, T. S. (Eds) (2004). *Educational Restructuring: International Perspectives on Traveling Policies*. Greenwich: IAP.

Lohr, S. (2012, February 11). The age of big data. The New York Times Sunday Review: The Opinion Pages. http://www.nytimes.com/2012/02/12/sunday-review/big-datas-impact-in-the-world.html?pagewanted=all

Luttrell, W. (2000). 'Good enough' methods for ethnographic research. *Harvard Educational Review, 70*(4), 499–523.

Matthiessen, C., Teruya, K., & Lam, M. (2010). *Key Terms in Systemic Functional Linguistics.* London: Bloomsbury Publishing.

Meyer, H. D., & Benavot, A. (Eds) (2013). *PISA, Power, and Policy: The Emergence of Global Educational Governance.* Oxford: Symposium Books.

Nespor, J. (2002). Networks and contexts of reform. *Journal of Educational Change, 3*(3–4), 365–382.

New London Group (1996). A pedagogy of multiliteracies: Designing social futures, *Harvard Educational Review, 66*(1), 60–93.

Ozga, J., Dahler-Larsen, P., Segerholm, C., & Simola, H. (Eds) (2011). *Fabricating Quality in Education: Data and Governance in Europe.* New York: Routledge.

Pahl, K., & Rowsell, J. (Eds) (2006). *Travel Notes from the New Literacy Studies: Instances of Practice* (Vol. 4). Clevedon: Multilingual Matters.

Pennycook, A. (2006). *Global Englishes and Transcultural Flows.* London: Routledge.

Peterson, S. S., & McClay, J. K. (2010). Assessing and providing feedback for student writing in Canadian classrooms. *Assessing Writing, 15*(2), 86–99.

Reckhow, S. (2013). *Follow the Money: How Foundation Dollars Change Public School Politics.* Oxford: Oxford University Press.

Reckhow, S., & Snyder, J. W. (2014). The expanding role of philanthropy in education politics. *Educational Researcher, 43*(4), 186–195.

Rhodes, R. A. W. (1996). The new governance: Governing without government. *Political Studies, 44*(4), 652–667.

Rizvi, F., & Lingard, B. (2009). The OECD and global shifts in education policy. In Cowen, R., & Kazamias, A. M. (Eds), *International Handbook of Comparative Education* (pp. 437–453). Dordrecht: Springer Netherlands.

Rizvi, F., & Lingard, B. (2013). *Globalizing Education Policy.* New York: Routledge.

Rose, N. (1999). *Powers of Freedom: Reframing Political Thought.* Cambridge: Cambridge University Press.

Rose, N., O'Malley, P., & Valverde, M. (2006). Governmentality. *Annual Review of Law and Social Science, 2*, 83–104.

Steiner-Khamsi, G., & Waldow, F. (Eds) (2011). *Policy Borrowing and Lending in Education.* London: Routledge.

Street, B. V. (2005). *Literacy and Development: Ethnographic Perspectives.* London: Routledge.

Street, B. V., Pahl, K., & Rowsell, J. (2009). Multimodality and new literacy studies. In C. Jewitt, G. Kress, & D. E. Mavers (Eds), *The Routledge Handbook of Multimodal Analysis.* London: Routledge (pp. 191–200).

Tamboukou, M., & Ball, S. J. (Eds)(2003). *Dangerous Encounters: Genealogy and Ethnography.* New York: Peter Lang.

Torrance, H., & Pryor, J. (1998). *Investigating Formative Assessment: Teaching, Learning and Assessment in the Classroom.* Maidenhead: McGraw-Hill International.

Van Leeuwen, T. (2005). *Introducing Social Semiotics.* London: Routledge.

1

Regimes of Literacy

Mary Kalantzis and Bill Cope

This book is about regimes of literacy – an ancien régime of print literacy, and an emerging regime of multiliteracies. It is about changes in our social practices of meaning-making and changes happening in the institutions of education where learners are socialized to mean. Or, more to the point, it is about changes that might happen, or are not happening but perhaps should, as well as changes that are in fact underway. Regime change is an opportunity to think prospectively, to imagine something different from, and better than, pasts which have been less than ideal.

We'll start with a brief sketch of the old regime of literacy, by way a counterpoint to our case for multiliteracies, a story which we tell at length in our book, *Literacies* (Kalantzis & Cope, 2012). Not until the rise of compulsory, mass-institutionalized education in the nineteenth century was literacy posited as an essential capacity for workers and citizens. Of the proverbial three 'r's, reading and writing were two-thirds – literacy was that important. Its purposes were in part functional to the world of industrial modernity – so that workers could read signs and memos in the workplace, and so that citizens could share a common civic and cultural life through newspapers and books. Literacy served an essential functional purpose, and this often translated into moral and nation-building imperatives in the discourse of educators.

The substance of literacy consisted of the phonics of transliteration of speech into writing, correcting spelling and grammar, reading texts in order to comprehend what the writer meant to tell, writing as a memory aid and to communicate with immediate others and developing an awed respect for the greats of the national literary canon. The characteristic modes of acquisition of literacy were a bureaucratic apparatus that prescribed content areas to be learned in the syllabus, the textbook which laid out the content, teacher recitation, teacher–student question and answer routines, filling out answers in workbooks, reading texts and answering comprehension questions, writing short texts and literacy taking tests to check what had been learned. The patterns of practice were predictable and straightforward. Often today, we find that not much in schools has changed.

If we are to ascribe to this literacy setup the full weight of the word 'regime', what do we make of it? What are its roles, rules, structures of governance and disciplinary logics? The teller (the teacher) is positioned over the told (the student). The teacher, in turn, is positioned in a bureaucratic line of control (syllabus, to textbook, to recitation). Administrative audit requirements are put in place, checking that both students and teachers have performed (the test). This is essentially a regime of epistemic discipline, a moral economy. We characterize this mode of literacy pedagogy as 'didactic'.

It is also a regime that systematizes inequality. Students are rated in such a way that they are spread across a normal distribution curve, where normal means that a few can excel because the centre is mediocre and the tail must fail outright. This maps perfectly onto a very unequal society, rationalizing that inequality. If you didn't excel at school, you only have yourself to blame and live with the consequences. This disciplinary regime of literacy mapped onto labour markets, where very few skilled and highly paid workers are needed. The majority could get by at work with only the most basic of functional literacies. It mapped well onto the domineering states of the twentieth century – 'welfare' states as well as totalitarian ones. It mapped well onto the textual relations of mass media and literature, where most were readers, consumers of mass culture, and only an elite few were writers. It is hardly surprising that, when the all-important time came to test literacy, reading 'comprehension' often became a proxy. The reason for this was partly pragmatic – it was cheap to mark reading comprehension with standardized bubble tests. However, this also aligned with a narrow view of literacy's moral purposes, to test whether the student has heard what the author must really have meant to say without interpretation.

The school also standardizes culture. It creates the 'imagined community' (Anderson, 1991) of the homogenous nation-state. Through literacy, colonized people and immigrants learn the standard form of the national language, and if to excel proves too challenging, it becomes their own fault, and so according to the logic of schooling, they are further marginalized.

Foucault's notion of 'governmentality' can be made to work for us as we interpret this regime (Foucault, 1982/2011) – a regime in which literacy is complicit. It explains how people are positioned and position themselves in structures of power. In Gramsci's terms, it becomes part of a 'common sense' of resignation to inequality (Gramsci, 1971). In Althusser's terms, it explains how people become 'bearers' of roles in unequal structures (Althusser, 1970). Or, in Lukács' terms, it is part of a process in which people assume passive stances in relation to social structures which are contrary to their objective interest (Lukács, 1923/1972). Foucault, however, is bleaker than his twentieth-century peers. He describes in graphic detail the mechanisms by which the prison of modernity incarcerates. He shows the microdynamics of power at work in ordinary social institutions and everyday practices. However, in his archaeology of power he offers no suggestion that there could be a way out, no suggestions of strategies for resistance nor more broadly that there might be a way to ameliorate the cruel injustices of modern life.

Now, stuff is happening in the twenty-first century that is dramatically different. The shapes of the changes are at times unclear, as we are caught in cross-currents from the past. To make sense of the new takes some effort because the present is complex, fluid and emergent.

The notion of multiliteracies is designed to capture two aspects of the new in the realm of human meaning-making, as a counterpoint to the characteristic features of the old regime of literacy. The first aspect is the substance of literacy – the things we do to mean in an era where communications are increasingly multimodal. The second aspect is a new regime of social power, and new structures of agency emerging in the meaning-making process.

To address the first of these aspects of multiliteracies, a key issue in our contemporary communications environment, is the phenomenon of multimodality. On the one hand, with the rise of the new, highly personalized media, we see the proliferation of still and moving image as modes of expression, displacing messages that would once have been expressed in oral or written language. Gunther Kress has characterized this as the rise of an image culture, displacing at least to some degree an earlier modern culture dominated by language and literacy (Kress, 2009).

At the same time, we also witness a dramatic extension of the sites of writing and reading, and in new or hybrid genres. Our television screens, our shopping malls and our smart phones are full of writing. We navigate both virtual and physical worlds with writing, from the 'tags' that support discovery to the requests and responses we get from GPSs. Arguably, we are doing more writing and reading than ever; and it is taking new forms.

Despite these convergences, we have a limited range conceptual tools for describing the shared and integrally connected aspects of meaning-making across modes. Grammars of various sorts describe the structures and functions of language. The psychology of perception and the analytic techniques of arts analysis help us to account for the workings of the image, to mention just two of a range of conceptual frameworks for analysing visual meanings (Kress & van Leeuwen, 1996). But rarely do our analyses of the parallels and the differences between these modes of meaning break out of disciplinary confines of 'linguistics' or 'visual communications'.

Why do we need to extend the grammar and interpretative frame of print literacy, with a grammar of multimodality? To answer this question, let's take a brief historical journey through modern technologies and media for the transmission of meanings across distances of time and space.

Letterpress printing technology, invented in the mid-fifteenth century, positioned the character the smallest unit of manufacture of machine-reproducible meaning (Eisenstein, 1979). For five centuries, the typesetter laid out these 'types' one by one on the printer's forme. Images could be reproduced by lithographic processes, but this was a different technology. Text and image could not be easily brought together, which is why until then newspapers had no photos and books needed separate sections for 'plates'.

A centuries-long enforced separation of formal, written-textual meaning from other modes followed. This did not significantly change until the application of the new technologies of photolithography in the mid-twentieth century, when image and text could conveniently be overlaid – hence the rise of magazines and illustrated books and the near-complete eclipse of letterpress in the third quarter of that century. But still, reproducible sound and orality happened in their own technologies (and thus cultural spaces): the gramophone record, radio, telephone.

Digital technologies for the production and transmission of meaning bring the modes together. Digital characters are made of little dots, which are now the smallest elementary modular units in the manufacture of writing. Digital pictures are made of the same thing – pixels or picture elements. As still and moving images and fonts are now made of the same raw materials, they can easily be combined. By the first decade of the twenty-first century, we had digital video that streamed more and more writing over image, in business or sports television, for instance, further extending effects that had only commenced with photolithography.

In these ways, the digital intensifies the multimodality in our contemporary media for representation and communication. We can now do all of text, still image, moving image, sound and calculation/data manipulation together, on one recording/transmitting device. The common elementary modular unit in the manufacture of meaning is binary encoding. So, we can speak, write and image across time and space using the same tools we have for listening, reading and viewing. We are now more appropriately called generic 'users' than writers and readers because, when we interact with communicated meanings, we write over them, reuse them, and manipulate them in the case of datasets and apps.

Taking this half-millennium long view, we can see that technological shifts in our meaning-making tools underpin the deep multimodality of today's communications environment. The social processes that follow we call 'affordances' – a 'can' rather than a 'must'. But because we 'can', we mostly find that we do.

In this understanding of the context of contemporary meaning-making, for the most pragmatic of reasons, we need to expand the focus of traditional literacy learning to encompass multimodal meaning-making. We do this by revising Halliday's three semiotic metafunctions (Halliday, 2004) and extending them with two more. All meaning-making, across all modes, operates at five levels, with five purposes. We to *refer* to things, events, processes and abstractions (Halliday's 'ideational' function). We *dialogue*, with ourselves and others (Halliday's 'interpersonal' function). We *structure* our meanings in ways which are both conventional and always innovative to the extent that every remaking is uniquely modulated (Halliday's 'textual' function). We *situate* our meanings in contexts, or at least find that they are situated by default (what we call a 'contextual' function). And we *intend* when we position and/or encounter meanings in webs of intention or agency (a metafunction we call 'interest').

What do meanings refer to? This is the first of five questions we want to ask about meaning-making. Referring may delineate particular things, in writing or speaking in the form of nouns to represent things or verbs to represent processes. In images, particular things may be delineated with line, form and colour; in space by volumes and boundaries; in tactile representations by edges and surface textures; in gesture by acts of pointing or beat. Referring may also be to a general concept for which there are many instances: a word that refers to an abstract concept; an image that is a symbol; a space which is characterized by its similarity with others; or a sound that represents a general idea. Referring can establish relations: prepositions or possessives in language; collocation or contrast in image. It can establish qualities: adjectives or adverbs in language; or visual attributes in images. It can compare, including juxtapositions or metaphors of all kinds, in words, image, sound or space.

These are the parallels. 'The mountains loomed large', says the sentence, then the image provides an entirely similar yet entirely different expression of the same thing – complementary, supplementary or perhaps disruptive. However, we also want to highlight the irreducible differences that account for the variations and disruptions, and offer evidence of the complementary value of multimodality. Writing, for instance, consists of sequential meaning elements, moving forward in English one word relentlessly at a time, left to right, line to line. It requires of us a composing and reading path that prioritizes time, because the progression of the text takes us through time. The image, by contrast, presents to us a number of meaning-elements simultaneously. Its viewing path prioritizes space. When we do both, we may attain a fuller, more nuanced meaning, or for that matter, a less settled meaning.

How do meanings connect the participants in meaning-making? Interaction is the second of our metafunctions. Here we establish roles: speaker/listener, writer/reader, designer/user, maker/consumer, gesturer/ observer and sound-maker/hearer. We direct or encounter orientations: in language first/second/third person and direct/indirect speech; in image, placement and eyelines; in gesture, pointing to self, others and the world. We also encounter agency: in language, voice, mood and transitivity; in image, focal planes of attachment and engagement; in space, openings and barriers. And we discover a range of interpretative potentials: open and closed texts; realistic and abstract images; directive or turn-taking gestures; spaces which determine flows deterministically and others that allow a range of alternatives.

How does the overall meaning hold together? Through this metafunction we analyse the devices used to create internal cohesion, coherence and boundedness in meanings. Each mode composes atomic meaning units (morphemes, picture elements, physical components, structural materials in the build environment, strokes in gesture) in a certain kind of order. This order is both conventional (using what we call 'available designs' for meaning) and inventive (the process of 'designing'), a consequence of which no two designs of meaning are ever quite the same. There are internal pointers: pronouns or connectives in language; keys and arrows in images; wayfinding markers in space; cadence and rhythm in sound. There is idea arrangement: sequence in text; positioning of picture elements in images; the functional mechanics of tangible objects. And there are the tangible forms of media: handwriting, speaking, drawing, photographing, making material objects, building, making music or gesturing. Here we also want to highlight some of the enormously significant and underplayed differences between the grammars of speaking and writing, as well as the hybrid forms of speaking-like writing and writing-like speaking that emerge in the new media.

Where is the meaning situated? Meaning is as much a matter of where it is, as what it is. To the extent that context makes meaning, it is a part of the meaning. A label on a packet points to the contents of the packet, and speaks to the supermarket where it is for sale. A text message speaks to the location of the conversants and the images that are posted with it. A kitchen relates to living areas in a house which in turn fits into larger patterns of everyday suburban life. Bells and electronic 'dings' can mean all manner of things, depending on their context. Across all modes, meanings are framed. They refer to other meanings by similarity or contrast (e.g. motif, style, genre). They assume registers according to degrees of formality, profession, discipline or community of practice.

Finally, whose interest is a meaning designed to serve? In this metafunction we interrogate the meanings we encounter or make for evidence of motivation. How does rhetoric work, in text, image or gesture? How do subjectivity and objectivity work in written and visual texts? In these and other explorations of interests, we might interrogate meanings for their cross purposes, concealments, dissonances or a variety of failures to communicate. We can explore the dynamics of ideologies, be these explicit or implicit, propagandistic or 'informational'. For this we need critique, or the methods used to uncover interests that may have been left unstated or deliberately concealed in text, image, gesture, sound or space.

This multimodality also involves the process of mode shifting, or transitions in our meaning-making attentions from one mode to another: oral, written, visual, audio, gestural and spatial. We use the word 'synesthesia' to describe this mode shifting, defining the word in broader sense than is commonly the case in psychology or neuroscience (Ramachandran, 2011). We conjure up an image, and then say the word for the same thing. We describe a feature of the natural world in scientific language and then show a diagram of that process. Each time, the meaning is at once the same (that mountain) and irreducibly different by virtue of the affordances of each mode (what words and images differentially tell of that mountain). In these ways, each mode becomes supplementary or complementary to others. Mode shifting is an integral part of our thinking. It is also an invaluable thinking tool when used in support of learning.

If the cognitive business of switching modes is to be called synesthesia, then the process of transferring meaning from one mode to another is called 'transliteration'. To be practical, the logistics of transliteration are now central for students reading and writing in science; designers creating products that 'speak to' their users; teachers who want to develop and implement contemporary academic pedagogies; web designers and web users … indeed, in all manner of meaning-making situations in today's deeply multimodal communications environment.

So, multiliteracies is a much bigger agenda than traditional print literacy. But to turn now to its second aspect, how might it represent a change in regimes of power? At this point, we move from the pragmatics of 'getting on' in the new communications environment to a phenomenon that we call changing the 'balance of agency'.

Let's examine just one aspect of the new media, as an instance in a change in the balance of agency, compared to the old, mass media. Journalists, television producers, radio announcers and authors were the producers of cultural and informational messages in the old media, a small creative elite in the 'culture industries', in the employ of a small controlling and owning class. The consumers of their products were their readerships, audiences and patrons. Culture flowed from a few producers to many consumers, a relationship that had been prefigured in the epistemic relations of the didactic classroom.

The new media, the social media, are by comparison 'participatory' (Jenkins, 2006). The balance of cultural and epistemic agency is transformed. Tweets and smart phone images become the news because everyone is a reporter. No need to send a camera crew to a news event. (They'll get there too late most of the time, anyway.) Someone will be there to take a picture, or make a video or tweet an observation, and share it with the world. Everyone is a reporter now. And it's not just the big news. It's the micro news of the meal I am just having, the people I am with, the thing-of-note I just saw or read on the web and my opinions and my feelings of the moment. The old, hierarchical role divisions of cognitive and cultural labour are blurred. Readers are simultaneously writers; viewers are simultaneously image makers.

New reciprocities, new sociabilities emerge: to like in order to be liked; to follow in order to be followed; to friend in order to be friended – a discourse that is by turns, mutually affirmatory and narcissistically exhibitionist. Of course, the situation is not all good, only different and complicated. After all, these same new media that invite us to participate also watch our every move – cravenly in order to sell us stuff, or chillingly as they watch us with suspicion. They take our intellectual work and our lives and make piles of money out of us. Divide today's Facebook or Twitter capitalization by the number of users and you'll be surprised what you're worth to them. You're doing the cultural and epistemic work. They're not paying you for the work you do, but your participatory fortune has become their monetary fortune.

Foucault's pessimism about governmentality – a regime without exit, without opening for agency – may have been in part a product of the horrors of twentieth century, when dreams of societies of more equal association were also shattered. The shapes of governmentality in the twenty-first century reflect the fact that the domineering state has withered away, to be replaced by the minimalist state of neoliberalism (Harvey, 2005) or no state at all, where totalitarianisms have been replaced by collapsed states. This brings us to the challenge of developing a pedagogy of renewed agency, of resilient self-governance. How do we infuse resilient agency into learning, such that learners are meaning makers not just meaning receivers, knowledge producers and not just knowledge consumers?

In multiliteracies theory, we use the word 'design' to describe the patterns of meaning and action that constitute representation, communication and interpretation. We use this word because it has a fortuitous double meaning. On the one hand, any meaning that is made has a design. Its parts can be identified, and these parts fit together in distinctive ways – nouns and verbs, hyperlinks and navigation paths, visual frames and focal points. Design in this sense is the study of form and structure in the meanings that we make. This is 'design' used as a noun. We spoke about these kinds of design when we described the phenomena of multimodality.

On the other hand, design is also a sequence of actions, a process motivated by our purposes. This is the kind of design that drives representation as an act of meaning-for-oneself, message-making as an act of communication oriented to others and interpretation as a process of making sense of communications. Design now refers to a certain kind of agency. It is something you do. It is a form of governance, of taking control in a more widely distributed balance of agency. This is 'design' used as a transitive verb.

In this conception of meaning-as-design, we move away from meaning-as-artefact, either intrinsic to the world or attributed to it by persons. Rather, it is about meaning-making as an activity. It is an act of agency. In this activity, we use our minds as well as our bodies (for instance, to speak, to see, to move, to use media). We use socially inherited cognitive tools (for instance, language, imagery, gestures, spatial movement). And we use physical media (for instance, voices, text-entry tools, cameras). The result is an effect on the world, a transformed meaning and a transformed world.

These meaning-making activities can serve a range of purposes. One is to communicate – we are by nature social creatures. Another is to represent without necessary communication – to undertake these activities and use these meaning-making tools as a kind of cognitive prosthesis, either as a preliminary to communication, or simply to provide support for our thinking. Still another activity is to interpret, or to add re-represent communicated meanings so they make sense to oneself. Still another is to refigure oneself as an agent, as someone who can change the world in small ways, and participate with others to change the world in larger ways.

References

Althusser, L. (1977). Ideology and ideological state apparatuses: Notes toward an investigation. In L. Althusser (Ed.), "Lenin and Philosophy" and other Essays (pp. 121–176). London: New Left Books.

Anderson, B. (1991). *Imagined Communities: Reflections on the Origin and Spread of Nationalism.* London: Verso.

Eisenstein, E. L. (1979). *The Printing Press as an Agent of Change: Communications and Cultural Transformation in Early-Modern Europe.* Cambridge: Cambridge University Press.

Foucault, M. (1982/2011). *The Government of Self and Others: Lectures at the College de France, 1982–1983.* London: Picador.

Gramsci, A. (1971). *Selections from the Prison Notebooks.* New York: International Publishers.

Halliday, M. A. K. (2004). *An Introduction to Functional Grammar.* London: Hoddler Arnold.

Harvey, D. (2005). *A Brief History of Neoliberalism.* Oxford: Oxford University Press.

Jenkins, H. (2006). *Confronting the Challenges of Participatory Culture: Media Education for the 21st Century.* Chicago: John D. and Catherine T. MacArthur Foundation.

Kalantzis, M., & Cope, B. (2012). *Literacies.* Cambridge: Cambridge University Press.

Kress, G. (2009). *Multimodality: A Social Semiotic Approach to Contemporary Communication.* London: Routledge.

Kress, G., & van Leeuwen, T. (1996). *Reading Images: The Grammar of Visual Design.* London: Routledge.

Lukács, G. (1923; 1972). *History and Class Consciousness.* Cambridge: The MIT Press.

Ramachandran, V. S. (2011). *The Tell-Tale Brain.* New York: WW Norton.

2

Beyond Governmentality: The Responsible Exercise of Freedom in Pursuit of Literacy Assessment

Sharon Murphy

The literature on the assessment of multimodal literacies is an emergent literature (e.g. Jewitt, 2003; Burke & Hammett, 2009; Chan & Choo, 2009; Stornaiuolo et al., 2009; Daly & Unsworth, 2011; Curwood, 2012; Cumming et al., 2012; Towndrow et al., 2013). In part, this state of affairs exists because the idea of multimodal literacies, the 'new literacies' (e.g. Kress, 2003; Unsworth, 2006; Walsh, 2010), is relatively new – the stuff of the new millennium (Alverman & Hagood, 2000).

First, consider the term multimodal literacies. The signification work of multimodal literacies is captured in images, movements, words, sounds and their interrelationships; multimodal literacies are seen as *in situ*, energetic, dynamic, creative and beyond the 'print-centric' (Wyatt-Smith & Kimber, 2009, p. 70). Contrast this understanding with, for instance, the scope of the opening statement made by Adams (1990) in an influential report about beginning to read in which she states, 'before you pick this book up, you should understand fully that the topic at issue is that of reading words' (p. 30). Such a statement leaves no doubt that other signification forms were not considered as forms to be read. Not only is the definition of what constitutes a signifier at stake in multimodal literacies, but the modalities of signification are at stake because they are seen as co-constitutive of the signification. Additionally, multimodal literacies often bundle a breadth of signification forms with the time-scaling advantages, production ease and dissemination possibilities afforded by digitization and global inter-connectivity. When juxtaposed against the less malleable paper-based print forms of signification typically associated with the literacy described by Adams (1990), multimodal literacies are seen as a challenge to convention or tradition.

Next consider the term assessment. Assessments are bound up in values, which in turn are bound up in shared systems of knowing (Murphy, 2013). Even though assessments and acts of judging are part of the everydayness of life, and can seem to be quite simple, they can have very complex architectures and are often repurposed to serve ends for which they were never designed (e.g. FairTest, 2013). The scope, scale and repurposing of assessments associated with governmental oversight of education and use of education for political purposes has led to sustained critique (e.g. Hillocks, 2002; McDonnell, 2004; Thomas, 2005; Valli et al., 2008; Nathan, 2009; McDermott, 2011). One critique is that educational assessments have become political tools with the potential to be inscriptive rather than descriptive, and to regulate rather than open up possibilities for learning.

Once this new way of conceptualizing literacy is invoked in relation to assessment, as indicated in the term 'multimodal literacy assessment', both theoretical and practical tensions ensue. In this chapter, I will work at harmonizing some of these tensions by first of all considering one possible framing, that of governmentality theory (Foucault, 1991/1978). Next, I will introduce an alternate theoretical framing that positions individuals as agentive, a framing that I argue that resonates with multimodal literacy theory. Finally, I will consider the implications of this alternate perspective for the assessment of multimodal literacies. By drawing on and highlighting values driven by principles of potentiality, plurality and openness to unpredictability and unconventionality, I believe that multimodal literacy assessment can become an example of an epistemically responsible (Code, 1987, 2006) assessment, one that offers the possibility for multimodal literacy educators to engage in ethical assessment driven by principles that recognize the scope of contemporary literacy practices in meaningful ways.

Situating contemporary assessment

Although many acts of assessment occur daily inside (e.g. Björklund, this book) and outside of classrooms, educational assessment, within societal discourse in general, is increasingly associated with large-scale standardized assessment forms. For example, at the OECD, the Program for International Student Achievement (PISA) offers to the world the proposition that it assesses a suite of skills necessary for the future, among which are literacy skills (Murphy, 2010). Individual nation-states or regions within nation-states have created their own large-scale assessments with math and literacy skills identified as core (e.g. in Ontario, Canada – Educational Quality and Accountability Office, n.d.; in the United Kingdom – Testing and Assessment, n.d.; and any number of state-wide assessment programs in the United States; see also Volante & Earl, 2013). The results of these and other large-scale tests are newspaper headlines, government policy changes and business reports which represent the work of education in aggregated statistical data that are removed from the nature of what is being assessed (Murphy, 2010). Why has educational assessment moved in this direction?

While there are many explanations for the pull of these types of assessments and their uses (e.g. Murphy, 2010), one theoretical framing used to understand this state of affairs is based on the work of the French philosopher, Michel Foucault (1991/1978). Governmentality 'captures the way governments and other actors draw on knowledge to make policies that regulate and create subjectivities' (Bevir, 2010, p. 423). Foucault (1991/1978) argues that governmentality involves the use of a suite of tactics to exercise power over the actions of individuals. In essence, governments have particular social objectives in mind and use statistics to turn society towards those objectives. Much has been written about the use of the tactic or technology of statistics in the exercise of power (Hacking, 1990; Kerr, 1999; Sokhi-Bulley, 2011). Within a governmentality framing, when statistics are used in combination with assessments or examinations, they have a transformative power – they 'make possible a knowledge of the subject but also ... they make objects visible, shap[e] them into forms that are calculable and able to be regulated' (Sokhi-Bulley, 2011, p. 141). Examinations are specifically referred to by Foucault (1995) in discussing the subjugating nature of the power of social institutions:

> The examination combines the techniques of an observing hierarchy and those of a normalizing judgment. It is a normalizing gaze, a surveillance that makes it possible to qualify, to classify and to punish. It establishes over individuals a visibility through which one differentiates them and judges them. That is why, in all the mechanisms of discipline, the examination is highly ritualized. In it are combined the ceremony of power and the establishment of truth ... We are entering the age of the infinite examination and of compulsory objectification. (pp. 184 and 189)

Foucault's (1995) words anticipate what is now being called 'the age of big data' (Lohr, 2012; see also, Anderson, 2008; World Economic Forum, 2012) –

an age where 'hidden predictive information from large databases' (Wang, 2003, p. vii) can be extracted through the process of data mining. Large-scale educational assessments represent one example of big data. These assessments now make education not merely an interest of students, teachers and parents, but they also make it the focus of nations and of the world (Murphy, 2010; Meyer, 2013). The mining of the data from such assessments presents particular visions of education (Raptis, 2012) that enter into social discourse; the assessments become both the means for and the ends of the engineering of education. The data from assessments, constructed by governments, render visible a state of education which at first glance appears to be the consequence of individual students' efforts within the educational system. However, through layers of encoding (Murphy, 2009), both through numbers and value-laden language, the statistical reports of assessments result in the 'making up of people' (Hacking, 1990, p. 6), which affects 'the ways in which we conceive of others and think of our own possibilities and potentialities' (Hacking, 1990, p. 6).

Educational assessment, when viewed at these macro-levels through the theoretical lens of governmentality theory, is managerialist (Goddard, 2010) and operates on a market economy approach (Meadmore, 2001; Pongratz, 2006; Rautalin & Alasuutari, 2009). In that governmentality theory allows us to 'see' this aspect of educational politics at work, it seems to have extraordinary explanatory potential in terms of the analysis and critique of education in general (e.g. Simons & Masschelein, 2006; Brass, 2010), and educational assessment in particular (e.g. Meadmore, 2001; Graham & Neu, 2004; Gruenewald, 2005; Gunzenhauser, 2006; Raptis, 2012). However, governmentality theory has a socially deterministic (Kerr, 1999) aspect to it; little space is left for action in the face of a subjugation so nuanced and powerful that, as Foucault (1995) suggests, subjects embrace the disempowerment while it is happening. As Kerr (1999) argues, Foucauldian governmentality theory 'gives rise to the notion that humanity can never escape from systems of power and governmentality' (p. 175). Although some (e.g. Levitt, 2008) suggest that Foucault offers the possibility of revolution 'by joining forces or "regrouping", and forming a "network of power relations"' (p. 56), readings of Foucault in relation to educational assessment tend towards the critique of subjugation rather than to the exploration of agency.

To move beyond the sensibility of powerlessness that, rightly or wrongly, is linked to Foucauldian governmentality theory, I will focus on the idea of agency first of all because it has a strong affinity with multimodal literacies and secondly because it offers a point of departure for thinking about assessment.

Agency and multimodal literacies

If multimodal literacies represent a move away from convention, then, by their nature, they counter some of the elements of governmentality theory. The multimodally literate individual is much more agentive than the individual imagined in governmentality theory who not only is subjugated but also is a participant in self-subjugation. How might such an agency be theoretically situated? One source for a theoretical framing of the agentive individual within a social world can be found in the work of Hannah Arendt. Though Hannah Arendt (1998/1958) was a political philosopher who drew as a reference point, the totalitarianism of the Holocaust, her ideas about individual freedom as expressed by agency can be read to complement theoretical understandings of multimodal literacies. Three concepts will be explored here and related to multimodal literacy in terms of theoretical synchronicity. These concepts are potentiality, plurality and openness to unpredictability and unconventionality.

Potentiality

Potentiality is at the heart of much of the theorization in multimodal literacies. The idea of semiotic potential, an idea drawn from the work of Halliday (1978), is about the meaning of potential of signs. By framing signs in terms of meaning potential, the role of social interpretation in literacy events is foregrounded. Building on this foundation, multimodal literacies (Kress, 2000, 2003) extend our recognition of the range and nature of signs such that the idea of literacy is much more capacious and offers many different possibilities in terms of the signification of meaning.

Potentiality is also invoked by Arendt (1998/1958) when she argues that our *natality* offers a 'new beginning [for the world] ... because the newcomer possesses the capacity of beginning something anew, that is, of acting' (p. 9). She goes on to argue that 'the miracle that saves the world ... from its normal, 'natural' ruin is ultimately the fact of natality ... the action they [human beings] are capable of by virtue of being born' (p. 247). Rather than position human beings as doomed to a normalizing gaze that ultimately would lead to a stagnant, managed and tyrannical civilization, Arendt (1998/1958) starts out with hope and potential which are fundamental to agency. Yet, Arendt (1998/1958) does not dismiss the influence of the social but recognizes that when we enter the world we become part of 'the human condition. The impact of the world's reality upon human existence is felt and received as a conditioning force' (p. 9). How, then, is the potential we all have for action realized in relation to the human condition?

Plurality

Arendt (1998/1958) does not believe that we are ever conditioned absolutely (p. 11). Action and speech, Arendt (1998/1958) argues, are bound up in human plurality, which 'has the twofold character of equality and distinction' (p. 175). Taking her lead from the Greek word *archein*, Arendt (1998/1958) sees action as 'set[ting] something in motion' (p. 177) that is both unanticipated and that cannot be controlled.

In an unabashed burst of hope, Arendt (1998/1958) observes that 'the new always happens against the overwhelming odds of statistical laws and their probability, which for all practical, everyday purposes amounts to certainty' (p. 178). She invokes the social-relational when she argues that action and power happen only in relation to others, in other words, in relation to the many that exist on the earth. When people come together and act and speak together, a 'space of appearance' (Arendt, 1998/1958, p. 199) is realized by which they make known to others 'who' they are, as opposed to 'what' they are. Rather than being normalized, and assigned to particular categories, individuals have the room to reveal themselves.

Multimodal literacy theorist Gunther Kress (2003) also locates the starting point of his thinking about literacy with the idea of '*text* as the product of social action' (p. 84). Others too have written about the dynamic quality of multimodalities within social spaces. For instance, Baguley et al. (2010) observe that new communications technologies encourage multimodality and make literacy apparent

in many different formats many of which encourage multiple authorship through sites such as blogs and wikis. The social context of literacy has evolved from lone author/reader with a portable print based text to multimodal sites which can be created, constructed and shared with large numbers of people. (p. 7)

Plurality is at the centre of multimodality but this plurality also means an openness to others' ideas and expressions as a complementary part of multimodal thinking, something somewhat different than the unwitting embrace of individual subjugation suggested by Foucault's ideas of governmentality.

Openness to unpredictability and unconventionality

Whereas Foucault (1990) asks that 'power be understood … as the multiplicity of force relations immanent in the sphere in which they operate', (p. 92),

Arendt (1998/1958) sees power as 'always…a power potential and not an unchangeable, measurable, and reliable entity like force or strength' (p. 200); power can only be realized in the space of appearance, in the relationships among people. Arendt (1998/1958) argues that taking action is not making something…it is not 'merely a means to an end' (p. 179); rather, taking action is engaging in the plurality, in taking a chance on the unpredictability of action, in 'sharing a common human world with others who look at it from different perspectives [which] can enable us to see reality in the round and to develop a shared common sense'. (Canovan, 1998, xix)

This aspect of the unpredictability of multimodal literacies and their relation to communal power is captured by Kress (2010) when he states that:

> Previously 'convention' – the sedimentation of social power over time – could ensure adherence to practices in representation, for instance, the question in what mode canonical knowledge should be represented: whether as image…or in writing…or, what should count as official knowledge. Now these frames have virtually disappeared in many domains, including in the domain of formal education. (p. 25)

Theoretically, then, the combination of potentiality, plurality and an openness to unpredictability and unconventionality, drawn from the philosophy of Hannah Arendt, offers a view of the agentive individual who, instead of embracing the subjugation of convention and tradition, moves through the world in hope and with the possibility of taking action. This theoretical framing is in keeping with multimodal literacies as they have been described in the literature.

From agency to assessment?

Situating multimodal literacies in relation to educational assessment requires several moves to be made. These moves conceptualize educational assessment professionals as being epistemically responsible (Code, 1987, 2006); that is educational professionals must not only know well but must also 'do well' with what they know. In this positioning, educational professionals should continuously struggle with the question of thinking about what makes any assessment 'good enough' because they recognize that all assessments bear flaws and are, at best, partial ways of understanding whatever is being assessed (Murphy, 2009, 2013).

To understand what makes an assessment good-enough, the warrantability of the claims is paramount. Assessment professionals must martial argumentation and evidence in relation to a claim and evaluate the proffered argumentation and evidence of others making claims. Inevitably, questions arise about one's ethical responsibility in considering individual situations in relation to the warrants being offered because, as Code (1987) suggests, 'in some sense, ethical responsibility is founded upon epistemic responsibility, even if it is not identifiable with it' (p. 95).

Given the positioning of the agentive individual within multimodal literacies, what implications are there for multimodal literacy assessment? An epistemically responsibilist view would attempt to account for the idea of agency in multimodal literacy assessment by assuming particular stances towards potentiality, plurality, unpredictability and unconventionality. These stances, outlined below, would then form part of warrantability arguments about what makes a good-enough multimodal literacy assessment.

Remaining open to potential

Being open to potential in multimodal literacy assessment means that the architecture of multimodal literacy assessment must provide room for defensible novel (new) readings and constructions of multimodal texts. In other words, the normalizing gaze so associated with governmentality theory is replaced; instead, there is an expectancy that the newcomer to these literacies, because of their nature, has the potential for utilizing existing or new semiotic resources to engage in novel kinds of meaning-making. This conceptualization might seem a little radical, but it isn't.

One argument that might be launched against it is that the potential for newness cannot reside in the young or the novice because these individuals do not know the ways of the world; they are not familiar with multimodal literacies. Three responses can be offered to such comments.

1.   Such comments rely on the idea that insight is the province of the experienced. Yet, studies of modern contemporary artists reveal that some of these artists retain in their collections works of art by children from whom they borrow (Fineberg, 1997), which raises questions about the ethical stances towards the intellectual and aesthetic property of the young and the proposition that they do not have new things to say visually.

2.   The capacity of novices to create anew has not been focused upon because the dominant goal of the educational literature is on documenting moves *towards* convention; however, when the capacity to create anew is revealed it can be quite provocative. Consider the example of the development of the sadlamation point

(Goodman, 2003). This is a punctuation mark developed in graphic form and assigned a name by a young child who had written it in a composition about the death of a pet. Its teardrop-like shape with a circle underneath it illustrates that the child appropriated novel signification resources to punctuate and represent into national and affective meaning. This example illustrates that invention is well within the province of the young or inexperienced, but educational assessment professionals need to be attentive to that possibility; educational assessment professionals need to see the novice as being engaged in meaning-*making* rather than meaning *reproduction*.

3. The relatively rapid development of multimedia software means that there is considerable room for invention by meaning makers because conventions are not yet firmly established. Consider, for example, that according to Zickuhr (2013), in 1995 only 14 per cent of American adults 18 years of age and older used the Internet whereas in May, 2013 the near inverse was true with only 15 per cent of adults 18 years of age and older *not* using the Internet.

A deterministic multimodal literacy assessment – one which has specified in advance appropriate ways of interpreting and representing – would not be ethically responsible given the framing of multimodal literacies. In terms of assessment architecture, assessment forms that involve educational assessment professionals in 'reading' or 'interpreting' instances of students engaged in semiotic readings and representations and then providing argumentation in support of these readings and interpretations would be more in keeping with the epistemic base of multimodal literacies.

Recognizing plurality within semiotic interpretation and representation

If texts are inherently social (Kress, 2003), then an epistemically responsible assessment would include in it not only a way of recognizing the social aspects of text interpretation and production, but also of finding the distinctiveness of the individual within the social. Of course, recognition of the social underpinnings of the reading and the creation of texts would destabilize the individualistic orientation underpinning much typical educational assessment practice; it would complicate understandings of accountability as the individual would always need to be considered in relation to the specificity of the social – not in the grand normative sense but in the sense of recognizing how any particular instance and context could make possible particular ways of interpreting texts and representing meanings.

Recognition of the social does not mean erasure of the individual; rather it would draw on Arendt's (1998/1958) idea of the 'twofold character of equality and distinction' (p. 175). The individual has the opportunity to create interpretations and representations but these interpretations and representations are considered in relation to others. This task may seem impossible in a time of standards, however an example of embedding these ideas into standards can be found in a subset of the Alaska Standards for Culturally Responsive Schools (Alaska Native Knowledge Network, 1998):

[Standard] B. A culturally-responsive curriculum recognizes cultural knowledge as part of a living and constantly adapting system that is grounded in the past, but continues to grow through the present and into the future. (p. 14)

[Standard] D. A culturally-responsive curriculum fosters a complementary relationship across knowledge derived from diverse knowledge systems.

A curriculum that meets this cultural standard … engages students in the construction of new knowledge and understandings that contribute to an ever expanding view of the world. (p. 15)

These descriptions mean that multimodal literacy assessments must have sufficient flexibility and elasticity in them to stretch towards appreciating the new practices offered by the individual while maintaining a critical understanding of the accepted practices of interpretation or representation, and yet understand that each text represents a layered social history (Rowsell & Pahl, 2007). These ideas of flexibility and elasticity very much hinge on what multimodal literacy knowledge is.

Viewing multimodal literacy knowledge as open to the unpredictable and unconventional

To situate the unpredictable and unconventional with respect to multimodal literacies, a logical point of departure is to juxtapose it with the predictable and conventional. Do multimodal literacies have conventions? Are they predictable? Jewitt (2008), in a review essay on multimodal literacies, argues that 'how knowledge is represented, as well as the mode and media chosen, is a crucial aspect of knowledge construction' (p. 241) and a foundational epistemic premise of multimodal literacies. She goes on to talk about the ways in which modes have been studied in terms of 'semiotic resources, their material affordances, organizing principles, and cultural referents' (p. 246), noting that 'all modes are partial ... [and] contribute to the construction of meaning in different ways' (p. 247). Some aspects of multimodal literacies have been highly specified. For example, one semiotic resource noted by Jewitt (2008) is Kress and van Leeuwen's (1996, 2006) grammar of visual design which draws upon Halliday's (1978) ideas of describing language in use. Similar aspects of multimodal literacies as those itemized by Jewitt (2008) are described by Stornaiuolo et al. (2009), who focus on 'the coordination of modes, interplay of process and product, and everyday contexts' (p. 386), and Wyatt-Smith and Kimber (2009), who identify six central concepts of multimodality: design, visualization of literacy, modes and modal affordances, transmodal operation, cohesion and staged multimodality.

These descriptions of structure, relations and context are about language in use (Halliday, 1978). As such, because of the centrality of language in use to multimodal literacy theory, there will always be an openness to the unpredictable and unconventional. Just as the idea of multimodal literacies evolved from new understandings about the visual in the reading of word-based texts and about the relation between image and word in the texts for children (e.g. Fabrizio et al., 1967; Wendt, 1979; Haber, 1981; Gilreath, 1993; Laspina, 1998; Seki, 2000; Walker, 2012), our understandings of what multimodal literacies are, the ways meaning can be signified and the potential that resides in this way of thinking about literacy continue to evolve (e.g. Provenzo et al., 2011). Yet, even with this context of the knowledge of multimodal literacies as evolving, Kress and van Leeuwen (2006) observe that because 'visual communication is coming to be less and less the domain of specialists ... this will lead to ... more formal normative teaching' (p. 3) and 'only a small elite of experimenters is allowed to break the rules' (p. 3). Such formal normative approaches to teaching, and assessment in particular, can close down the possibility of the emergence of the unpredictable and unconventional in semiotic interpretation and representation as well as eliminate the possibility for distinctiveness amid the social, and essentially eliminate the 'space of appearance' (Arendt, 1998/1958, p. 199) in which individuals make known who they are.

Even though, as noted earlier, Kress (2010) observed that multimodal literacies have had a tremendous effect on destabilizing 'convention', the worry lurks that somehow multimodal literacies will become the new handmaiden of governmentality. Just as worded texts on paper were, to borrow a phrase from Hannah Arendt (1998/1958), the 'common world' of literacy in that 'everybody ... [was] always concerned with the same object' (pp. 57–58), multimodal texts are set to become the common objects of contemporary society. Assessment efforts that do not recognize that multimodal literacies differ from earlier conceptualizations of literacy will err in representing the knowledge of those assessed.

What can be done about this state of affairs? First of all, the knowledge about what multimodal literacies are must inform assessment without overly inscribing it. To date, efforts to incorporate the visual into assessments have not recognized the layers of signification within multimodal representations. For instance, in one study of tests which incorporated images, Unsworth and Chan (2009) report that questions with images accompanying them were much more difficult tasks than those without images because, depending upon the particular test question, the images bore different relations to the word based texts and therefore demanded different reading and interpretation strategies for each type of signification.

Because multimodal literacies are epistemically rooted in a situated way of knowing, they need to be assessed in a way that affords meaning makers the opportunity to defend their interpretations and representations. This type of assessment is demanding as it means that the *a priori* all-knowing 'other' of the large-scale assessment who sits with 'the correct' responses must be replaced by persons who carefully consider interpretations and representations, make sense of them and also provide warrants as to their sense making. This type of assessment is a discursive one which sees both the assessed and the assessor as staking out and defending claims about interpretation and representation. It also demands of assessors a strong ethical stance (see Murphy, 2013) which:

- Understands that assessments may have consequences for students and single assessments should not bear extraordinary consequences

- Understands that 'the representational possibilities for knowing offered by assessment designs should be acknowledged as limiting some representations while enabling others' (p. 563)

- Understands that one's own epistemic location has limits and that these limits are bounded by practices within the epistemic community which has its own set of values

- Understands one's own interests within any assessment and takes steps to ensure that these interests do not impinge on the ways in which we are working with ideas of multimodal literacies

- Remains open to the new in terms of thinking about assessment as a form of the interpretation and representation of knowledge.

Towards action

What motivates action? What stirs one to take one's place among the many and to engage in the possibility of beginning something new? That action is already occurring within multimodal literacies but needs to be more present and articulated more clearly in terms of the assessment of multimodal literacies. Arendt (1978/1971) suggests that the 'motives for action may be certain designs, desires, passions, and goals' (p. 180), or as Thompson (2012), drawing on Frankfurt (1998) suggests, the motives for action are found in what we care about. The prevalence of multimodal literacies suggests that we value or care about them. Given the description of the agentive individual that I have argued underlies multimodal literacies, I think that the field of assessment may well learn the same types of values dispositions in representing multimodal literacies in educational systems.

References

Adams, M. J. (1990). *Beginning to Read: Thinking and Learning about Print.* Boston: MIT Press.

Alaska Native Knowledge Network. (1998). *Alaska standards for culturally responsive schools.* Anchorage, Alaska. Retrieved from http://ankn.uaf.edu/publications/standards.html

Alverman, D. E., & Hagood, M.C. (2000). Critical media literacy: Research, theory, and practice in "New Times." *Journal of Educational Research, 93*(3), 193–205.

Anderson, C. (2008, June 23). The end of theory: The data deluge makes the scientific method obsolete. *Wired.* http://www.wired.com/science/discoveries/magazine/16-07/pb_theory/

Arendt, H. (1978/1971). *The Life of the Mind.* Orlando: Harcourt.

———. (1998/1958). *The Human Condition* (2nd edition). Chicago: University of Chicago Press.

Baguley, M., Pullen, D. L., & Short, M. (2010). Multiliteracies and the new world order. In D. L. Pullen & D. R. Cole (Eds), *Multiliteracies and Technology-Enhanced Education: Social Practice and the Global Classroom* (pp. 1–15). New York: Information Science Reference.

Bevir, M. (2010). Rethinking governmentality: Towards genealogies of governance. *European Journal of Social Theory, 13*(4), 423–441.

Björklund Boistrup, L. Governing through implicit and explicit assessment acts: Multimodality in mathematics classrooms. In M. Hamilton, R. Heydon, K. Hibbert, & R. Stooke (Eds), *Negotiating Spaces for Literacy Learning.* London: Bloomsbury/Continuum.

Brass, J. (2010). The sweet tyranny of creating one's own life: Rethinking power and freedom in English teaching. *Educational Theory, 60*(6), 703–717.

Burke, A., & Hammett, R. F. (Eds) (2009). *Assessing New Literacies: Perspectives from the Classroom*. New York: Peter Lang.

Canovan, M. (1998). Introduction. In H. Arendt, *The Human Condition* (2nd edition, pp. vii–xx). Chicago: University of Chicago Press.

Chan, C., & Choo, S. (2009). *Introducing a multimodal framework in English language reading assessment*. Proceedings of the Second International Conference of Teaching and Learning, INTI University College, Malaysia. 1–17. Retrieved from http://ictl.intimal.edu.my/ictl2009/proceedings/index.html

Code, L. (1987). Epistemic *Responsibility*. London: University Press of New England.

———. (2006). *Ecological Thinking: The Politics of Epistemic Location*. New York: Oxford UP.

Cumming, J., Kimber, K., & Wyatt-Smith, C. (2012). Enacting policy, curriculum and teacher conceptualisations of multimodal literacy and English in assessment and accountability. *English in Australia, 47*(1), 9–18.

Curwood, J.S. (2012). Cultural shifts, multimodal representations, and assessment practices: A case study. *E-learning and Digital Media, 9*(2), 232–244, http://dx.doi.org/10.2304/elea.2012.9.2.232.

Daly, A., & Unsworth, L. (2011). Analysis and comprehension of multimodal texts. *Australian Journal of Language and Literacy, 34*(1), 61–80.

Educational Quality and Accountability Office. (n.d.). Retrieved from http://www.eqao.com/

Fabrizio, R., Kaplan, I., & Teal, G. (1967). Readability as a function of the straightness of right-hand margins. *Journal of Typographic Research, 1*(1), 90–95.

FairTest. (2013). *Why teacher evaluation shouldn't rest on student test scores*. Retrieved from http://www.fairtest.org/why-teacher-evaluation-shouldn%E2%80%99t-rest-student-test

Fineberg, J. (1997). *The Innocent Eye: Children's Art and the Modern Artist*. Princeton: Princeton University Press.

Foucault, M. (1990/1978). *The History of Sexuality* (Trans. by R. Hurley). London: Penguin.

———. (1991/1978). Governmentality. In G. Burchell, C. Gordon, & P. Miller (Eds), *The Foucault Effect: Studies in Governmentality* (pp. 87–104). Chicago: University of Chicago Press.

———. (1995). *Discipline and punish* (Trans. by A. Sheridan, 1977). New York: Random House.

Frankfurt, J. G. (1998). *The Importance of What We Care About*. Cambridge: Cambridge University Press.

Gilreath, C. T. (1993). Graphic cueing of text: The typographic and diagraphic dimensions. *Visible Language, 27*(3), 337–361.

Goddard, R. (2010). Critiquing the educational present: The (limited) usefulness to educational research of the Foucauldian approach to governmentality. *Educational Philosophy and Theory, 42*(3), 345–360. doi: 10.1111/j.1469-5812-2008.00456.x

Goodman, Y. (2003). *Valuing Language Study: Inquiry into Language for Elementary and Middle Schools*. Urbana: National Council of Teachers of English.

Graham, C., & Neu, D. (2004). Standardized testing and the construction of governable persons. *Journal of Curriculum Studies, 36*(3), 295–319.

Gruenewald, D. A. (2005). Accountability and collaboration: Institutional barriers and strategic pathways for place-based education. *Ethics, Place and Environment, 8*(2) 261–283. doi: 10.1080/13668790500348208

Gunzenhauser, M. G. (2006). Normalizing the educated subject: A Foucauldian analysis of high-stakes accountability. *Educational Studies, 39*(3), 241–258.

Haber, R. N. (1981). Visual components of the reading process. *Visible Language, 15*(2), 147–182.

Hacking, I. (1990). The *Taming of Chance*. Cambridge: Cambridge University Press.

Halliday, M. A. K. (1978). *Language as Social Semiotic: The Social Interpretation of Meaning and Language*. London: Edward Arnold.

Hillocks, G. W. (2002). *The Testing Trap: How State Writing Assessments Control Learning*. New York: Teachers College Press.

Jewitt, C. (2003). Re-thinking assessment: Multimodality, literacy and computer-mediated learning. *Assessment in Education, 10*(1), 83–102. doi: 10.1080/0969594032000085767

Jewitt, C. (2008). Multimodality and literacy in school classrooms. *Review of Research in Education, 32*, 241–267. doi: 10.3102/0091732X07310586

Kerr, D. (1999). Beheading the king and enthroning the marked: A critique of Foucauldian governmentality. *Science and Society, 63*(2), 173–202.

Kress, G. (2000). Design and transformation: New theories of meaning. In B. Cope & M. Kalantzis (Eds), *Multiliteracies: Literacy Learning and the Design of Social Futures* (pp. 153–161). London: Routledge.

———. (2003). *Literacy in the New Media Age*. London: Routledge.

———. (2010). *Multimodality: A Social Semiotic Approach to Contemporary Communication*. New York: Routledge.

Kress, G., & Van Leeuwen, T. (1996). *The Grammar of Visual Design* (1st edition). London: Routledge.

———. (2006). *The Grammar of Visual Design* (2nd edition). London: Routledge.

Levitt, R. (2008). Freedom and empowerment: A transformative pedagogy of educational reform. *Educational Studies, 44*, 47–61.

Laspina, J. A. (1998). *The Visual Turn and the Transformation of the Textbook*. London: Routledge.

Lohr, S. (2012, February 11). The age of big data. The New York Times Sunday Review: The Opinion Pages. http://www.nytimes.com/2012/02/12/sunday-review/big-datas-impact-in-the-world.html?pagewanted=all

McDermott, K. A. (2011). *High-stakes Reform: The Politics of Educational Accountability*. Washington: Georgetown University Press.

McDonnell, L. M. (2004). *Politics, Persuasion, and Educational Testing*. Cambridge: Harvard University Press.

Meadmore, D. (2001). Uniformly testing diversity? National testing examined. *Asia-Pacific Journal of Teacher Education, 29*(1), 19–28.

Meyer, H. (2013, Dec. 19). OECD's PISA: A tale of flaws and hubris. Teachers College Record. http://www.tcrecord.org ID Number: 17371

Murphy, S. (2009). Matters of goodness: Knowing well and doing well in the assessment of critical thinking. In J. Sobocan & L. Groarke (Eds), *Critical*

Thinking Education and Assessment: Can Higher Order Thinking Be Tested? (pp. 331–339) London, ON: Althouse Press.

———. (2010). The pull of PISA: Uncertainty, influence, and ignorance. *Inter-American Journal of Education for Democracy, 3*(1), 28–44.

———. (2013). Towards knowing well and doing well: Assessment in early childhood education. In N. Hall, J Larson, & J. Marsh (Eds), *Handbook of Early Childhood Literacy* (2nd edition; pp. 561–574). London: Sage.

Nathan, L. F. (2009). *The Hardest Questions* aren't *on the Test: Lessons from an Innovative Urban School.* Boston: Beacon Press.

Pongratz, L. A. (2006). Voluntary self-control: Education reform as a governmental strategy. *Educational Philosophy and Theory, 38*(4), 471–482.

Provenzo, E. F., Goodwin, A., Lipsky, M., & Sharpe, S. (Eds) (2011). *Multiliteracies: Beyond Text and the Written Word.* Charlotte: Information Age.

Raptis, H. (2012). Ending the reign of the Fraser Institute's school rankings. *Canadian Journal of Education, 35*(1), 187–201.

Rautalin, M., & Alasuutari, P. (2009). The uses of the national PISA results by Finnish officials in central government. *Journal of Education Policy, 24*(5), 539–556.

Rowsell, J., & Pahl, K. (2007). Sedimented identities in texts: Instances of practice. *Reading Research Quarterly, 42*(3), 388–404.

Seki, Y. (2000). Using lists to improve text access: The role of layout in reading. *Visible Language, 34*(3). 280–295.

Simons, M., & Masschelein, J. (2006). The learning society and governmentality: An introduction. *Educational Philosophy and Theory, 38*(4), 417–430.

Sokhi-Bulley, B. (2011). Governing (through) rights: Statistics as technologies of governmentality. *Social and Legal Studies, 20*(2), 139–155. doi: 10.1177/0964663910391520

Stornaiuolo, A., Hull, G, & Nelson, M. E. (2009). Mobile texts and migrant audiences: Rethinking literacy and assessment in new media age. *Language Arts, 86*(5), 382–392.

Testing and Assessment (n.d.). Retrieved from http://www.education.gov.uk/schools/teachingandlearning/assessment

Thomas, R. M. (2005). *High Stakes Testing: Coping with Collateral Damage.* Mahwah: Erlbaum.

Thompson, M. (2012). *Goodness, promise, and importance: Perspectives on cultivating democratic education in an age of accountability.* Ph.D dissertation, Graduate Program in Education, York University, Toronto, Canada.

Towndrow, P. A., Nelson, M. E., & Yusef, W. F. B. M. (2013). Squaring literacy assessment with multimodal design: An analytic case for semiotic awareness. *Journal of Literacy Research, 45*(4), 327–355.

Unsworth, L. (2006). Towards a metalanguage for multiliteracies education: Describing the meaning-making resources of language-image interaction. *English Teaching: Practice and Critique, 5*(1), 55–76.

Unsworth, L., & Chan, E. (2009). Bridging multimodal literacies and national assessment programs in literacy. *Australian Journal of Language and Literacy, 32*(3), 245–257.

Valli, L., Croninger, R. G., Chambliss, M. J., Graeber, A. O., & Buese, D. (2008). *Test Driven: High-stakes Accountability in Elementary Schools.* New York: Teachers College Press.

Volante, T., & Earl, L. (2013, June). Standards, accountability, and student assessment systems: An international overview. Education Canada. Retrieved from http://www.cea-ace.ca/education-canada/article/standards-accountability-and-student-assessment-systems

Walker, S. (2012). Describing the design of children's books: An analytical approach. *Visible Language, 46*(3), 180–199.

Walsh, M. (2010). Multimodal literacy: What does it mean for classroom practice? *Australian Journal of Language and Literacy, 23*(3), 211–229.

Wang, J. (2003). Preface. In J. Wang (Ed.), *Data Mining: Opportunities and Challenges* (pp. vii–xii). Hershey: Idea Group Publishing.

Wendt, D. (1979). An experimental approach to the improvement of the typographic design of textbooks. *Visible Language, 13*(2), 108–133.

World Economic Forum. (2012). Big data, big impact: New possibilities for international development. Retrieved from http://www.weforum.org/reports/big-data-big-impact-new-possibilities-international-development

Wyatt-Smith, C., & Kimber, K. (2009). Working multimodally: Challenges for assessment. *English Teaching: Practice and Critique, 8*(3), 70–90.

Zickuhr, K. (2013, Sept. 25). *Who's not online and why.* Washington: *Pew Research Center's Internet and American Life Project.* Retrieved from http://www.pewinternet.org/~/media//Files/Reports/2013/PIP_Offline%20 adults_092513_PDF

3

Re-centring the Role of Care in Young People's Multimodal Literacies: A Collaborative Seeing Approach

Claire Fontaine and Wendy Luttrell

As globalized educational policy increasingly incorporates multimodal literacies into the definition of an educated person and estimations of human capital (Rizvi & Lingard, 2010), particular literacies are valued and privileged while others are devalued. For instance, expertise in the processes of digital media production – animation, video editing, sound engineering, game design – is prized, while that in more socially oriented practices – like the use of social networking sites and video chatting programs – is stigmatized by educators (Sims, 2014). Engaging in valued digital media practices, those most likely to be framed as multimodal literacies, allows young people to locate themselves on the 'right' side of the 'participation gap' (Jenkins et al., 2006) or 'participation divide' (Hargittai & Walejko, 2008).

Meanwhile, technological developments are leveraged to support narrow assessments of young people's knowledge and identities, and young people's goodness, normalcy and value are distorted through the force of educational standards and measures – as if these standards are given not made. There are complex metrics-based systems for classifying, labelling, evaluating, ranking and monitoring children and their knowledge, but schools have rarely devised equally meaningful and useful strategies for hearing, seeing, knowing and understanding children as full human beings and knowing subjects. Far too often, schools are simply 'voicing over' children's experiences from 'adultist' perspectives (Thorne, 2002).

Collaborative seeing is an iterative and reflexive practice of inquiry that combines elements of visual and narrative analysis (Lico & Luttrell, 2011; Luttrell, 2010) to address the structural imbalance of power between children and adults (James, Jenks & Prout, 1998). It aims to preserve the multiplicity of meanings that are co-constructed between researchers and researched, teachers and learners. In the *Children Framing Childhoods* project, thirty-six young people were given cameras and invited to take photos of what matters in their lives over a period of eight years. The participants were afforded numerous opportunities to construct meaning around these photographs. Among the salient themes in the resulting archive of data were images and narratives of young people's digital media practices, including their gaming, blogging, video-making, computer usage at home and in school and diverse uses of mobile devices. Following a structured, sequenced immersion intended to catalyse researcher/adult reflexivity about what is seen and interpreted about working class children and working class childhoods, researchers engaged in 'stereophonic listening' (Charon, 2006) to pick up on young people's resistance to regulation and their claims of value and worth. This helped attune our eyes and ears to the role of longing, constraint, difficulty, complexity and contradiction in inspiring what young people do when they spend time online.

This methodology illuminates often-unseen dynamics of young people's own understandings of their digital media practices and the ways that these understandings are shaped by the context of the contradictory tensions produced by digital technologies and globalized educational policies. We found that young people represent their practices in relation to their care worlds and ambivalently position themselves relative to dominant cultural discourses about limiting screen time and risky behaviour online. The forces of care and love, generally neglected in politics and scholarship (Feeley, 2009; Lynch, Baker & Lyons, 2009), are also under-theorized in relation to multimodal literacies. This understanding provides a useful counterbalance to overly instrumental assessments of kids' time online, which typically focus on how human capital is enhanced by mastery of particular modes of digital media practice.

Three elements of collaborative seeing

Although the *Children Framing Childhoods* project (2003–2012) coincides with the explosion of 'giving kids cameras' research (Clark, 1999; Orellana, 1999; Rasmussen, 1999; Rich & Chalfen, 1999; Clark-Ibanez, 2004; Burke, 2005; Tinkler, 2008; Luttrell & Chalfen, 2010; Yates, 2010; Pini & Walkerdine, 2011; Kaplan, 2013; to name a few), three features of the collaborative seeing approach distinguish it from these other projects. The first is the extent of the iterative and co-constructed flow of meaning-making generated by numerous audiencing opportunities. Second is the particular analytic approach – a sequenced immersion in the visual and audio-visual material intended to catalyse researcher/adult reflexivity about what is seen and interpreted about children and childhood. Third is a way of looking with and listening to the children.

Iterative and co-constructed meaning-making

In the early phase of the project (2003–2009), thirty-six elementary school students in Worcester, Massachusetts were given a disposable camera (now an ancient technology) with twenty-seven exposures and had four days to photograph their everyday lives, at home, school and in their communities and 'whatever matters most'.[1] Students participated in the project as fifth graders and again as sixth graders. The project was originally designed to bring the children's experiences and perspectives about immigration, social and cultural differences and family–school relationships more fully into view. A microcosm of Worcester and its century-long history of diverse and shifting waves of immigration, the school enrolled 370 students, of whom 92 per cent were eligible for free school lunch, 37 per cent were white, 10 per cent were black, 18 per cent were Asian and 35 per cent were Hispanic;[2] the children who participated represented the linguistic, racial and ethnic diversity of the school.

After the photographs were developed, Wendy or a research assistant met with each child to talk about her/his images, asking why she/he had taken them, what pictures she/he wanted to take but couldn't, to select personal favourites, and to select photos to share with teachers and a larger public. Then we met in small groups with the children to discuss each others' photos. In these groups, the adults held back from directing the conversations, letting the children direct their questions, comments and 'noticings' to each other. All the interviews and small group conversations were audio and video recorded so that we would be able to trace how context mattered. For example, when speaking with the interviewer about a photograph he had taken of his church, 10-year old Gabriel turned to the video camera and spoke directly to his mother, 'Mommy, I took this picture for you, I'm sorry it is blurry'. This was one of several photographs he had taken to express his love and gratitude for his mother, 'I love her so much I could explode from too much'. But in conversation with his peers, Gabriel emphasized that he had taken the picture because it is where he goes to 'hang with the teenagers' who invite him to join their activities even though he is 'only in fifth grade', highlighting the dual worlds children inhabit as they seek status with peers.

In the later phase of the project (2009–2012), the young people had spread out and only some could be contacted through school. Many were connected through Facebook, however, and Wendy was able to track down twenty-six of the thirty-six original participants. Most greeted her with astonishment: 'I can't believe you really came back!' was a familiar refrain. All agreed to be interviewed about their childhood photographs and to reflect upon the ways in which they and their lives had and had not changed. These audiotaped interviews were rich with memories, laughter and sometimes embarrassment about a 'past self' or 'child self' as some put it. Most of the participants agreed to continue by taking photographs to document their contemporary life-worlds. The four young people who decided not to continue participating gave varied reasons, including work and family care-giving responsibilities.

In this next phase of the project, each young person was again given an analogue disposable camera and asked to photograph 'what matters most'. Analogue cameras were chosen over digital cameras for two reasons. First, although young people now had cameras on their phones, not all of them did, and over the course of the year, some had to cancel their phone service because of limited finances. Second, using analogue cameras allowed us to keep the imposed limitation of twenty-seven exposures. Participants selected their five favourite photographs, which they assembled and narrated using VoiceThread, a programme that allows users to upload photographs and create audio and text-based commentary. To facilitate dialogue among participants in different school settings, VoiceThreads were shared among group members, and the young people posted questions and comments on each other's 'threads'. Participants were also given Flip video cameras to record themselves at home, with family, at school, in their neighbourhoods and with friends. The decision to introduce video – the youth participants' preferred medium – was grounded in a recognition of the benefits of involving young people in decisions about representing their lives, an insight from Wendy's research with pregnant teens (Luttrell, 2003). We presented the project in open-ended terms 'Make a short video about you, your world, or your life' and provided no instructions or guidance with regard to composition, light, narrative or camera work. Ethical considerations were discussed at length, building upon the project's earlier role-playing about issues related to intrusion, embarrassment and consent. This later phase of the project was similarly informed by a commitment to providing multiple spaces and opportunities for the young people to speak about their image making.

Collaborative seeing is thus distinguished by the extent of the iterative and co-constructed flow of meaning-making generated by numerous audiencing sessions – *between* a child and his/her intended audience; *between* the child and the interviewer; *among* the children themselves; *between* the children and an intended teacher/public audience; and finally *the self as audience over time*, as a particular strength of this study lies in its longitudinal orientation.

A structured, sequenced immersion

Our analytic approach, which involves a sequenced immersion in the visual and audio-visual material, is intended to catalyse researcher/adult reflexivity about what is seen and interpreted about working-class children and working-class childhoods. Wendy developed this approach to structure graduate students' introduction to the images, first at the Harvard Graduate School of Education (HGSE) (2004–2009) and later at the CUNY Graduate Center (2010–2015). In these courses, students begin by looking across the images, taking time to identify where they fix their eyes and what questions they have. Then students develop a categorization scheme for the photos. These schemes inevitably vary but frequently include descriptive groupings like 'people, places, things'; settings like 'school, family, community'; activities such 'work, consumption, leisure, literacy'; as well as more interpretive groupings like 'what I am proud of, what I am concerned about'. What is most salient about the images varies by student. For Claire, who took the course in the spring of 2011, the sheer quantity of screen photos attracted her attention. Indeed, an early content analysis conducted with the HGSE students had found that screens – boxy televisions of various sizes, tiny screens on flip-style cell phones, shared home computers and many almost identical photos of the new school computer lab – were the most frequently photographed category of items in the children's image galleries at ages 10 and 12.

Following the categorization exercise, students move more deeply into the practice of looking by drawing on Howard Becker's guidelines (1986, p. 232) for working with images. He writes:

> Don't stare and thus stop looking; look actively ... you'll find it useful to take up the time by naming everything in the picture to yourself and writing up notes.

After building up capacity for attention to detail, he encourages observers to engage in

> a period of fantasy, telling yourself a story about the people and things in the picture. The story needn't be true, it's just a device for externalizing and making clear to yourself the emotion and mood the picture has evoked, both part of its statement.

Immersed in these retro-seeming images from the pre-smartphone pre-touchscreen era, Claire noted her own discomfort with the many photos of televisions and gaming consoles perched atop cabinets and makeshift stands in children's bedrooms, often amid elaborate arrangements of toys, figurines and other collectibles. Particularly troubling were the plentitude of photos of televisions in Mesha's fifth-grade gallery, suggestive of the ways television is popularly conceived of and portrayed, 'as an addiction, as a passive, individual activity which precludes direct communication with others, as an impediment to fulfilling family relationships … [all of which] are thought to increase in direct proportion to the amount of time the television is turned on in the home' (Seiter et al., 1989, p. 1). Absorption in these images led to Claire's imaginings of 'lonely and unsafe after-school hours' (Strandell, 2013, p. 1), and contrasted with a nostalgic ideal of a 'good' childhood, meaning a less mediated and commercialized one, filled with grass and bikes, suntanned faces and dips in the kiddy pool.

Recalling Becker's (1986) advice to use storytelling to externalize and 'make clear to yourself the emotion and mode the picture has evoked', Claire thought of her own youth, coming up in the 1980s, in a neighbourhood of working folks, modest ranch houses and old cars, in the tiny city of Portland, Maine, noshing on fresh-plucked lettuces, ears of corn, and heirloom tomatoes from the backyard garden and roaming the streets with the neighbourhood kids until the sun set. These imaginings were accompanied by a certain melancholy and a sense of loss of the Rousseauian 'free child' – the child who enjoys spatial and temporal autonomy, and plays unstructured by adults (Hart, 1979). At the same time, Claire noted her own subtly positive reaction to other types of screen photos across the galleries, especially those of the newly installed school computer lab and of home computers. She imagined these represented the children's, and their parents', pride, upward mobility and valuing of schooling.

Reflecting on the emotions raised by this disciplined practice of looking, naming, fantasizing and storytelling, Claire became aware that she was drawing implicitly on a good screen/bad screen dichotomy, rooted not only in nostalgia but also in an evaluative teacher identity, reflecting a germ of belief in a 'strong theory' of media effects (Seiter, 1999), typical of teachers and childcare professionals. This realization highlighted the ways that screens can function as symbolic scapegoats and saviours, with the wrong kinds, or wrong uses, linked in adult imaginations, popular perception and paediatric knowledge to the potential degrading of young people's brains, bodies and educational trajectories (American Academy of Pediatrics, 2011). Meanwhile, the right kinds and uses are linked to white-collar work and 'the power to control information' (Scheck, 1985, p. 284), upward mobility (Persell & Cookson, 1987) and enhanced human capital (Keeley, 2007), particularly for girls and women (AAUW, 2000; Margolis & Fisher 2002).

Only after completing this activity do graduate students view the video clips of the children speaking about their images. Upon hearing what the children have to say, there are moments of surprise, pride (for 'getting it right') and embarrassment or guilt for making 'wrong' assumptions – especially a tendency to see the photographs through the lens of their own (predominantly white, middle-class) childhoods; to see deficiencies in the student's lives; to misrecognize strengths; and, at times to assign blame. It is this structured, sequenced immersion that makes adult viewers (as teachers or researchers) aware of, and able to reflect upon, their own projections onto children's images, knowledge and intentions.

Stereophonic listening

The third distinguishing element of collaborative seeing is its commitment to a way of looking with and listening to the children, inspired by what Rita Charon calls 'stereophonic listening' (2006, p. 97). Charon is writing about narrative medicine, and what is needed in the exchange between patients who are speaking about their illnesses and medical professionals who are committed to caring for the sick. To listen fully means being able to 'hear the body and the person who inhabits it'. Charon suggests that there has been 'an odd diminishment of the status of storytelling in medicine ever since we decided we knew enough about the body by virtue of reducing it to its parts that we did not need to hear out its inhabitant' (2005, p. 261). This is a fitting metaphor for what has happened in contemporary educational policy and practice – the reduction of children's knowing, being and doing to its measurable parts.

André Turmel (2008), among others, has written about the changing social technologies (recording methods, graphs, charts, tables, etc.) that focus attention on children in specific ways, as if these ways were the only way to know, understand or value a child. The everyday classroom activities of classification, 'standardization' and identifying how a child measures up (or not), is the water in which children swim in school. Insofar as processes of standardization have narrowed the spaces for diverse expressions of young people's everyday informal practices, interests and funds of knowledge (Gonzalez et al., 2005), it is all the more important that we are able to hear the 'student' body and the young person who inhabits it.

Listening stereophonically to the children's narrations of their many screen photos, we attended especially to regulation and resistance, and tried to hear the ways that the children were making their worth visible and thus intelligible. For instance, Mesha's fifth-grade image gallery was dominated by photos of a muscular female character captured during 'cut scenes', or cinematic interludes between sections of game play. In conversation with Wendy about these images, Mesha spoke longingly of past afternoons with her father, who now works in the night shift and 'he's so busy, we don't have that time to go play together anymore'. Mesha recounted taking pleasure in after-school gaming sessions with friends and how they 'used to have a lot of fun together', and described the rituals that framed these gatherings – cleaning up wires, organizing the controllers – as a kind of social glue that bound them together. As she explained that the game is fun because 'you get to beat up monsters' and 'you get to be any character you like', we realized that what we had originally read as photos *of* television screens, were meant to be photos of what was *on* the screen, in this case, Yuna, the female protagonist, practitioner of healing magic and one of the main playable characters in the role-playing game Final Fantasy Ten.

This realization opened up new possibilities and questions about Mesha's digital literacy. Perhaps she took the photographs to document her advanced skill and high level of achievement in this male-dominated niche interest (Cassell & Jenkins, 1998; Taylor, 2009; Kafai et al., 2008). Or was she making an identity claim by signalling her identification with this powerful female protagonist? Maybe these photos were references to the social contexts of her gaming, rather than the solitary ones. Or perhaps this was the first step in her process of articulating a critique, echoed by radical feminist gaming scholars (Bucholtz, 1998, 2002; Sunden, 2009) of the gendered structuring of geek identity. From this perspective, girls' and women's claims of time and space to develop esoteric, specialized expertise in domains like gaming, where such expertise is typically linked to constructions of hegemonic masculinity (Connell & Messerschmidt, 2005), are regarded as resisting a patriarchal order that is predicated on women's and girls' moderation in pursuing such focused endeavours, while permitting men's and boys' enthusiastic escape into arenas of geek pleasure.

The answers to these questions would become clearer over time and with more probing into Mesha's use of gaming as a multimodal literacy practice and marker of her gender identity as a 'strong woman'. Indeed, when invited by Claire to participate in a follow-up project about 'what teenage girls know about technology that adults don't know that they know', she immediately exclaimed, 'You've come to the right person!' With an imitation of an upper class British accent, Mesha invited Claire to her family house to play games and share 'tea and crumpets'. Mesha's adaptation of the research protocol, which originally called for the youth-led digital media tutorial to be held in a school conference room, was noteworthy in at least three ways. First, it signalled that Mesha felt comfortable and trusting enough of Claire to invite her into her home as the site of her digital literacy practices. Second, it reinforced the idea that Mesha understands her technological expertise as an outside-of-school activity. Third, her 'tea and crumpets' comment recalls Pini and Walkerdine's (2011) account of the way working-class girls put on more 'posh' accents and middle-class affects in their video diaries. It suggests an awareness of the intimacy of having a researcher in one's home across race-, class-, age- and education-based differences and how these differences might shape expectations of the encounter. On the appointed day, Mesha answered the door wearing dark-washed blue jeans and a deep black, freshly laundered and impeccably ironed black t-shirt, emblazoned in white lettering with the prominent logo, 'Strong, Smart, Bold', a choice of clothing perhaps reflecting her desire to be seen just in those terms. And indeed, as she launched into a two and a half hour, enthusiastic and extensively detailed introduction to six of her favourite games on the Play Station 3 gaming console, she schooled Claire in the politics of gender, power and value that attend in these virtual spaces, and their intersections with the pressing financial, emotional and familial challenges of her daily life described in the next section.

Care networks, governmentality and multimodal literacy

Well-designed games are considered valuable spaces for negotiating literacy (Gee, 2003; Gee & Hayes, 2011), requiring gamers to navigate complex environments, learn by doing and produce themselves as flexible learners, thus demonstrating competencies that are in line with the criteria of being a 'lifelong learner' – a neoliberal form of governmentality. A lifelong learner works actively in 'communities of learners' and engages in a 'continuous course of personal responsibilities and self management of one's risks and destiny' (Popkewitz & Lindblad, 2004, p. 238). These values – of being thoughtful and 'productive' about one's uses of time and aiming towards continuous self improvement – are deeply embedded in global educational policy and schooling ideologies.

Mesha's identity as a gamer was already well established when she began participating in *Children Framing Childhoods* as a fifth grader. She sustained her avid gaming practice through her high school graduation, but her ways of narrating her gaming shifted over these eight years. Ten-year-old Mesha accounted for her daily after-school routine by emphasizing first doing her homework before playing games, watching movies or engaging in other 'leisure' activities. This is exemplary of the ways the children made identity claims through their photography (Tinkler, 2008), as a 'good' student (reading or doing homework); as a grateful/loving son or daughter (Luttrell et al., 2011);

as 'boys' or 'girls' (Luttrell, 2012); and as soon-to-be teenagers. However, eighteen-year-old Mesha offered a more nuanced accounting of her gaming time:

> It's kind of like my getaway, like from reality. You don't have to be stressed out about anything, just get on. You don't have to worry about anything, just get on and go. But you still have to be worried. You have to think about who you're talking to and make sure you don't give a bad impression, you know? Before my dad passed he said that a lot, that I was spending too much time on it. But I told him, 'You know what? In a few years, I'm gonna be majoring in this exact same thing that I love doing now, playing video games and drawing. And I'm gonna prove you wrong, that I can do something with this.' [Extended pause.] So hopefully I can support my mom with that too.

Her beloved father recently deceased, her mother disabled and bedridden, her two older brothers out of the family house and living with their respective girlfriends, Mesha faces the transition from the relatively defined and structured life of a high school student living at home to a more uncertain future. She bears the responsibility for caring for her ailing mother, maintaining the house and paying the bills with the proceeds from her part-time, minimum wage job. Against this gendered and classed backdrop, she represents her gaming in relational terms as well as in career terms. Referencing her long-standing ambition to find gainful employment as a game designer, she frames it as a passion, as something she loves, not just a job. Speaking as if in direct dialogue with her father from beyond the grave ('I'm gonna prove you wrong'), she acknowledges his disapproval of her gaming, at the same time countering the broader cultural discourses of limiting screen time and avoiding risky behaviour in networked spaces. And in declaring her intention to support her mother, she establishes a claim to a carer identity, while narrating her gaming as an investment of time that she will make good on.

Mesha asserts that her gaming and drawing – activities that she perhaps fears will be seen as unproductive, or as a waste of time – have in fact been part of a concerted effort to cultivate herself against the odds into a productive, employable knowledge worker. To bolster this identity claim, she also highlights the school-based, domestic and extracurricular contexts of her digital literacy development. Speaking retrospectively of her younger self, she recounts being singled out by teachers for placement into an advanced computer class in the first grade because 'I was learning so much'; taking on the role of the tech expert among her family and being called upon 'at such a young age' by her mother, father and grandmother to troubleshoot the home computers and programme the VCR; and learning how to build a computer 'from scratch' as a middle school student participating in an intervention programme designed to increase the representation of girls of colour in STEM fields. In these three examples, she draws attention to her mastery of valued and privileged digital literacies like that of computer programming while drawing on the neoliberal governmental discourse of the lifelong learner to establish her own value and worth.

And yet there is also, embedded in the nuanced accounting for her gaming time quoted in full above, an implicit critique of the overly instrumental emphasis of the lifelong learner discourse for its framing of learning and working as divorced from the dynamics of responsibility and obligation to particular intimate others, as opposed to the state. This way of making meaning from her gaming practice is another example of the young people's *counter-narratives of care* (Luttrell, 2013) and suggests an alternative economy of valuing young people's multimodal literacies, one that re-centres the shaping force of care worlds and networks.

This analysis of what Mesha values about her gaming and digital literacy complicates the implicitly individualized and instrumental terms – a *children as human capital and social investment* discourse (Kjørholt, 2013) – through which multimodal literacies are often seen. By practising the three dimensions of collaborative seeing described in this chapter, we have grown aware of the under-recognized role of care and care relations in young people's perceptions of their engagements with digital technologies. First, the iterative and co-constructed flow of meaning-making generated by numerous audiencing sessions gives young people multiple opportunities to bring to light various valued aspects of their experience. Second, the structured, sequenced immersion, first in the visual, and then in the audio-visual data, helps to guard against the adult/researcher voicing over children's perspectives. And third, the practice of stereophonic listening, tunes us into both the regulatory discourses (such as the 'productive' use of time) as well as the resistant possibilities (such as the value of care and care relations).

Other young people in the project, like Mesha, used their cameras to make visible and thus place value on aspects of their multimodal literacy practices, to make identity claims and to participate in their social worlds. Like Allison Pugh who has argued that children use their knowledge of commodified goods (whether they own these goods or not) to 'transform themselves into citizens of their public sphere' (Pugh, 2009, p. 52), we found that the young people used screens, and access to and knowledge of digital technologies in a similar way, to position themselves as carers and cared for, as valued and valuable, as agents of their own making and as worthy citizens of broad publics.

Notes

1   See Luttrell (2010) for the prompt and how we addressed issues of consent.

2   These are the labels and percentages provided by the school; they do not publish records of the immigrant status of the children. Students are eligible for 'free and reduced lunch' in US schools if their family income is at or below 185 per cent of the Federal poverty line. The percentage of students in a school receiving free and reduced lunch is an indicator of the socio-economic status of a school.

References

American Academy of Pediatrics. (2011 July). Council on communications and media. Policy statement. Children, adolescents, obesity and the media. *Pediatrics, 128*, 201–208.

American Association of University Women. (2000). *Tech-savvy: Educating Girls in the Computer Age*. Washington: Educational Foundation of the American Association of University Women.

Becker, H. S. (1986). *Doing Things Together: Selected Papers*. Evanston: Northwestern University Press.

Bucholtz, M. (1998). Geek the girl: Language, femininity, and female nerds. In N. Warner, J. Ahlers, L. Bilmes, M. Oliver, S. Wertheim & Melinda Chen (Eds), *Gender and Belief Systems: Proceedings from the Fourth Berkeley Women and Language Conference*. Berkeley: Berkeley Women and Language Group.

Bucholtz, M. (2002). Geek feminism. In S. Benor, M. Rose, D. Sharma, J. Sweetland & Q. Zhang (Eds), *Gendered Practices in Language* (pp. 277–307). Stanford: CSLI.

Burke, C. (2005). 'Play in focus': Children researching their own spaces and places for play. *Children, Youth and Environments, 15*(1), 27–53.

Cassell, J., & Jenkins, H. (1998). *From Barbie to Mortal Kombat: Gender and Computer Games*. Cambridge: MIT Press.

Charon, R. (2005). Narrative medicine: Attention, representation, affiliation. *Narrative, 13*(3), 261–270.

———. (2006). *Narrative Medicine: Honoring the Stories of Illness*. Oxford: Oxford University Press.

Clark, C. D. (1999). The autodriven interview: A photographic viewfinder into children's experiences. *Visual Sociology, 14*, 39–50.

Clark-Ibanez, M. (2004). Framing the social world with photo-elicitation interviews. *The American Behavioral Scientist 47*(12), 1507–1527.

Connell, R. W., & Messerschmidt, J. W. (2005). Hegemonic masculinity: Rethinking the concept. *Gender & society, 19*(6), 829–859.

Feeley, M. (2009). Living in care and without love: The impact of affective inequalities on learning literacy. In K. Lynch, J. Baker, & M. Lyons (Eds), *Affective Equality: Love, Care and Injustice* (pp. 199–215). New York: Palgrave Macmillan.

Gee, J. P. (2003). *What Video Games Have to Teach Us About Learning and Literacy*. New York: Palgrave Macmillan.

Gee, J. P., & Hayes, E. R. (2011). *Language and Learning in the Digital Age*. New York: Routledge.

González, N., Moll, L. C., & Amanti, C. (2005). *Funds of Knowledge: Theorizing Practice in Households, Communities, and Classrooms*. Mahwah: L. Erlbaum Associates.

Hargittai, E., & Walejko, G. (2008). The participation divide: Content creation and sharing in the digital age. *Information, Communication & Society, 11*(2), 239–256.

Hart, R. A. (1979). *Children's Experience of Place*. New York: Irvington Publishers.

James, A., Jenks, C., & Prout, A. (1998). *Theorizing Childhood*. Cambridge: Polity Press.

Jenkins, H. et al. (2006). *Confronting the Challenges of Participatory Culture: Media Education for the 21st century*. Chicago: The John D. and Catherine T. MacArthur Foundation.

Kafai, Y. B., Heeter, C., Denner, J., & Sun, J. Y. (2008). *Beyond Barbie(r) and Mortal Kombat: New Perspectives on Gender and Gaming*. Cambridge: MIT Press.

Kaplan, E. B. (2013). *"We Live in the Shadow": Inner-city Kids Tell Their Stories Through Photographs*. Philadelphia: Temple.

Keeley, B. (2007). *Human Capital: How What You Know Shapes Your Life*. Paris: OECD Publishing.

Kjørholt, A. (2013). Childhood as social investment, rights and the valuing of education. *Children & Society, 27*(4), 245–257. doi:10.1111/chso.12037

Lico S., & Luttrell W. (2012). An important part of me: A dialogue about difference. *Harvard Educational Review, 81*(4), 667–686.

Luttrell, W. (2003). *Pregnant Bodies, Fertile Minds: Race, Gender and the Schooling of Pregnant Teens*. New York: Routledge.

———. (2010). A camera is a big responsibility: A lens for analyzing children's visual voices. *Visual Studies, 25*: 224–237.

———. (2012). Making boys' care worlds visible. *Thymos: Journal of Boyhood Studies, 6*(2), 185–201.

Luttrell, W. (2013). Children's counter-narratives of care: Towards educational justice. *Children & Society, 27*, 295–308.

Luttrell, W., & Chalfen, R. (2010). Hearing voices: An introduction to dilemmas in visual research. *Visual Studies*, Special Issue: *Visual Research Methods and Issues of Voice*.

Luttrell, W., Dorsey, J., Shalaby, C. & Hayden, J. (2011). Transnational childhoods and youth media: Seeing with a learning from one immigrant child's visual narrative. In J. Fisherkeller (Ed.), *International Perspectives on Youth Media: Cultures of Production and Education*. New York: Peter Lang.

Luttrell, W., Restler, V., & Fontaine, C. (2012). Youth video-making: Selves and iden tities in dialogue. In E. J. Milne, C. Mitchell, & N. de Lange (Eds), *Participatory Video Handbook*. Latham: AltaMira Press.

Lynch, K., Baker, J., & Lyons, M. (2009). *Affective Equality: Love, Care and Solidarity Work*. New York: Palgrave Macmillan.

Margolis, J. & Fisher, A. (2002). *Unlocking the Computer Clubhouse: Women in Computing*. Cambridge: MIT Press.

Orellana, M. F. (1999). Space and place in an urban landscape: Learning from children's views of their social world. *Visual Sociology, 14*, 73–89.

Persell, C. H., & Cookson, P. W. (1987). Microcomputers and elite boarding schools: Educational innovation and social reproduction. *Sociology of Education, 60*(2), 123–143. doi: 10.2307/2112587.

Pini, M., & Walkerdine, V. (2011). Girls on film: Video diaries as 'autoethnographies.' In Reavey, P. (Eds), *Visual Methods in Psychology: Using and Interpreting Images in Qualitative Research*. New York: Routledge, 139–152.

Popkewitz, T. S., & Lindblad, S. (2004). Historicizing the future: Educational reform, systems of reason, and the making of children who are the future citizens. *Journal of Educational Change, 5*(3), 229–247.

Pugh, A. J. (2009). *Longing and Belonging: Parents, Children, and Consumer Culture*. Berkeley: University of California Press.

Rasmussen, K. (1999). Employing photography and photos in research on childhood. *Dansk Sociology, 10*(1): 63–78.

Rich, M., & Chalfen, R. (1999). Showing and telling asthma: Children teaching physicians with visual narrative. *Visual Sociology, 14*(1), 51–71.

Rizvi, F., & Lingard, B. (2010). *Globalizing Education Policy*. Milton Park, Abingdon: Routledge.

Scheck, D. C. (1985). Promoting computer literacy in schools: Some humanistic implications. *Humanity and Society, 9*, 280–92.

Seiter, E. (1999). *Television and New Media Audiences*. Oxford: Oxford University Press.

Seiter, E., Borchers, H. Kreutzner, G., & Warth, E.-M. (Eds) (1989). *Remote Control: Television, Audiences, and Cultural Power*. London: Routledge.

Sims, C. (2014). From differentiated use to differentiating practices: Negotiating legitimate participation and the production of privileged identities. *Information, Communication & Society, 17*(6), 670–68.

Strandell, H. (2013). After-school care as investment in human capital: From policy to practices. *Children & Society, 27*(4), 270–281.

Sunden, J. (2009). Play as transgression: An ethnographic approach to queer game cultures. In Barry Atkins, Helen Kennedy and Tanya Krzywinska (Eds), *Breaking New Ground: Innovation in Games, Play, Practice and Theory: Proceedings on the 2008 Digital Games Research Associations conferences*, London.

Taylor, T. L. (2009). *Play between Worlds: Exploring Online Game Culture*. Cambridge: MIT Press.

Thorne, B. (2002). Editorial: From silence to voice: Bringing children more fully into knowledge. *Childhood, 9*(3), 251–254.

Tinkler, P. (2008). A fragmented picture: Reflections on the photographic practices of young people. *Visual Studies, 23*(3), 255–266.

Turmel, A. (2008). *A Historical Sociology of Childhood: Developmental Thinking, Categorization, and Graphic Visualization*. Cambridge: Cambridge University Press.

Yates, L. L. (2010). The story they want to tell, and the visual story as evidence: Young people, research authority and research purposes in the education and health domains. *Visual Studies, 25*(3), 280–291.

4

Multimodality and Governmentality in Kindergarten Literacy Curricula

Rachel Heydon

Kindergarten literacy curriculum has become a nexus for questions about multimodality and governmentality. Certain early childhood education and care (ECEC) approaches have long recognized the semiotic heterogeneity of children's meaning-making. The ECEC approach of Reggio Emilia, Italy, for instance, has as one of its foundations the *one hundred languages of children* (e.g. Edwards et al., 2012), a metaphor for the myriad modes through which children can make sense of the world and share it with others. The approach sees even the youngest children as competent explorers of semiotic resources (e.g. Fraser, 2012). Lately, ECEC is becoming increasingly formalized; examples include ECEC being governed within education portfolios (Kaga et al., 2010), stand-alone kindergarten programmes moving into schools (e.g. Mella, 2009), and full-day kindergartens (e.g. British Columbia Ministry of Education, 2010). Such reforms do not presuppose governmentality, but they raise the questions of how governments are involving themselves in ECEC and with what consequences.

This chapter explores multimodality and governmentality through three case studies. Focusing on the *classroom* (literacy) *curricula* (i.e. what actually happens in the teaching and learning circumstances) (Doyle, 1992), the studies asked, *How are literacy curricula produced? What part might children's interests and funds of knowledge play in their production and practice? What are the implications for children's literacy and identity options?* The studies map kindergarten literacy curriculum networks located along different points in ECEC reform in Ontario, Canada. The province introduced strategies to produce 'continuity of early learning experiences' within children's days by moving child care into schools and providing full-day learning for kindergarten-aged children (3.8–5 years) (Pascal, 2009, p. 16). One hoped-for outcome of the changes was the creation of 'literate citizens' (p. 4), signalling the importance of literacy curricula. The first two cases concern kindergartens at the cusp of the reform: an ECEC programme for kindergarten-aged children offered by a child care centre and a half-time kindergarten in a school. Both cases offer knowledge of what was in existence before the ECEC reform, and case three, the literacy curricula of full-day kindergarten, offers what is now in place. Together, the cases document how differences in networks can produce radically different effects and provide talking points linked to ideas of multimodality and governmentality. They also produce side notes concerning how actor-network theory (ANT) can be a tool for (re)viewing these ideas.

Background

The studies are premised in understandings of the relationships between literacies, children and curriculum.

Multimodal literacy may be of central concern to ECEC curricula when viewed within the context of the United Nations Convention on the Rights of the Child (UNCRC) (1990) which establishes children's rights *to be heard* (Article 12) and *to have freedom of expression.* Freedom of expression is defined as children having the right to communicate 'either orally, in writing or in print, in the form of art, or through any other media of the children's choice' (Article 13). The UNCRC legitimizes the communicative potency of children's multimodal practices which by extension suggest that ECEC curricula provide children with *literacy options* (Heydon, 2013). The importance of freedom of expression is evident given the connection between literacy and identity. Identity has been described as 'a sense of self' (Pahl & Rowsell, 2005, p. 7) that is instantiated within literacy practices, and a reciprocal relationship has been identified between literacy options and the possibilities children have for the formation of their *identity options* (Cummins, 2001).

Curricula can forward children's rights with Nutbrown (1996) signalling to the import of curricula that are locally developed by discerning educators in response to children:

adults with experience who respectfully watch children engaged in their process of living, learning, loving and being are in a better position to understand what it is these youngest citizens are trying to say and find ways of helping them to say it. (cited in Watson et al., 2012, p. 55)

'Giving voice' is here construed as a semiotic practice predicated on adults having the tools to listen and may also require opportunities for children to exercise responsibility through choice in daily living:

Giving people a voice … is an active process of communication involving hearing, interpretation and construction of meanings that is not limited to the spoken word. It is also a necessary stage in participation in daily routines and in wider decision-making processes. (Watson et al., 2012, p. 112)

This stance demands for children to be *curricular informants* (Harste, 2003) and requires a critical contemplation of curriculum.

Multimodal curriculum and pedagogy have been variously defined, although they tend to have in common the provision of spaces for learners to engage with an array of semiotic resources, understand what these resources afford (or not), acquire and expand facility with them and identify and play with the relationships between modes (e.g. Walsh, 2011). In Canada, where the studies took place, every programmatic literacy curriculum (Doyle, 1992) (i.e. curriculum document) includes some mention of all of reading, writing, speaking, listening, viewing and representing (including through digital media), suggesting an acceptance of multimodality. However, assessment policies privilege print literacy (Bainbridge & Heydon, 2013) creating a tension also felt outside of Canada (e.g. Sanders & Albers, 2010). True multimodal curricula (and pedagogy) may however require more than the simple inclusion of diverse modes and a change in assessment policy. Stein's (2008) version is a vehicle to democratic classrooms based in students' interests and *funds of knowledge* (Moll et al., 1992) (i.e. their linguistic and epistemic resources).

Literacy curriculum was conceptualized in the studies through ANT which offers 'material-semiotic tools … and methods of analysis that treat everything in the social world as a continuously generated effect of the webs of relations within which they are located' (Law, 2009, p. 141). Networks are 'contested and precarious multiplicities which order practices, bodies, and identities' (Fenwick, 2010, p. 119) and are composed of *actors* (i.e. 'any person or object involved in forming a network' (Bleakley, 2012, p. 464)). In ANT curricula are plural and dynamic and the effects of networks. 'Change', or the production of curricula, is 'a series of complex negotiations at micro-levels setting in motion complex dynamics that reconfigure systems' (Fenwick et al., 2012, p. 7). ANT analyses are thus useful in highlighting 'questions about the politics' of networks or the curricular constituents 'that constrain, obscure, or enable certain enactments' (Fenwick, 2010, p. 119) such as literacy and identity options. ANT and the analytic tools of governmentality are employed to respond to the studies' questions.

Rose's (1999) take on governmentality is suggestive of asymmetries of power whereby 'strategies' may be mobilized by governments to 'conduct the conduct of their citizens and achieve their objectives while governing in a liberal fashion' (Rutland & Aylett, 2008, p. 628). The exertion of power is omnipresent and couched as 'care' (p. 630) exemplified through Foucault's (e.g. 1981) allegory of the shepherd. The shepherd cares for/controls his flock by having 'clear and precise knowledge of each of its members' which 'allows him to guide them as he wishes' (Rutland & Aylett, 2008, p. 630). Knowledge allows a 'governing body to properly orchestrate the various elements of the state' and is the 'primary vehicle through which the state spreads its particular priorities and goals among the population' (p. 630). Knowledge, however, is always an interpretation and structured by the kinds of questions asked and tools used, thus rendering some 'courses of action' more possible than others (p. 631). Inscription devices (e.g. statistics) can be used to accumulate knowledge with 'aspir[ations]' to 'shap[e] conduct' (Rose, 1999, p. 52) and render 'constituents of a system visible and therefore calculable' (Fenwick & Edwards, 2010, p. 115). Devices can be 'internalize[d]' as a form of 'self-regulation', such that people 'make themselves into calculable subject[s]' (pp. 115–116). As will be shown, when coupled with ANT, the ideas of governmentality become more liquescent.

Methodology

Three classroom literacy curricula from three sites formed the cases. Table 4.1 describes the sites, educators and child participants. Ethnographic tools, which have been tapped as useful in ANT enquiries (e.g. Latour, 2005), were used to collect data on the programmes' spatial (e.g. layout of room), temporal (e.g. timetables) and physical (e.g. contents of classroom) composition. Data concerning what happened in the curriculum, how and with what effects were also collected through interviews with educators (e.g. teachers,[1] early childhood educators[2] (ECE) and administrators) and focal children, and participant observation over the course of at least one cycle of activity (e.g. a term). Observation focused on literacy *events* and *practices* and the texts they engendered (e.g. children's writing and artwork).

Table 4.1 Sites and Participants

Site	Programme	Locale	Educators	Children
Child care	– full- and part-time programming – not for profit – fee for service but municipal subsidy available	– neighbourhood in medium size city characterized by mixed socio-economic status and cultural and linguistic diversity	– classroom staffed by 2 ECEs: 'Lisa' (+5 years' experience; part of leadership programme) and 'Denise' (+20 years' experience)	– 20 children in class – not all children present at the same time as 15 children participated in half-time kindergarten in school (morning or afternoon), thus attended child care programme either morning or afternoon, respectively – 3 children identified as culturally and linguistically diverse (CLD)
Half-time kindergarten	– 5 days a week (1:00–3:30) – publically funded school	– neighbourhood in medium-sized city home to post-secondary institution with mixed middle to upper income housing interspersed with student housing – students largely children of post-secondary institution students (many international)	– classroom staffed by 1 teacher: 'Judy' (20 years' experience)	– 16–18 children in class – 6 children CLD

Site	Programme	Locale	Educators	Children
Full-day kindergarten	– 5 days a week (9:00–3:30) – publicly funded school	– neighbourhood in large city often first stop for immigrants – school identified as 'high needs' (half student population living in 'lower income households')	– classroom staffed by 1 teacher: 'Rhea' (less than five years' experience) and 1 ECE, 'Lori' (recent ECE graduate; approximately 20 years' experience as educational assistant) – 1 child with special education needs qualified for support by educational assistant	– 31–32 students in class – approximately 50% children CLD

Data analysis took a 'looking down' (Fenwick et al., 2011, p. 124) approach to detect the constituents of the networks, what actors did to produce literacy curricula, the form of those curricula and their effects. The 'relations, connections or associations between actors' were employed as 'the signals … used to trace and describe the characteristic embedding and embedded by curriculum' production and its effects (Perillo & Mulcahy, 2009, p. 45).

Findings

The most salient finding across cases concerned the way in which opportunities for multimodality were network effects, and these opportunities were radically different across networks. No one actor accounted for all the differences, although certain actors were imbued at times with more power than others.

Literacy curriculum in a child care centre

Case one, the classroom literacy curricula in a child care centre, was a flexible curricular network characterized by educator attempts to *listen to children* and the provision of expansive multimodal literacy learning opportunities. Curricula were produced through a process of *provocation/investigation*, *observation*, *documentation* and *interpretation*, guided by an emergent curricular philosophy supported by the organization's provision of professional learning. Children's interests and knowledge were key actors that *informed* and *were informed by* actors from in and out of the classroom. The network was coloured by what administrator Carolyn called a 'Reggio-inspired' philosophy which she described by focusing on the children: '[children] are not citizens of tomorrow, they are citizens of today. They already know so much and our job is to learn what they know and allow that to impact our space'.

The child care centre was governed by the Government of Ontario's Day Nurseries Act (2010) which left many programme decisions affecting classroom curriculum to the provider. Educators were required to comply with generous child-to-adult ratios and supply learning opportunities within broad areas which they listed in a programme planner (i.e. 'social emotional, creative, language, intellectual, and motor'), but overall Carolyn was able to say of the organization, 'We have tremendous choice! … [our] leadership has incredible autonomy … Day Nurseries Act and health and safety are taken as minimum and are not daunting at all … There is really little that we have to follow at all and that is empowering'. The Centre developed an emergent approach to classroom curricula which it promoted through print information to educators, a leadership programme where interested educators were provided release time to mentor in other classrooms, a resident artist and ongoing professional learning that included multimodal sense-making opportunities for educators and whose artefacts were displayed throughout the Centre. The study educators enacted emergent curriculum as a recursive process of provoking children's meaning-making by stimulating children's thinking through provocations such as texts or objects, assessing and documenting effects and interpreting documentation which included sharing it with others (e.g. families and children). Provocations could turn into larger and longer investigations and the interpretation of documentation then fed into the next provocation.

What Denise and Lisa, the ECEs, called 'novel study' was primary in organizing the classroom curriculum. Educators selected novels to read aloud to the children based on their understanding of the children's interests and knowledge. During data collection, two novels were studied: *Charlie and the Great Glass Elevator* (Dahl, 1972) and *Charlotte's Web* (White, 1952). The novels were provocations and anchors for investigations and provided opportunities for the children to pursue multimodal practices; for instance, in *Charlie* there was a potion called Wonka Vita which decreased a person's age. As a provocation, the educators invited the children to express what would happen if they consumed Vita-Wonk, a potion that *increased* a person's age. All of the children elected to participate and therein used a variety of modes (e.g. writing and drawing) to express ideas like ageing and dying. The children were also provided increased identity options as they engaged with imagined futures within their literacy practices. Figure 4.1, one child's expression of herself after ageing from Vita-Wonk, is representative, for example, of the care the children took to deal with the big ideas and technical aspects of the modes so that they could convey their messages. Of note is the attention to spelling, letter formation and spacing, complementary relationship between the semantics in the illustration and writing, precise drawing and colouring and accuracy in calculating the age after the Vita-Wonk.

Other actors, like 'Gilly' the tadpole, were *enrolled* in the network. Noticing that the children were interested when the letter carrier arrived at the Centre, the educators created a Centre-wide mail system through which members could correspond. One day, a message arrived in the classroom saying that a surprise was waiting for them. A parent had sent in an aquarium containing a tadpole. Concurrent with their reading of *Charlie*, the children became enthralled with Gilly and all he could teach them (e.g. metamorphosis and life cycles). The children, supported by the educators, elected to observe, sketch

Figure 4.1 *Vita-Wonk*

and write about Gilly on a daily basis, again practising multimodal literacies in the pursuit of their interests and new knowledge.

Through their documentation during *Charlie*, the educators discerned that *Charlotte's Web* would be an opportunity to build on the children's interests in life cycles and animals. The data suggest that the novel content (e.g. Wilbur the pig's fear of death), its connection to the themes already explored in the classroom and the ideas it sparked from the children (e.g. is killing spiders okay?) formed links with new actors to provide multimodal explorations. The new actors arose from the spring season. Specifically, one of the children started making paper birds; soon all the children were folding paper birds. Around this time, Denise noticed birds nesting by her home; she shared photos of this, and the class observed the progress. Class members then brought in nests and other bird paraphernalia. These additions prompted fresh lines for the exploration of life cycles. By the close of data collection, the class had engaged in observing, reading, discussing, sketching, writing and representing through plasticine and photography all things to do with birds.

Literacy curriculum in a half-time kindergarten

Case two, the literacy curriculum of a half-time kindergarten, is an example of a sometimes tightly knit network characterized by *listening to programmatic curriculum, assessments and the market, after which children could be listened to*. Assessments and outcomes often directed classroom literacy curriculum away from multimodal literacy and produced identities formed in relation to them. Still, there were slippages in the network that creates spaces for multimodal practice.

Under the responsibility of the Ministry of Education, in contrast to the child care centre, this kindergarten was beholden to an outcomes-based programmatic curriculum (Ontario Ministry of Education, 2006) that had an effect on the network. Children were required to meet dozens of outcomes (called 'expectations') for each of reading, writing, oral language and media literacy. Though the ends of the programme were prescribed and standardized, the means to achieve them were not, thus the curricular paradigm fell within an *adaptable* (Heydon & Wang, 2006) range. When Judy, the teacher, described how she planned with Mary, a teacher from a neighbouring kindergarten, she stated, '[we] follow the kindergarten documents by the province and then basically our philosophy is that's our guideline and just to take the children to wherever they can go'. Other data indicate that the expectations were foundational to the creation of classroom curricula. For example, though Judy said she could 'individualiz[e]' the curriculum, she had to select expectations from the kindergarten document or a document for another grade. She could not create her own expectations and the children could not inform them. The expectations were also a lynchpin in the planning process; for instance, when reviewing a worksheet while planning a unit for the book *Rosie's Walk* (Hutchins, 1968), Judy stated, 'I know what I liked… this is a map so [Rosie]… walks around the pond, climbs over the haystack… it's good for sequencing.' In the programmatic curriculum, sequencing is an expectation in oral communication and reading (e.g. 'retell stories in proper sequence' (Ontario Ministry of Education, 2006, p. 37)). The mapping activity did allow for multimodality in the form of the children reading a map and tracing Rosie's route in a sandbox; however, a standardized provincial report card monitored each child's achievement relative to the expectations and when enrolled with other actors, translated the classroom literacy away from multimodal literacy, especially with regard to children's ability to be curricular informants.

Literacy assessments translated the expectations and other constituents of the network to produce a classroom literacy curricula that operated outside of the children's interests, funds of knowledge and multimodal potentiality. When, for instance, Judy and Mary planned, they monitored themselves to ensure they covered what they called 'must-dos' before planning from the children. Judy explained,

> We talk about must-dos … we're getting too much … this week we're doing [an abridged version of] *Charlotte's Web*, I got a must-do with the writing but I know I'll get something really cool for science or craft and I'll want everybody to do [it] and then I'll be going why did I do this?

Curricular plans that might provoke the children had to be reserved for after the must-dos which were connected to expectations and assessments where there was monitoring. Exerting force within the network were school district enterprises aimed at predicting student achievement relative to the provincial grade 3 test of literacy and identifying children whose literacy acquisition was not following a prescribed trajectory as set out by district officials. A mandatory, district-constructed phonological awareness screening was a chief actor in this regard.

The screener was a must-do, for example Judy said to Mary during planning, 'one thing for sure in literacy that we have to work on is how many sounds do we hear in a word, because our phonological screening is coming up'. Wanting her students to do well required that Judy prepare the students even though most of them were reading short picture books independently, and the school had been lauded for its high achievement on the grade 3 test. The teachers were concerned about the screener as they explained that the children's literacy proficiency and scoring well on the screener were two different things. When explaining to Mary that they needed to plan lessons to help the children count sounds in words, a skill on the screener, Judy lamented,

> Today [I asked the children to count the sounds in 'dog'] and again [they] keep wanting to give me the letter … if I said dog and [they] went d-o-g, [I had to say] no I don't want [you to spell], I want the sound. They're just so used to spelling.

The children's knowledge actually interfered with their achievement on the screener.

The commercially produced Developmental Reading Assessment (DRA) (e.g. Beaver, 2001) also created barriers to multimodal pedagogy and children's interests enrolled in the network. The district had adopted the DRA to quantify children's reading achievement. To administer it, children were individually asked to read progressively more difficult books aloud to the teacher, retell the text and answer standardized questions about text features and content. The district had identified benchmarks for the children to reach at prescribed points, and teachers had to report children's levels to the district. The DRA mobilized children to regulate their literacy practices and constrained identity options. The children's text selections for home reading were largely commercial-level texts or texts where publishers ascribed a level to the text after its initial publication. A conversion chart was used to correlate different publishers' levels. In the classroom, the texts were organized in tubs with the levels marked on them, and Judy asked the children to select daily from the tubs and keep a log of the text title, level and number of books read.

Levels were a ubiquitous topic of conversation amongst the class. The following conversation I had with child participant Lucy exemplifies how children were inducted into becoming calculable subjects.

> Rachel: Do you learn to read and write at school?
> Lucy: Yeah. I can read, because … I've read 63 books.
> Rachel: 63 is a very big number, isn't it?
> Lucy: Yes. And that's all you need to read … get to [level] Q and then you can read like Ramona books.
> Rachel: How do you learn to read and write at school?
> Lucy: With your mom and dad, you go home, you borrow a book from school … [from the levelled] basket, and I'm in B books. You have to get all the way to Q.

Lucy wanted to read the Beverly Cleary series *Ramona* (e.g. 1955). Publishers had put these books at a level beyond where she was assessed. Lucy's identity as a reader was formed in the face of her aspiration to be permitted to access the texts that she desired and was phrased in terms of quantity which found her *lacking*.

The network produced the greatest opportunities for children to be curricular informants and practice multimodal literacies when the literacy events were informal such as during open centre time. Daily, the children selected amongst centres where Judy had laid out various literacy materials and invited the children to interact with them as they wished. The centres often corresponded with other literacy events such as a dramatic play centre stocked with costumes/puppets corresponding to *Charlotte's Web* and an overhead centre made up of a projector, pens, and transparencies (some blank and others that showed maps of *Rosie's Walk*). Findings indicate that the children pursued their interests while being provided learning opportunities related to expectations. Yet, even in more compactly wound centres, children sometimes found ways to satisfy the demands of the must-dos *and* their interests. For instance, all of the children were required to cycle through a centre where they had to add letters to a rhyme (e.g. '_at') to create a word family book. Lucy completed the requirement and went beyond it: she made words from the rhyme, but on the first page, after the inclusion of a 'th' to the rhyme, Lucy filled the page with other marks resembling letters and complex drawings. When I asked her about the book, she pointed to the marks on the first page and began to recount her day at kindergarten: 'I come to school. When I come to school, I sing O' Canada.' Lucy then turned the page and continued to tell the story despite these pages containing only the word families with a discrete little picture in the box supplied by the teacher in which to illustrate the word: 'Then I do stuff on the smartboard. Then I go to music. After I came back, I have snack when I'm done centre.' The assigned task may have been about phonics, but Lucy had found a way to also make it something she wanted to communicate.

Literacy curriculum in full-day kindergarten

Case three was one of *not being able to listen for the noise* and showed how a network can produce a curriculum where literacy events are based in *regulatory* language (Halliday, 1975) related to the establishment and enforcement of rules and routines and the maintenance of children's behaviour—most commonly through attempts to control their expressive communication. Here, children barely had the space to split off to create alternate assemblages to pursue their interests and funds of knowledge, including those related to multimodal literacies. This case is presented last, as it was produced by the most recent configuration of kindergarten in the Ontario reform. Class size, the direct result of legislative changes that were made to the permissible number of children in a full-day kindergarten class, in relation to other actors in the network was the predominant producer of this curriculum.

The classroom literacy curriculum was replete with events that were taken over by the teacher, Rhea's, attempts to manage the children or by events explicitly directed towards managing the children's behaviour. For example, Read-Aloud was one of the most regular events in the literacy curriculum. Most salient, however, were the children's attempts to assert their interests and engage in discussions and Rhea's attempts to control what was said while organizing the children's bodies. As the following sample of transcript from a Read-Aloud of a non-fiction book on Remembrance Day illustrates, most of the time in the events was directed towards management and there was considerable waiting which interfered with the flow of reading:

Rhea: Shhhh Yanni
      (2 sec)
Rhea: Remembrance Day takes place on November 11th each year –
      Yanni back to your spot
      (5 sec)

Rhea: Rowan come sit up at the front by me I think you need to
         hold my hand
         (8 sec)
Rhea: I am going to start again
         (1 sec)
Rhea: Remembrance Day takes *place* on November 11th each year (.)
         On this day – Sarah please stop being rude
         (2 sec)
Rhea: Harriet *again*
         (2 sec)
Rhea: on this day Canadians honour the men and
         (6 sec)
Rhea: *Karen* (.) I'm over here
         (3 sec)
Rhea: Remembrance day – Harriet leave the carpet go sit on a chair
         (2 sec)
Rhea: On this day Canadians honour – oh I'm going to start from the
         very beginning
         (1 sec)

Read-Aloud contained repeated teacher appeals to manage children's expressions. Other events were even more overt in their attempts to direct children's behaviour; an example is the daily routine of reading aloud the rules of the classroom.

Reading the rules aloud was a lesson for the children in listening. In an interview about the literacy curriculum, we asked child participant, Akil, 'Do you learn to talk at school?' Akil, who was being interviewed in his classroom, answered, 'I am talking right now.' When asked the question again with a different emphasis, 'But do you *learn* to talk at school?' Akil shook his head 'no'. He nodded 'yes' to the question of whether he learned to 'listen' at school. To explain how he understood this as happening, he instructed, '[the teacher] puts up a board', and he pointed to signs of rules Rhea had posted in the classroom. Handwritten by Rhea, the signs were sometimes illustrated by icons or images of children engaged in the target behaviours (see Figure 4.2), and sometimes structured as a rubric with rewards/punishments listed. Each afternoon, Rhea pointed to the rules of rest time and read them with the children. Transcripts of this type of event was almost identical to each other.

Rhea: Rule number one (1 sec)
Rhea: shoes?
Students: stay on

Figure 4.2 *Rest Time Rules*

Rhea: Rule number two (teacher pause for Joshua to settle: 1 sec)
Rhea: m[ats stay still(.) So Joshua broke rule number two (teacher pause
         for Robert and Matthew to settle: 1 sec)
Rhea: as did Robert and Matthew
         (1 sec)
T: so they've all gotten (.) a minute off their playtime (2 sec)
Rhea: thank you for fixing it (.) Rule number three
         (1 sec)
Rhea: blankets stay still
         (1 sec)

The data suggest that over thirty young children in one classroom trumped all other actors and directed the classroom curriculum towards events that might help to keep them safe. Given the numbers, Rhea expressed that she and ECE Lori had to forgo the full-day kindergarten programmatic curriculum (Ontario Ministry of Education, 2010–2011):

I felt like we're just gonna try and make it through…one of the things the Ministry envisioned…is children choosing centres and going and deciding where they're going to play and having an opportunity to work at somewhere for an hour if they want or not, and we tried it that way. But with the needs of the students in our class…having self-regulation and choosing their own things and deciding what choices to make while walking from one side of the room to another or moving from one centre to another that was not something they were equipped to handle yet. Some of them could, but it wasn't safe for the ones that could. Because the ones that couldn't were jumping off of tables.

An effect of the network was that the children had scant literacy learning opportunities and could not inform the curriculum.

Class size in relation to other network actors produced the classroom literacy curriculum. A lack of physical space coalesced with weak class size policies to create a classroom with too many children. The principal explained that the school was declared high needs, yet that did not qualify it for smaller class sizes. Once full-day kindergarten was initiated, there was no provincial hard cap on class size, and the soft cap from the district (approximately thirty-one) could not be invoked, because, as he said, 'I didn't have the classroom space…The structure, the physical layout of this building…it doesn't give me a lot of flexibility around [class] size.' Other physical plant issues such as toilets created increased stress on time that might have been spent on literacy. There was, for instance, only one often-clogged toilet for the classroom, resulting in long lines and accidents requiring educator resources. Educator resources were also engaged with helping young children to dress for Canadian winters, be fed and move safely en masse from one part of the building to another to attend programming such as library. Other actors that exacerbated the pejorative effects of the class size included a mismatch between the children's funds of knowledge and the knowledge necessary to get along in the school. For instance, Rhea stated that instead of 'teaching' the children 'to read', she had to spend her time 'teaching them…how to be in a room with people'. Expanding on this, Lori explained how having so many children in one place created 'chaos' from something as little as a child spilling water at a centre, so when Rhea was asked, 'What would you say if the Ministry says to you "there's two educators in the room, so it's really…a one-to-sixteen ratio?"' she replied, "I would say 'you try doing something with a four year old, when something is happening with another group of four year olds five feet away"'.

Discussion and conclusions

The main finding was that radically different classroom literacy curricula were produced depending upon the network. The juxtaposition of curricula that fall along different points in the Ontario kindergarten reform teaches that literacy curricula are not static and power is complex, circulating in networked configurations creating certain possibilities for multimodal literacy and constraining others. The network that created the curriculum in the child care centre was the loosest, focused on listening to children's knowledge and interests, and mobilized children as curricular informants. The network of the half-time kindergarten regulated literacy practices and identities through technologies of inscription and directed teachers to must-dos and sometimes away from children's voices. Nonetheless, there were some spaces for the children to pursue their interests and practise their preferred literacies. In the third case, the network, bogged down by too many children in difficult circumstances, produced a cacophonous classroom where the curriculum allowed children few opportunities for expression except for overt resistance.

The study findings demonstrate how ANT provides fresh lenses for contemplating issues of governmentality. The rights discourse has been critiqued for generating static binaries, where children are seen 'as either vulnerable and dependent or as autonomous and independent' (Kjorholt et al., 2005). Instead, a curriculum as network ontology rejects the view of children as being part of a reproductive process where they are simply 'induced to comply with the dominant ideologies and social practices' (McLaren, 1994, p. 191) of curriculum or resist them. Like other approaches born in the post-foundational age, the ANT-informed findings of the studies are compatible with the 'presumption that knowledge of any given concept is constantly in flux and situated' which 'permits novelties, difference and surprises to emerge' which can 'deflect normalizing master-narratives of children' (Watson et al., 2012, p. 115) such as those concerning cultural reproduction binaries such as powerful/powerless.

Through ANT, the studies temper governmentality from being understood as overly predictive and deterministic, and they caution against static dichotomies. They illustrate power and agency as themselves network effects rather than 'inherent and individually possessed' (Rutland & Aylett, 2008, p. 632), and as in other ANT studies (e.g. Fenwick & Edwards, 2010), the current studies illustrate how ANT can be used to investigate governmental relations in distinct manners by considering all actors 'at every point of a network' and how actors 'work upon each other' (p. 116). Governmentality supplied a way of identifying how governing ECEC bodies might reach their 'objectives by disseminating particular forms of knowledge to produce self-governing citizens' while ANT offers 'a complementary set of tools to help reveal how political priorities and the capacity to achieve them emerge *over time* from the dispersed energies of diverse actants, both human and nonhuman' (Rutland & Aylett, 2008, p. 633). The studies thus express a mobile and complex conception of power while identifying asymmetries in power in literacy curriculum production. Together, they suggest that the building of networks that forward children's rights to voice and expression involves the consideration of all actors in a network and their potential relationship to each other (e.g. optimum class size is not just about pupil-teacher ratio). This includes the material, leading to questions about the modal learning opportunities provided to children and ensuring that all parts of the network are supportive of multimodality and the opportunities that exist for children to be curriculum informants.

Acknowledgement

The author wishes to acknowledge the support of the Social Sciences and Humanities Research Council of Canada. This chapter brings together data reported on in three separate papers:

Heydon, R., Moffatt, L., & Iannacci, L. "Every day he has a dream to tell": Classroom literacy curriculum in a full-day kindergarten. *Journal of Curriculum Studies*.

Heydon, R., Crocker, W., & Zhang, Z. (2014). Nests, novels, and other provocations: Emergent literacy curricula in a child care centre. *Journal of Curriculum Studies, 46*(1), 1–32.

Heydon, R. (2013). Learning opportunities: A study of the production and practice of kindergarten literacy curricula. *Journal of Curriculum Studies, 45*(4), 481–510.

Notes

1 In Ontario, certification as a teacher requires the equivalent of four-years of post-secondary education including a field practicum (Pascal, 2009).
2 Qualifying as an ECE requires two years of community college including a field practicum (or equivalent) (Pascal, 2009).

References

Bainbridge, J., & Heydon, R. (2013). *Constructing Meaning: Teaching the Elementary Language Arts* (5th edition). Toronto: Thomson Nelson.
Beaver, J. (2001). *Developmental Reading Assessment: K-3 Teacher Resource Guide* (Revised edition). Parsippany: Celebration Press.
Bleakley, A. (2012). The proof is in the pudding: Putting actor-network-theory to work in medical education. *Medical Teacher, 34*, 462–467.
British Columbia Ministry of Education. (2010). Full school day kindergarten. Retrieved from http://www.bced.gov.bc.ca/early_learning/fdk/

Cleary, B. (1955). *Beezus and Ramona*. New York: William Morrow.

Cummins, J. (2001). *Negotiating Identities: Education for Empowerment in a Diverse Society* (2nd edition). Los Angeles: California Association for Bilingual Education.

Dahl, R. (1972). *Charlie and the Great Glass Elevator: The Further Adventures of Charlie Bucket and Willy Wonka, Chocolate-maker Extraordinary*. New York: Knopf.

Doyle, W. (1992). Curriculum and pedagogy. In P. W. Jackson (Ed.), *Handbook of Research on Curriculum* (pp. 486–516). New York: Macmillan.

Edwards, C, Gandini, L., & Forman, G. (Eds) (2012). *The Hundred Languages of Children: The Reggio Emilia Approach in Transformation* (3rd edition). Santa Barbara: Praeger.

Fenwick, T. (2010). (un)Doing standards in education with actor-network theory. *Journal of Education Policy, 25*(2), 117–133.

Fenwick, T., & Edwards, R. (2010). *Actor-network Theory in Education*. London: Routledge.

Fenwick, T., Edwards, R., & Sawchuk, P. (2011). *Emerging Approaches to Educational Research: Tracing the Sociomaterial*. London: Routledge.

Fenwick, T., Nerland, M., & Jensen, K. (2012). Sociomaterial approaches to conceptualising professional learning and practice. *Journal of Education and Work, 25*(1), 1–13.

Foucault, M. (1981). Omnes et singulatim: towards a criticism of 'political reason'. In S. McMurrin (Ed.), *The Tanner Lectures on Human Values Volume 2* (pp. 223–254). Salt Lake City: University of Utah Press.

Fraser, S. (2012). *Authentic Childhood: Experiencing Reggio Emilia in the Classroom*. Toronto: Nelson Education.

Government of Ontario. (2010). *Day Nurseries Act*. Toronto: Queen's Printer for Ontario. Retrieved from http://www.e-laws.gov.on.ca/html/statutes/english/elaws_statutes_90d02_e.htm

Halliday, M. A. K. (1975). *Learning How to Mean: Explorations in the Function of Language*. London: Edward Arnold.

Harste, J. (2003). What do we mean by literacy now? *Voices from the Middle, 10*(3), 8–12.

Heydon, R. (2013). *Learning at the Ends of Life: Children, Elders, Literacy, and Intergenerational Curriculum*. Toronto: University of Toronto Press.

Heydon, R., & Wang, P. (2006). Curricular ethics in early childhood education programming: A challenge to the Ontario kindergarten program. *McGill Journal of Education, 41*(1), 29–46.

Hutchins, P. (1968) *Rosie's Walk*. New York: Macmillan.

Kaga, Y, Barneynett, J., & Moss, P. (2010). *Caring and Learning Together: A Cross-national Study on the Integration of Early Childhood Care and Education within Education*. Paris: UNESCO.

Kjorholt, A. T., Moss, P., & Clark, A. (2005). Beyond listening: Future prospects. In A. Clark, A. T. Kjorholt & P. Moss (Eds), *Beyond Listening: Children's Perspectives on Early Childhood Services* (2nd edition) (pp. 175–188). Bristol: Policy Press.

Latour, B. (2005). *Reassembling the Social: An Introduction to Actor-network Theory*. Oxford: Oxford University Press.

Law, J. (2009). Actor-network theory and material semiotics. In B. S. Turner (Ed.), *The New Blackwell Companion to Social Theory* (3rd edition) (pp. 141–158). Oxford: Blackwell.

McLaren, P. (1994). *Life in Schools: An Introduction to Critical Pedagogy in the Foundations of Education* (2nd edition). New York: Longman.

Mella, P. J. (2009). *Every Child a Better Future* (Report No. 09EC35-23971). Charlottetown: Document Publishing Centre.

Moll, L. C., Amanti C., Neff, D., & Gonzalez, N. (1992). Funds of knowledge for teaching: Using a qualitative approach to connect homes and classrooms. *Theory into Practice 31*(2): 132–142.

Nutbrown, C. (Ed.) (1996). *Respectful Educators-capable Learners: Children's Rights and Early Education.* London: Paul Chapman.

Ontario Ministry of Education. (2006). *The Kindergarten Program.* Toronto: Queens Printer for Ontario.

Ontario Ministry of Education. (2010–2011). *The Full-day Early Learning-Kindergarten Program (Draft Version).* Toronto: Queen's Printer.

Pahl, K., & Rowsell, J. (2005). *Literacy and Education: Understanding the New Literacy Studies in the Classroom.* London: Sage.

Pascal, C. (2009). *With Our Best Future in Mind Implementing Early Learning in Ontario: Report to the Premier, Government of Ontario.* Toronto: Queens Printer for Ontario.

Perillo, S., & Mulcahy, D. (2009). Performing curriculum change in school and teacher education: A practice-based, actor-network theory perspective. *Curriculum Perspectives, 29*(1), 41–52.

Rose, N. S. (1999). *Powers of Freedom: Reframing Political Thought.* Cambridge: Cambridge University Press.

Rutland, T., & Aylett, A. (2008). The work of policy: Actor networks, governmentality, and local action on climate change in Portland, Oregon. *Environment and Planning D: Society and Space, 26*(4), 627–646.

Sanders, J., & Albers, P. (2010). Multimodal literacies: An introduction. In P. Albers & J. Sanders (Eds), *Literacies, the Arts, and Multimodality* (pp. 1–25). Urbana: NCTE.

Stein, P. (2008). *Multimodal Pedagogies in Diverse Classrooms: Representation, Rights and Resources.* London, New York: Routledge.

United Nations General Assembly. (1990). *Convention on the Rights of the Child.* New York: United Nations. Retrieved from http://www.ohchr.org/Documents/ProfessionalInterest/crc.pdf

Walsh, M. (2011). *Multimodal Literacy: Researching Classroom Practice.* Newtown: Primary English Teaching Association.

Watson, D., Emery, C., & Bayliss, P. (2012). *Children's Social and Emotional Wellbeing in Schools: A Critical Perspective.* Bristol: Policy Press.

White, E. B. (1952). *Charlotte's Web.* New York: Harper & Row.

5

Re-educating the Educator's Gaze: Is Pedagogical Documentation Ready for School?

Roz Stooke

Introduction

Set against a backdrop of ongoing reform in Ontario's early childhood education and care (ECEC) sector, this chapter draws on in-depth, qualitative interviews with fourteen Ontario-based early childhood educators to discuss ways in which they were learning about and mobilizing pedagogical documentation in their local practice settings. Pedagogical documentation has been employed in ECEC for several decades, but at the time of the study it had only recently been mandated for all Ontario ECEC settings and many practitioners were just beginning to learn about it. My study aimed to understand how diversely situated educators employed in an educational sector characterized by lack of coordination were learning about documentation, and how they were mobilizing documentation for pedagogical decision-making. In the chapter I critically examine what the educators told me about their experiences with documentation. The educators were unanimous in their enthusiasm for documentation and contrasted it favourably with traditional approaches to observation and assessment, especially mandated assessments such as the Ontario provincial report card. Moreover, although several participants confessed to feeling unsure about how to conduct documentations, no participant described the alienation that so often surfaces in conversations with teachers about standardized assessments (e.g. Parkinson & Stooke, 2012).

I contend nevertheless that documentation, like all technologies, is not neutral, but 'supports certain actions and reflections over others' (Arthur, 2012, p. xiii). Later in the chapter I present evidence that documentation's power to promote new ways of looking at practice and being with children is contingent on the curriculum in which it is situated. To put it another way, documentation practices, like all meaning-making practices, are 'located in particular times and places … [and] indicative of broader social practices' (Barton & Hamilton, 2000, p. 8).

In recalling their work with early childhood curriculum implementation in the Canadian province of New Brunswick, Rose and Whitty (2013) note the importance of 'a continuous process of reflection, dialogue, critical thinking and meaning making … within workshop spaces' (p. 36). The numerous references to 'Aha' moments in the interview data suggested to me that documentation enabled the educators to create workshop spaces in the interstices between planned activities. Reflecting on documentation encouraged them to take risks in their teaching and pleasure in their professional learning. They reflected on genre characteristics of documentations and linked visual design problems to ethical questions. On the other hand, the educators' accounts lend powerful support to Prochner and Pacini-Ketchabaw's (2013, p. 3) observation that 'core ideas in early childhood education' such as child development discourse are highly resilient and easily flow across domain boundaries to govern new spaces.

Background

Once described as the 'Cinderella of the education system' (Dalli et al., p. 3), ECEC currently receives an unprecedented amount of attention from policy makers. Canada has lagged behind many wealthy countries in the area of ECEC provision, but here too governments are working to transform a 'patchwork of disjunctive programs' (Friendly & Prentice, 2009, p. 5) into an early childhood system. In the province of Ontario, for example, a full-day early learning kindergarten programme is now available free of charge to four- and five-year-olds and all ECEC programmes and services are now administered by the Ministry of Education (OME). The ECEC community has welcomed the changes. Advocates worked long and hard to bring visibility to the field and they continue to lobby to improve access to affordable, quality programmes. Yet the notion of *quality* is itself a contested one. ECEC is a deeply contested field in which ideas from the 'new childhood studies' (Thomson, 2008) compete with 'a view of education that is strongly instrumental in rationality, strongly reproductive and transmissive in pedagogy, and strongly technical in practice' (Moss, 2013, p. 10). It is not surprising, then, that some members of the

ECEC community regard the enhanced visibility of their field to be a 'mixed blessing' (Moss, 2012, p. v). Enhanced visibility exposes ECEC practices 'to the gaze of external experts' (Shore, 2008, p. 281); closer ties with the school system make ECEC vulnerable to neoliberal schooling reforms. A powerful voice among critical early childhood scholars, Peter Moss, recently called for a 'counter-offensive of poetry' (2012, p. vii) in which educators emphasize 'participation, love, eagerness, and joy' (p. vi). For Moss and others, quality programmes for young children must create spaces for 'the surprising and unexpected, not just the predefined and normative' (p. vii).

Disentangling notions of quality from 'the predefined and normative' is a theoretical project grounded in critique of the modernist world view and a practical political project whose allies include innovative curricula and pedagogical practices that stress 'process, engagement, dialogue and co-construction…over routines, prescribed best practices, exclusivity and the safe haven of predetermined outcomes' (Pacini-Ketchabaw & Pence, 2005, p. 6). Notable among these innovative curricula and practices are the emergent curriculum approach developed in the Reggio Emilia preschools of northern Italy during the 1970s (Edwards et al., 2012) and pedagogical documentation (hereafter called documentation), a practice aligned with the principles of emergent curriculum in which educators and children collaborate as co-researchers to record, revisit and reflect on significant events and experiences. Variations of emergent curriculum and documentation have been adopted and adapted in many countries and educational settings, including Ontario. The following description of documentation appears in a recently published ministry guide for Ontario educators.

> We have always documented as a society – from cash register slips to medical records, family photo albums to report cards. But pedagogical documentation offers more than a record. It offers a process for listening to children, for creating artifacts from that listening and for studying with others what children reveal about their competent and thoughtful views of the world. To listen to children, we document living moments with images, video, artifacts, written or audio recordings of what children have said, or other digital traces. These documented traces of lived experience, when shared with others, become a tool for thinking together. (Wien, 2013, p. 1)

The above description articulates several foundational principles of the emergent curriculum approach. It represents children as curriculum informants with a right to participate in decisions about their education. It articulates a commitment to bring into view aspects of 'living moments' that traditional approaches to observation and assessment tend to disregard – what classification theorists, Bowker and Star, call the 'undifferentiated other'

(2000, p. 252) – and it makes a commitment to look with children rather than at them. The above description also reveals documentation's commitment to multimodal forms of expression and communication and to what Reggio-inspired educators call 'the hundred languages of children' (Edwards et al., 2012). The artefacts of documentation (e.g. Figure 5.1) orchestrate 'a variety of modalities – speech, writing, image, gesture and sound – to create different forms of meaning' (Hull & Evan Nelson, 2005, pp. 224–225). Missing from the above description, however, is an explicit reference to the ways in which documentation is situated in the broader set of social and material practices that make up a curriculum.

Overview of the study

Since the introduction of full-day kindergarten programmes (FDK) (see Ontario Ministry of Education, 2010), the Ontario government has been actively promoting documentation across the ECEC sector. However, at the time of the study, the government had provided little guidance and less monitoring. My study aimed to understand how educators were learning about and engaging with documentation and how their engagements with documentation were mediating their practice. To this end I distributed invitations to all Ontario College of Teachers (OCT), certified teachers and registered early childhood educators (RECEs) employed in the publicly funded kindergartens of two school districts and to the members of two local ECEC professional networks. Thirteen female educators and one male educator volunteered to participate in the study (see Table 5.1).

The participants were employed in a variety of ECEC settings located in a mid-sized Ontario city (population about 350,000).[1] They were employed in school-based kindergarten programmes, child care centres, preschool classrooms and one parenting centre. The male educator was employed in an infant–toddler setting, but all others worked with children between the ages of three and six years. Each participant had at least two years' professional experience in early childhood education and three educators had worked in the field for more than twenty years.

In the interviews, participants shared views about the nature and purpose(s) of pedagogical documentation and described their experiences of learning to conduct documentations. They also discussed ways in which the process of documentation informed their thinking about and interactions with children. They shared photographs of individual children and groups of children at work as well as examples of children's artwork and other artefacts. Most artwork and artefacts were annotated with short written narratives and interpretive

Table 5.1 Participants

Setting	Participants
Three full-day, school-based kindergartens for four- and five-year-olds (FDK)	Two OCT teachers (K2, K4) and their RECE teaching partners (E1, E2) One OCT teacher with preschool experience (K1)
One half-day kindergarten for four- and five-year-olds	One OCT teacher (K3)
One licensed preschool with resource programme	One RECE (E6) One specialist resource teacher/RECE (E7)
Three licensed child care centres	Two RECEs (E3, E4,) employed in preschool rooms One male OCT teacher employed in an infant–toddler room (E5)
Ontario Early Years Centre (OEYC)	One RECE (EY1) employed as playroom director
One child care organization	One RECE administrator (L1)

Primary teachers receive certification from the Ontario College of Teachers (OCT).
RECE = Registered Early Childhood Educator
OEYC = Ontario Early Years Centre
In Ontario there is one OEYC for each provincial electoral riding. The city in which the study took place has three OEYCs.

comments, but occasionally they were annotated with a question or a letter to the child from the educator. Larger documentation panels assembled a variety of images and texts. These were displayed in hallways and on classroom walls. The kindergarten teachers and early childhood educators employed in schools shared examples of portfolios compiled for each child and one team shared a portfolio in which they had documented their own learning journey with documentation over four years.

Learning to look: The pleasures of documentation

You know you're supposed to observe, but you don't know what you're supposed to observe for. And at the same time that I'm looking, I have to keep them safe, make sure people aren't in trouble. So how can we consider looking and thinking in useful ways? (L1)

In theory, the process of documentation begins with the decision to record an event or an activity deemed significant by a child or an educator. In practice, only the most experienced educators said they worked in this way. Less experienced educators took many more photographs than they actually used and then searched for a storyline to document.

> You can't learn how to walk every month…About half the time it's just looking at the photos and piecing together the different stories and being like, okay, this is where they've been going. This is what they've been doing all week, And you're like, Oh, okay! So that's one of the things that's remarkable, because you can really see how something's developing. (E5)

In theory, children participate in the documentation process and educators record their words verbatim. A child and an educator might revisit recordings together, sometimes several times, and educators are encouraged to keep children and their actions in focus throughout the process (Macdonald, 2007, Curtis & Carter, 2013). Again, stories of practice did not match the ideal. With the exception of one teacher who spoke about her students' enthusiasm for documenting 'everything and anything', participants talked primarily about what they themselves had done and said. But their accounts did suggest that they viewed documentation as a form of research with the children and, although one educator likened the process to scrapbooking, another was quick to point out that the children had never been as interested in the 'old-style scrapbook with all the artwork shoved in'.

The point of looking closely during documentation is to glean insights into a child's thinking in order to support deeper thinking. In the following excerpt from the data, a child care educator explains that if she had not been carefully documenting what she and the child were saying and doing, the child's deliberate and meaningful markings would have been overlooked as mere scribbles. Her comment serves as a reminder that making sense of children's multimodal representations often requires their multimodal assistance. This 'problem' can be a resource because it encourages dialogue and relationship building between educators and children.

> And so then he drew the tree. And this looks like scribblings, but it's very deliberate markings. He would really look at the photo of the house and he would show me the lines that would correspond with his drawing. And so, if I had not documented his experience, this would look very random and scribbly. (E3)

Participants' comments suggest that the benefits they personally experienced from documentation paralleled the benefits they desired for the children.

They found joy in documenting mundane events and small achievements – even achievements as routine as learning to hold a pencil – and encouraged children and their parents to find joy in discovery too. Witness this excerpt from a letter to parents written by a child care educator.

> Many children commented on how their drawing has changed in the past few months. Recognizing and identifying this growth helps to build self-esteem and promotes a positive attitude towards learning. Comparing and contrasting paint and pencil crayons gives children an opportunity to closely observe the properties of the materials they are using, and reflect on their experiences with each. (E4)

In their various ways participants appeared to be exploring the affordances of documentation for self-defined needs. Documentation is time consuming. School teachers were expected to add it to a long list of traditional assessments and all participants used personal time to complete documentations. The general enthusiasm for documentation was therefore quite striking. A preschool educator said that a high point for her was the discovery that she could actually use the children's words; teachers said they appreciated the school district's uncharacteristic lack of explicit direction because it gave them permission to play. However, one kindergarten teacher who worked alone in the classroom felt unable to manage her class in a way that would permit documentation and two other school-based participants talked of searching for more efficient ways to maintain the authenticity of the process without 'going crazy'. They were experimenting with a form of documentation that 'didn't look as pretty' but 'would still be useful to us'.

None of the participating educators voiced concerns about access to or use of mobile technologies for documentation, but less experienced educators confessed to feeling challenged by the style of writing they felt documentation demanded. One educator said his goal was to become 'less formal' and 'more creative'. Another recalled that her early documentations were not 'pulling out any of the learning that was happening'. They were just 'Here's a picture. Here's the story. And that's it'. The educator praised a colleague who could 'really paint a picture with the words that she was using, but not in a way that was fluffy and excessive'. Ironically, the two participants whose roles included hiring and training staff were unconcerned. One participant commented that she knew writing was difficult for many educators, but she believed success in documentation resulted from a disposition towards learning, reflection and collaboration rather than a pre-existing ability to write well. When I asked the other participant how she would support an educator in learning to conduct documentation, she related a story of 'thinking together' alongside a colleague for several weeks. As the colleague gained skills and confidence in her interactions with the children, the quality of the documentations improved without any explicit instruction. The educator said, 'Now she knows how it should feel, she's not going back to this place of surface again'.

Making learning visible: Multimodality, memories and mirrors

The claim that documentation makes learning visible raises questions about the kinds of learning that documentation brings into view. My first review of the data suggested that the types of learning mapped easily onto the curricular approach in each practice setting. For example, emergent (print) literacy learning surfaced in stories from a kindergarten where children were 'documenting themselves' and using portfolios to 'track' their progress in printing skills. And while all participants spoke of using documentation to name dispositional accomplishments such as staying committed to a difficult task, it was the child care educators who reflected most often on social and emotional dispositions such as shyness, kindness and courage.

A further review of the data revealed that all the interviews contained references to problem solving with multimodal resources. Before Jake could begin to draw his tree, he had to make room for the tree – and because the page was full, the educator had shown him that he could tape another paper to the original page. In another interview, a teacher and early childhood educator recalled an 'Aha' moment in which they experienced first-hand the pedagogical affordances of documentation and the extent to which the children's engagement had been deepened by an invitation to draw a solution.

> And the very next day we went on this field trip and we took some pictures and we documented what happened and we made a class book and we looked at it on the smart board and one of the pictures we were looking at (pause) ... [Child's name] said, 'One of the guys was trying to catch the chicken but the chicken was too fast.' So now we said, 'Hey. Well. How would you catch the chicken?' So then they all did a visual picture that was neat and we realized 'This is all documentation.' They were so very engaged. And it was just a pencil sketch. (K2, E1)

Another kindergarten teacher told a story about her cat, Gary. The teacher had moved Gary's food bowl, but because Gary was old and blind he was having trouble getting to his food. Every day for weeks the children had come up with new ideas for Gary, including food trails and treasure maps, and the class was documenting their success (or lack of it) in an ongoing story.

Using Blocks To Build Relationships

Tom - this morning while you were building with the blocks, I challenged you to build a tower that was as tall as the ceiling. You eagerly accepted this challenge and told me that you needed to "build a steady base" first. I watched with interest as you set a flat board on the ground, stood several tall blocks on top of it, and then balanced another flat board on top. Then you set two long blocks on their side across the board and laid more long blocks side by side across the top. You repeated this pattern until you expressed that you were running out of blocks. I asked you what you were going to do now and you replied, "smaller blocks". As you resumed building, I noticed that you changed your design so that you could use the smaller blocks to continue constructing in a similar way.

When Harry approached you and said that he wanted to help build, you said, "No. Not tall enough." You shared with him your fear that since he wasn't tall enough to reach the top of the tower, he might cause the tower to fall down when he tried to place a block on top. I was impressed with the way that you communicated your concerns to Harry, and then worked together with him to negotiate a solution that satisfied both of you. Together, you decided that Harry would hand you the blocks and you would place them on the tower. You continued building together until you could no longer reach the top using the step ladder. We searched the building, but couldn't find a bigger ladder, so I suggested that we save your tower and continue building later when we could borrow a big ladder. You agreed, but decided to place an X shaped block on each side of the base to warn the other children not to knock it down.

<u>What It Means</u>
Tom, I was very excited as I observed this experience. Not only did you demonstrate your knowledge and skill of building, but you held up our classroom values of respect, working together to solve problems, and forming relationships. Over the past few months you and Harry have been forming a strong relationship, as you are the only boys in the class on the days when you attend. Today when Harry wanted to join in your play, you showed him that you respect him by taking the time to figure out a way for him to be involved without giving up your own values. You considered Harry's feelings as well as your own. You were able to negotiate this process on your own, without having to seek help from the teachers.

Figure 5.1 *Building Blocks: A Learning Story*

Figure 5.1 shows an abridged version of a Learning Story written by a child care educator.[2] The educator documented the child's accomplishments in detail, naming the ways in which he approached challenges in the physical and social worlds of the classroom. By naming his accomplishments, she aimed to make them visible and replicable. Some participants used the phrase 'providing memories' to label this aspect of documentation, but the educator was also providing a mirror in which the child could look at himself through her eyes. She reflected back to him the kindness that he had shown towards his friends as well as the persistence he had demonstrated in building the tower. Tom got to see himself as a persistent learner, a competent builder *and* a good friend.

Thinking together within and across boundaries

Most opportunities for educators and children to think together arose within a single setting, but several educators spoke of participating in planned dialogue sessions with colleagues. For example, the staff of one child care centre scheduled regular photo-study sessions over the lunch hour. The educator who described these 'Nooners' valued the critical questions that other educators posed, noting that 'documenting with coworkers keeps you honest'.

> [W]e'll say things like 'I was so surprised you did this.' And the thing that was offered to me was, 'When you think of your image of the child and you're saying that you believe children are capable of doing these things and then you're shocked when they do them … Why were you shocked that they did this?' (E4)

Documentations were sometimes employed in classroom activity centres as provocations for the children to think together. Small format documentations were included in children's portfolios and stored in places that children could easily access individually or with another child. Large poster-size panels were usually displayed on classroom walls and in hallways and a few were annotated with questions such as 'What did we do?' Notable among the educators' stories of 'thinking together' was the story told by a kindergarten teacher (K2) and early childhood educator (E1) team who had compiled a portfolio to show the evolution of their documentation practices over four years of working together. The team brought the portfolio to the interview and leafed through it together, linking the evolution of their thinking about documentation to the evolution of their thinking about pedagogy. The two women disagreed often, but their lively disagreements communicated deep mutual respect and the collaborative retelling of their story was punctuated with laughter and comments such as 'I don't know why it took us so long to get to that place.'

The participants spoke about mobilizing documentation for 'thinking together' across domains as well as within them. The parent–child programme created documentation panels 'primarily *for* our families' and assigned space on the monthly planning sheet to consider documented conversations with parents. Several educators were experimenting with the Learning Stories approach (see Figure 5.1) and offering the story to the child's family for comments. The educator from the infant–toddler programme pointed out that documentation can support relationships in less elaborate ways too. He had been able to reassure the parents of one toddler by showing them a video-recording of their child.

> So they're worried about their child's communication skills. And you're like She's got this covered. She's not necessarily saying, 'I'd like my bottle please.' But that's okay. She's able to communicate the things that she needs. (E5)

A group of researchers in Aotearoa, New Zealand, have found that artefacts of documentation can facilitate the flow of knowledge across domain boundaries. In sociocultural theory, a boundary marks 'a sociocultural difference leading to discontinuity in action or interaction' (Akkerman & Bakker, 2011, p. 133) but a 'boundary' can 'simultaneously suggest a sameness and continuity in the sense that within discontinuity two or more sites are relevant to one another in a particular way' (p. 133). A boundary object supports the coordination of multiple perspectives across boundaries by being 'plastic enough to adapt to local needs ... yet robust enough to maintain a common identity across sites' (Star & Griesemer, 1989, p. 369). Carr (2013) proposes that a child's Learning Stories portfolio fulfils these requirements for although a kindergarten teacher and early childhood educator would attach locally specific meanings to the portfolio, each would recognize the structure and general purpose of the portfolio and each could contribute a Learning Story that would be acceptable to the other. Viewed in this light, boundaries are learning spaces that support rather than impede dialogue.

The interview data contain only a few examples of thinking together across boundaries. Most participants felt that 'coordinating multiple and conflicting viewpoints' (Carr & Lee, 2012, p. 8) was a good idea and a shared responsibility, but at the time of the study, ECEC organizations across the province were just beginning to develop inter-professional learning activities. There was some flow of knowledge and practices across boundaries and the flow was not unidirectional – that is not just flowing *from* schools. As this excerpt from an interview with a teacher shows, an ECE teaching partner's skills in documentation skills could be coveted by teachers.

> So I continued on my very curriculum focused way ... not necessarily paying much attention to what were the kids really doing ... So that's where we

started and then [the early childhood educator] started to do it. And I had to ask myself: How did you pick up all that information from just watching a child? And so she started to sell me on the idea that you could actually stop being so crazed about what comes in the curriculum document and start listening to the kids. And seeing how you can draw from the kids and how that becomes what you document. (K2)

The educators' unanimous enthusiasm for documentation suggests that it could be a powerful vehicle to support multidirectional flows of knowledge and practices across Ontario's ECEC sector. Its ability to adapt to local needs is well demonstrated and it is quickly becoming a recognized practice in schools as well as other ECEC organizations. However, the extent to which documentation can promote 'poetic ways of being with children' is less clear. As one participant put it, learning to look this way will take 'a tremendous amount of practice because, we have so much practice looking...from a different point of view'.

Instructing the educator's gaze

At some point, the society teaches them that they're not a miracle, that instead of looking in the mirror and thinking you're amazing, and looking at other people and thinking, wow, they're amazing too, we've suddenly started to look at ourselves in the mirror and go, ooh, this isn't right. (L1)

Early childhood educators are accustomed to observing and documenting children's sayings and doings, but traditional approaches to observation tend to place dominant discourses such as *school readiness* and *child development* 'centre stage' (Thomson, 2008, p. 2). Reggio-inspired approaches to documentation aim to de-centre dominant discourses, but without a coherent curriculum in which to situate documentation, educators are easily drawn back to familiar ways of looking.

School readiness refers to a policy goal for all children to arrive in grade one ready for academic and social success (Stooke, 2014). However, the participating educators framed their comments about readiness primarily in terms of academic skills. The early childhood educators were generally sceptical about the need to explicitly teach academics before school and one ECE pointed out that the early childhood education field has 'understood early years development for sixty years'.

Child development discourse is so entrenched in Western ways of looking at and acting towards children that we barely notice the extent to which everyday conversations depend on its categories. However, an increasing number of ECEC researchers now question developmental discourse. In *Governing the Soul*, the Foucauldian scholar, Nikolas Rose (1999) links the near universal adoption of child development discourse in the West to the growth in importance of psychology and psychiatry as disciplines. Rose pays particular attention to the famous continuum of child development created by Arnold Gesell during the 1920s. He proposes that the wide uptake of Gesell's continuum by human services professions during the latter half of the twentieth century ensured that '[a]ll who had dealt with children in their professional and personal life could now have their mind instructed through the education of their gaze' (p. 153).

Gesell inscribed the behaviours of actual children first through multiple photographs, then through stick figure drawings and captions. By so doing, he transformed the child into a 'visible, observable, and analyzable object' (Rose, 1999, p. 147). Rose argues that Gesell's continuum did not simply offer a technical aid for observing what was actually there but it also enshrined a particular vision of childhood and opened up new ways of acting towards children. Once the continuum was established, educators could confidently make judgments about normal and abnormal development and they mobilized those judgments for practical purposes such as referring 'abnormal' children to clinicians. The set of pedagogical principles known as developmentally appropriate practice (DAP) (Bredekamp, 1987) would be impossible without the norms first made visible by Gesell's continuum.

In Ontario early child development discourse is textualized in five continua in a government document entitled Early Learning for Every Child Today (ELECT) (Best Start Panel on Early Learning, 2007). The data revealed ELECT to be a powerful mediator of practices in the parent–child and preschool programmes. It was slightly less powerful in the kindergarten classrooms and played a small, but not inconsequential role in at least one child care setting.

The parent–child programme had adopted ELECT as a programme evaluation tool and planning framework. Programme leaders were not compelled to enact any formal curriculum, and as noted earlier, they saw documentation as being primarily for the parents. They developed a large planning template on which they recorded conversations with parents, but during planning meetings they translated what families had told them into activities that would 'cover' the ELECT domains and they created documentation panels that represented the activities as developmentally appropriate practices.

The preschool organization was making a transition from the High Scope[3] curriculum to an eclectic approach that included aspects of emergent curriculum. The educators developed an in-house version of the ELECT document and conducted ELECT-based assessments for each child twice during the academic year. They routinely conducted a variety of other types of documentation, but they described ELECT-based assessments as the most important forms of documentation.

School teachers in Ontario are less familiar with child development norms than with curricular expectations, but full-day kindergarten teachers are partnered with early childhood educators who are assumed to be knowledgeable about child development. In the first years of the kindergarten implementation the early childhood educators had taken the lead in documentation and one team showed me their first template, a letter-size page that featured a checklist based on the ELECT domains. The template seemed ill-suited to documenting the innovative practices that the team described during the interview. It left little room for detailed description, but neatly translated children's actions into developmental milestones. Over time, the team came to the same conclusion. The template had been a good starting point, but they were experimenting with a Learning Stories format which they found 'harder to write as well as time-consuming' but more authentic and rewarding.

The child care organization had adopted an emergent curriculum framework several years prior to the study. They were not obligated to work with ELECT, but one centre had begun to employ the document for marketing purposes. The educator explained that the centre was obliged to compete with publicly funded, school-based kindergartens. They had recently begun to keep a copy of the ELECT document on hand and to incorporate the language of ELECT in their documentations. For this educator ELECT was not so much a pedagogical resource as a form of image management since parents who were choosing between their programme and a school-based programme could now access comparable information. An additional advantage for the staff was that students on placement from the local colleges could now fulfil their course assignments that required references to ELECT.

> [S]o we've been really working on helping parents to see … [that] their children are not going to be worse off for staying here, … and we really know that the ELECT document is huge and is about much more than the Continuum, but parents really want to see that part of it. So what we've done is – we've started using the language of the Continuum, without specifically pointing out the numbers in the Continuum. (E4)

The educator's comments serve as a reminder that organizing early childhood education as a marketplace can actually promote standardization. Market policies encourage organizations to see themselves as enterprises and they encourage individual educators to override pedagogical principles to ensure the survival of the organization. The educator's comments resonate with Foucault's (1991) notion of governmentality, which shows how power is exercised indirectly and without regulations through the gradual alignment of individuals' subjectivities with the goals of powerful groups. Seemingly insignificant moments of translation (Callon, 1986) such as this one tend to go unnoticed, but as moments accumulate they threaten to undermine professional discernment. According to Fenwick and Edwards (2010, p. 115), this is exactly how '[a]countability is achieved' in the absence of regulations.

The educators' comments about ELECT suggest that it is easier to adopt the forms and formats of documentation than it is to implement the principles of emergent curriculum with which documentation is most closely associated. If educators engage in practices that resemble documentation, but continue to look at and act towards children with minds instructed by child development discourse, the consequences for children may be more 'predefined and normative' (Moss, 2012, p. vii) than they intend. The account from the child care setting is particularly disturbing because it shows how market strategies can enable old ideas to re-colonize a curriculum space in which those ideas long ago ceased to occupy centre-stage.

Conclusion

My inquiry into educators' experiences with pedagogical documentation in Ontario's ECEC sector considered the potential for documentation to promote ways of being with young children characterized by participation, love, eagerness and joy. There is no doubt that the educators who participated in the study were eager to promote and experience joyful ways of being with children. Inviting children to participate in documentation recognizes their right 'to have a say about things that concern them' (Thomson, 2008, p. 1). Inviting them to express their ideas in self-chosen ways recognizes them as capable meaning makers. Neither is there any doubt that the multimodal nature of documentation facilitates the sharing of ideas across settings and the creation of workshop spaces in which educators can engage in reflection and curriculum design processes. Yet the interview data suggest that documentation's ability to support a counter-offensive of poetry depends less on its multimodal affordances than on the curriculum approach in which it is situated. The fact that the ELECT document played such a visible role in the documentation process in all settings suggests that there is work to be done if documentation is to support new ways of looking at learning and acting towards children. The fact that the Ontario government promoted ELECT and documentation at the same time suggests that it has not yet committed to a coherent vision for ECEC in the province. It is there that the work must begin.

Notes

1 Interviews were conducted with a teacher and her early childhood educator teaching partner.

2 The original story contains photographs of the children and a section in which the educator invites the parents to add to the story. All names have been changed.

3 HighScope is a research-based approach to preschool education that stresses the importance of participatory learning.

References

Akkerman, S. F., & Bakker, A. (2011). Boundary crossing and boundary objects. *Review of Educational Research, 81*(2), 132–169. doi: 10.3102/0034654311404435

Arthur, C. (Ed.) (2012) *Financial Literacy Education: Neoliberalism, the Consumer and the Citizen*. Rotterdam: Sense.

Barton, D., & Hamilton, M. (2000). Literacy practices. In D. Barton, M. Hamilton & R. Ivanic (Eds), *Situated Literacies: Reading and Writing in Context* (pp. 7–15). New York: Routledge.

Best Start Panel on Early Learning. (2007). *Early Learning for Every Child Today*. Toronto: Ontario Ministry of Child and Youth Services.

Bowker, G. C., & Star, S. L. (2000). *Sorting Things Out: Classification and Its Consequences*. Cambridge: MIT Press.

Bredekamp, S. (1987). *Developmentally Appropriate Practice in Early Childhood Programs Serving Children from Birth through 8*. Washington: National Association for the Education of Young Children.

Callon, M. (1986). Some elements of a sociology of translation: Domestication of the scallops and the fishermen of St Brieuc Bay, In J. Law (Ed.), *Power, Action and Belief. A New Sociology of Knowledge?* (pp. 196–233). London: Routledge & Kegan Paul.

Carr, M. (2013). Making a borderland of contested spaces into a meeting place: The relationship from a New Zealand perspective. In P. Moss, L. Balduzzi et al. (Eds), *Early Childhood and Compulsory Education: Reconceptualizing the Relationship* (pp. 92–111). London: Routledge.

Carr, M., & Lee, W. (2012). *Learning Stories: Constructing Learner Identities in Early Education*. Los Angeles: Sage.

Curtis, D., & Carter, C. (2013). *The Art of Awareness: How Observation Can Transform Your Teaching*. St. Paul: Redleaf Press.

Dalli, C., Miller, L., & Urban, M. (2012). Early childhood grows up: Towards a critical ecology of the profession. In L. Miller, C. Dalli, & M. Urban (Eds), *Early*

Childhood Grows Up: Towards a Critical Ecology of the Profession (pp. 1–20). Dordrecht: Springer.

Edwards, C., Gandini, L., & Forman, G. (2012). *The Hundred Languages of Children: The Reggio Emilia Experience in Transformation*. Santa Barbara: Praeger.

Fenwick, T., & Edwards, R. (2010). *Actor-network Theory in Education*. Milton Park: Routledge.

Friendly, M., & Prentice, S. (2009). *Childcare*. Black Point: Fernwood.

Foucault, M. (1991). Governmentality. In G. Burchell, C. Gordon & P. Miller (Eds), *The Foucault Effect. Studies in Governmentality. With Two Lectures by and an Interview with Michel Foucault* (pp. 87–104). Chicago: University of Chicago Press.

Hull, G., & Evan Nelson, M. (2005). Locating the semiotic power of multimodality. *Written Communication, 22*(2), 224–261.

Macdonald, M. (2007). Toward formative assessment: The use of pedagogical documentation in early elementary classrooms. *Early Childhood Research Quarterly 22*, 232–242.

Moss, P. (2012). Foreword. In L. Miller, C. Dalli & M. Urban (Eds), *Early Childhood Grows Up: Towards a Critical Ecology of the Profession* (pp. v–viii). Dordrecht: Springer.

Moss, P. (2013). The relationship between early childhood and compulsory education: A properly political question. In P. Moss, L. Balduzzi, J. Bennett, M. Carr, G. Dahlberg, H. Gobeyn, P. Haug, S. L. Kagan, A. Lazarri, N. De Sterke, and M. Vandenbroek (Eds.), *Early Childhood and Compulsory Education: Reconceptualizing the Relationship* (pp. 2–50). London: Routledge.

Ontario Ministry of Education. (2010). *Full-day Early Learning – Kindergarten Program (Draft)*. Toronto: Ontario Ministry of Education.

Pacini-Ketchabaw, V., & Pence, A. (2005). The reconceptualizing movement in Canadian early childhood education, care and development. In V. Pacini-Ketchabaw & A. Pence (Eds), *Canadian Early Childhood Education: Broadening and Deepening Discussions of Quality* (pp. 5–20). Ottawa: Canadian Child Care Federation.

Parkinson, H., & Stooke, R. (2012). Other duties as assigned: The hidden work of reading and writing assessments in two primary classrooms. *Language & Literacy, 14*(1), 59–77.

Prochner & Pacini-Ketchabaw, V. (2013). Resituating early childhood education: Introduction. In V. Pacini-Ketchabaw & L. Prochner (Eds), *Resituating Early Childhood Education* (pp. 1–14). New York: Peter Lang.

Rose, N. (1999). *Governing the Soul: The Shaping of the Private Self*. London: Free Association Books.

Rose, S., & Whitty, P. (2013) Valuing subjective complexities: Dumping the tyranny of time. In V. Pacini-Ketchabaw & L. Prochner (Eds), *Resituating Early Childhood Education* (pp. 35–52). New York: Peter Lang.

Shore, C. (2008). Audit culture and neoliberal governance: Universities and the politics of accountability. *Anthropological Theory, 8*, 278–298. doi: 10.1177/1463499608093815

Star, S. L., & Griesemer, J. R. (1989). Institutional ecology, 'translations' and boundary objects: Amateurs and professionals in Berkeley's Museum of Vertebrate Zoology, 1907–39. *Social Studies of Science, 19*, 387–420.

Stooke, R. (2014) Producing neoliberal parenting subjectivities: ANT-inspired readings from an informal early learning program. *Canadian Children, 39*(1), 22–46.

Thomson, P. (2008). Children and young people: Voices in visual research. In P. Thomson (Ed.), *Doing Visual Research with Children and Young People* (pp. 1–19). London: Routledge.

Wien, C. (2013). *Making Learning Visible Through Pedagogical Documentation.* Toronto: Queens Printer for Ontario. Retrieved from http://www.edu.gov. on.ca/childcare/Wien.pdf

6

Regulatory Gaze and 'Non-sense' Phonics Testing in Early Literacy

Rosie Flewitt and Guy Roberts-Holmes

Chapter overview

In the context of increasing political intervention in early years and primary assessment in England, this chapter discusses how the power of 'highly prescriptive systems of accountability' (Ball, 2013, p. 173) has drawn early literacy into the state's regulatory and disciplinary gaze through a process of 'datafication' (Roberts-Holmes, 2014). We examine the disciplinary effects of assessment technologies upon early literacy pedagogy through the focussed perspective of one inner-city primary head teacher discussing the impact of the statutory 'Phonics Screening Check' (DfE, 2012a). We critique the multimodal design of this assessment tool for 5- to 6-year-old children in England, and discuss how some practitioners have 'cynically complied' (Bradbury 2013, p. 124) to new literacy regulations through a process of accommodation and resistance. Whilst the Phonics Screening Check will no doubt disappear in time from early literacy assessment in England, it serves as an example of how discourses of power infiltrate from political ideology to literacy policy and education practice, undermining professional judgement and moulding children's multimodal experiences of literacy in the primary classroom. As education assessment technologies come and go, it is highly likely that teachers' work will continue to be constrained by the political need to produce 'appropriate' data (Bradbury 2013; Roberts-Holmes, 2014). We therefore close the chapter by suggesting that Foucault's conceptualization of 'care of the self' (Foucault, 1988) can create spaces for teachers to resist imposed regimes of governmental 'truth' and to plan motivating, creative and multimodal activities that nurture young students' long-term engagement with literacy learning.

Regimes of truth and the regulation of English education

In a global context of international economic competition, national governments in the developed world have increasingly heralded education as being the key to a country's long-term economic and social well-being. Discourses of economy have dominated neoliberal national and global arguments for education transformation, with 'effective' early education, literacy and numeracy in particular cited as long-term cures for the social ills of poverty, unemployment and poor health, and for enabling effective participation in the workforce (Organisation for Economic Cooperation and Development (OECD), 2006). On the political stage in England, economic ideologies have explicitly become the bedrock for government education policy and the justification for curriculum intervention, in a socio-economic discourse where the need to be competitive in a global marketplace is presented as an unquestionable truth. For example, in the first statement of the Foreword to the coalition government 2010 White Paper *The Importance of Teaching* (DfE, 2010), the Prime Minister David Cameron and Deputy Prime Minister Nick Clegg asserted:

> … what really matters is how we're doing compared with our international competitors. That is what will define our economic growth and our country's future. The truth is, at the moment we are standing still while others race past. (DfE, 2010, p. 3)

The White Paper goes on to compare England's performance with that of the highest ranking countries in the OECD Programme for International Student Assessment (PISA) surveys, and argues that certain attributes in those education systems contribute to their success. Applying a form of logic akin to association fallacy,[1] the document then suggests that importing those attributes into England's education would ensure its greater success in the PISA charts. From a necessarily wide choice of possibilities, given the diversity and complexity of education provision in the PISA top-performing countries, the particular criteria for success selected in the White Paper include: ensuring the high quality of teaching staff; allocating teacher training roles to outstanding schools; boosting teacher authority in the classroom with increased powers for detention and other instruments of child control; devolving power 'to the front line' (DfE, 2010, p. 3) while retaining accountability; and having high expectations of all children, including those 'on free school meals' (DfE, 2010, p. 4). Curriculum reforms were subsequently developed following a dominant discourse of 'a firm grip of the basics' (DfE, 2012a, p. 13), and premised on an ideological model of education driven by economics and international competitiveness.

As Foucault asserts, every society has a 'general politics' of truth, with particular discourses which are accepted and enacted as true by those who have the status to define what counts as true (Foucault, 1980, p. 131). The meanings implied by these discourses shape social reality as embodiments of the dominant 'regimes of truth' which operate in and regulate a country's political, economic and social institutions. In turn, the discourses govern the relationships between people in those institutions, such as head teachers, teachers and children, and ensure that these relationships are constrained by the dominant discourses (see Dahlberg et al., 2013). The teaching of reading in England is a case in point, where, influenced by the position of UK literacy in international league tables, government policy has become increasingly prescriptive, as evidenced in a series of initiatives such as the National Literacy Strategy (NLS), the Rose Report (DfES, 2006) and the current phonics testing regime (DfE, 2012a). Underpinning these interventions lie definitions of literacy as the acquisition of a set of neutral, universal and transferable skills. This approach stands in contrast to established work in the field of New Literacy Studies, which promotes a holistic, child-centred literacy curriculum and pedagogy that recognizes how literacy is woven into the fabric of children's daily lives in diverse social settings (Marsh, 2011; Flewitt, 2012). Current literacy policy in England also ignores international visions for literacy as the multimodal ability 'to identify, understand, interpret, create, communicate, compute and use printed and written materials associated with varying contexts' (UNESCO, 2013). Yet teachers in England have little option but to honour policy intervention in the classroom, as their practice is inspected, regulated and disciplined by often unannounced government inspection in the form of OFSTED (Office for Standards in Education),[2] as discussed later in this chapter.

As one example of the pervasive nature of the particular regime of truth presented in the 2010 White Paper, we focus on the introduction of the statutory 'Phonics Screening Check' (DfE, 2012a) for 5- and 6-year olds in English primary school education, on the official justification for its existence, the process of its development, its multimodal design and its disciplinary impact on teacher autonomy and children's literacy learning in early primary education. We begin with some background information about this statutory assessment which was first imposed on all mainstream primary schools in England during the academic year 2011–2012.

The Phonics Screening Check

In September 2011, the Department for Education in England announced that a new, statutory Phonics Screening Check (PSC) would be introduced for all Year 1 primary school children (aged 5–6 years depending on their birth date) during the summer term of the same academic year. A pilot was conducted in 296 schools in June 2011 (Townley & Gotts, 2013) and a statutory assessment framework was subsequently published (DfE, 2012a) with the dubiously reassuring assertion that the PSC had been devised by an unspecified 'group of phonics experts' (DfE, 2012a, p. 6). Driven by the political goal of ensuring high aspirations for all children, the stated purpose of the check was 'to confirm that all children have learned phonic decoding to an age-appropriate standard' (DfE, 2012a, p. 4).

We now fast forward to Monday, 18 June 2012, the week when all Year 1 children in England, regardless of their age in calendar months during that particular week, sat for the PSC. The check required them to read aloud forty isolated words, working one-to-one with their teacher in the classroom. Children were allowed some practice words before completing the assessed task, where explicit and detailed scoring criteria were provided for practitioners (see Appendix A). Official guidance suggested the check was likely to take '4–9 minutes to complete per pupil' (Coldwell et al., 2011) and a pass score was set in advance at thirty-two out of forty correct pronunciations.

To ensure 'the purest assessment of phonic decoding' (DfE, 2012a, p. 8), the check contained twenty real words and twenty 'pseudo-' or 'non-sense' words, that is words that had been invented to represent grapheme-phoneme correspondence but which carried no meaning. The stated purpose of the nonsense words was to ensure there would be 'no unintended bias based on visual memory of words or vocabulary knowledge' (DfE, 2012a, p. 8). During the consultation phase for the test, it was pointed out that for early readers who regularly encounter real words that are new to them, the juxtaposition of real and pseudo-words could cause confusion. This potential flaw was resolved by presenting a picture of an imaginary creature alongside the pseudo-words (see Figure 6.1) but not alongside the real words, with the following guidance for practitioners:

> The pseudo-words will be presented with a picture prompt (a picture of an imaginary creature) and children will be asked to name the type of creature. This approach makes it clear to children that they are reading a pseudo-word, which they should not expect to be able to match to their existing vocabulary. (DfE, 2012a, p. 8)

Figure 6.1 *Extract from 2012 Phonics Screening Check 'pseudo-words'*

The communicative clarity and disciplinary impact of the PSC's multimodal design is critiqued in the following section. For now, we return to the selection of real words, which intentionally included a high proportion of uncommon words (between 40–60 per cent of those presented in the PSC), on the basis that 'the majority of children will need to decode using phonics rather than rely on sight memory of words they have seen before' (DfE, 2012a, p. 8).

To briefly recap: to succeed in this test, each child was required correctly to read aloud a minimum of thirty-two out of forty isolated, de-contextualized words, half of which were pseudo-words and half real words, most of the latter being intentionally unknown to them. The pseudo or real status of the words was indicated by the presence or absence of an imaginary creature, drawn in cartoon form. During the test, the children were told the pseudo-words had no meaning, and the creatures were imaginary. The children were then invited to 'name the type' of imaginary creature, even though the creature did not exist and therefore did not belong to an identifiable type. Perhaps at this stage the reader might care to try naming the types of creature illustrated in Figure 6.1, or reading aloud the pseudo-words: 'vus' is particularly interesting, with /ʌ/ or /ʊ/ possible for the vowel sound, depending on the reader's interpretation and/or regional accent. In cases such as these, decisions about the correctness or incorrectness of the responses were left to the interpretation of individual teachers, in accordance with the official guidance shown in Appendix A.

Once the check had been completed by all pupils and the results dispatched, parents were informed by teachers of their child's success or failure, national results were published and the media lost no time in reporting the controversial status of the PSC, with headlines such as 'Spelling test "a load of bunkum"' (*Times*, 18 June 2012) and 'Phonics literacy test for young children "a waste of time and money"' (*Guardian*, 21 May 2013). The Statistical First Release of the PSC results (DfE, 2012b) revealed that only 58 per cent of all children met the 'expected standard of phonic decoding'. Girls outperformed boys in the test with 62 per cent meeting the required standard compared to 54 per cent of boys, with wide ethnic variation in achievement: the highest scoring groups were Indian (70 per cent) and Chinese (69 per cent); 58 per cent White British children passed the check, with the lowest scoring groups Gypsy/Roma (17 per cent) and travellers of Irish Heritage (16 per cent) (for detail see Townley & Gotts, 2013, p. 10). Socio-economic background also appeared a significant predictor of success with 44 per cent of pupils eligible for Free School Meals (FSM) achieving the expected standard, compared to 62 per cent of pupils not eligible for FSM. Likewise, date of birth was significant, with 75 per cent of the oldest boys and 55 per cent of the youngest achieving a pass standard, and a corresponding 81 per cent and 64 per cent of girls. Interestingly, linguistic background showed more equitable results, with 58 per cent of pupils with English as a first language achieving the required standard and 58 per cent of pupils whose first language was not English. Independent survey analysis of the 2012 Screening Check (UKLA, 2012) showed that many students already deemed by their teachers to be fluent and successful readers underperformed in the test, with 73.4 per cent of teachers (from a total of 494 responses) reporting that one or more of their 'good readers' failed to meet the expected standard. Fluent readers in particular were confused by the pseudo-words, often sounding out phonemes correctly but then blending them incorrectly as they tried to make sense of what they read, such as sounding out the pseudo-word 'thend' as 'θ - ɛ - nd' but then reading aloud 'the end'. Consequently, many highly competent young readers were labelled failures by the PSC regime.

There are many aspects of the PSC which lend themselves to critique, not least its title 'screening check' – a term associated with the medical diagnosis of disease which situates the check as a scientific instrument for diagnosing children's literacy ills. There is also scant research evidence to support a phonics-led approach to literacy teaching, as made clear in the negative findings of *A Systematic Review of Experimental Research on the Use of Phonics Instruction in the Teaching of Reading and Spelling* (Torgerson et al., 2006) and in subsequent research (see Wyse & Goswami, 2008; Ellis & Moss, 2014). The DfES commissioned Systematic Review, which is incompatible with the current government 'regime of truth', appears to have been ignored during literacy policy development, while other conclusions have been based on research that has had little or no external validation (Clark, 2006). Furthermore, the forms of statistical modelling used to present the national results of the check are highly questionable, as is the statistical distribution of the 2012 and 2013 phonics test results (see Clark, 2013b), which both showed a conspicuous spike in the distribution at a score of thirty-two, that is, the required standard for pupils to succeed (see Figure 6.2). This spike suggests that in the first years of its delivery, teachers may have erred towards a pass mark for children whose performance lay at the pre-determined pass/fail boundary.

Overall, the check has been rebuked as failing to add meaningfully to information that teacher assessment already provided; as inaccurate for incorrectly labelling 'good readers' as 'failing'; and as unethical for not offering guidance on how to support children who are identified as underperforming

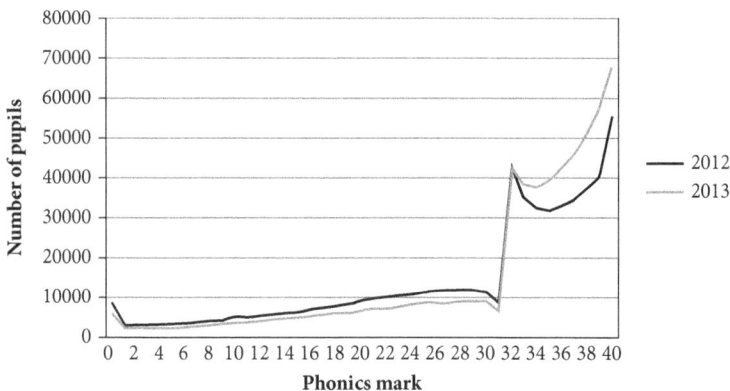

Figure 6.2 *Year 1 phonics screening check mark distribution*

(Clark, 2013a,b). Yet, despite deep reservations expressed by education professionals, leading public figures and researchers about the purpose, accuracy, validity, ethics and value of the check (see Clark, 2013a,b), it has continued to be administered to all Year 1 students, with consequences for children's education that reach far beyond literacy learning, and beyond the classroom. To explore these consequences in more depth, we now scrutinize the PSC as one example of how the design of a nationwide testing system enforces a particular political disciplinary regime and has a profound impact on professional judgement.

The Phonics Screening Check as multimodal literacy artefact

A central consideration in the design of any text is which mode (such as written language and/or image in printed texts) is the most apt resource for expressing a particular meaning. As mentioned, during the 2011 PSC Pilot children were confused by the juxtaposition of real and pseudo-words, and the design of the test was consequently changed to include images of imaginary creatures alongside the pseudo-words, as shown in Figure 6.1.

As Kress and van Leeuwen (2001) discuss, for a semiotic resource (such as an image) to count as a communicative mode, it must be used regularly for meaning-making within a community, and fulfil the purpose which that community expects to be fulfilled by that mode. Following Halliday's theorization of language as social semiosis (1984), a mode fulfils three semiotic functions, namely to deal with ideational, interpersonal and textual meanings. Each of these semiotic functions is an essential aspect of a representational and communicational resource: to be able to account for states of affairs in the world; to convey meanings about the social relations of those who are engaged in interaction; and to be able to form complete semiotic entities, which display coherence internally and externally with the environment in which they occur (Kress, 2014).

Images have particular affordances, such as their position on a page, their size, colour, shape and their spatial relation to other communicative modes. Sign makers can draw on the socially and culturally established uses of images to realize their rhetorical intentions and to meet the needs of their audience (for further discussion, see Bezemer & Kress, 2008). In written texts, particularly texts for early readers, images are conventionally used to add meaning to words – to give clues, to supplement the words or sometimes to offer different possible interpretations, so that meanings are read across multiple modes. However, in the PSC the way images are used breaks away from these established modal conventions in two significant ways. Firstly, using a series of different images (and each pseudo-word had a different image) to denote the same meaning is a significant departure from the conventions of visual sign-making, where, for instance, the repetitious use of a single image or icon is more conventional, as in the sign of a white horizontal bar on a red circular background which is used consistently to denote 'No entry' to a road.

Secondly, there is the meaning that readers were expected to understand from each image in the PSC, that is, 'the word next to this image is not a real word and has no meaning'. This creates an ideational relationship between the written word and the image (the presence of the image means that the co-present word has no meaning) and an interpersonal relationship between the image and the young readers, who were encouraged to attribute a name and a meaning to each image by suggesting which type of creature it represented, but not to attribute the same meaning to the word. This in itself is a highly unconventional use of semiotic resources, which is confusing for any reader, but perhaps particularly so for emerging readers, whose semiotic landscapes are highly likely to be populated with similar-looking commercially created creatures (such as Monsters, Inc. or Peppa Pig). Hence, it can be argued that the flawed multimodal design of the PSC is bound almost inevitably to confuse young children taking the assessment. The low scores achieved by many able readers bear testament to this likelihood.

Productive power of the Phonics Screening Check

Despite its evident flaws, within the dominant political discourse of 'a firm grip of the basics', the PSC continued to be perceived as *the* panacea for young children's early literacy development, with the former coalition Minister for Education stating that such assessment constituted 'proper testing you can trust' (Gove, 2011, Speech to Ofqual Standards Summit 13 October 2011, cited in Ozga, 2013). In the following interview with an inner-city primary school head teacher, the impact of this pedagogical 'gaze' and 'proper testing' was clear:

Assessment affects pedagogy and I had the prime example of Year 1 children who didn't pass the phonics screen check now in Year 2 having additional phonics in the afternoon once a week. Those children were being withdrawn from the foundation subjects like art and all the other subjects that are going to be helping them to be holistic learners. The teachers have a real conflict with the fact that the children should be having an entitlement to those subjects but being withdrawn. I, as the headteacher have to say to them that in the grownup world OFSTED are not really interested that those children are not getting this and that. They want to know that 58% of the children passed so what are we doing about the other 42% who didn't pass in the subsequent year so we have got to have measures in place. We can't say that by osmosis they will pick it up.

(Head teacher, London Primary School, 2013)

In Foucauldian terms, the power of the flawed Phonics Screening Check produces children (and teachers, head teachers and schools) who are either 'successful' or 'failures'. It attempts to ensure that all young children conform to 'the same universal, comparable and centralised standards' (Moss, 2014, p. 41) and at the same time it excludes complexity and diversity. Hence the PSC enacts a critical piece of developmental assessment, normalizing certain children and categorizing others as being outside developmental norms. Within the particular regime of truth behind the phonics check, the arbitrary pass mark of thirty-two out of forty becomes the developmental norm, with particular learners deemed to be successful and others labelled unsuccessful. By informing parents of their children's performance in the PSC, this technology of governmentality includes a process of responsibilization, whereby parents are also made to feel responsible by comparing themselves and their children to the norm and correcting any of their mutual 'deficits'. As noted earlier, learners who are labelled unsuccessful by the PSC are over-proportionally children from disadvantaged socio-economic backgrounds, from particular ethnic groups, and summer-born children, particularly boys. Also amongst the unsuccessful are a significant number of children deemed by their teachers to be fluent and successful readers.

Within such normalizing, exclusionary and competitive assessment regimes, failure rarely goes unmarked and unpunished hence specific, detailed and disciplinary processes are put into effect to 'correct' such failure. Following the principle of high aspirations for all, the PSC included the directive that all children 'with below expected progress in phonic decoding' would 'receive extra support from their school to ensure they can improve their decoding skills, and will then have the opportunity to retake the phonics screening check' (DfE, 2012a, p. 4). In addition to this 'opportunity', OFSTED regulates and questions schools on their procedures for re-testing, so that children deemed to be phonic 'failures' can become phonic 'successes'. In this way, OFSTED's governing of the phonics testing is coercive, disciplinary and threatening for the school, the teachers and the children. In effect, the 'opportunity to retake' has for most children become a *requirement* to *pass* a similar test the following year. As mentioned, no official guidance is given to schools about how to enable children to pass the check, other than encouragement to purchase more commercial programmes, and schools have consequently developed their own strategies for delivering further synthetic phonics instruction to the high percentage of children who are required to retake the check.

Governing the child

The head teacher cited earlier in this chapter noted the harsh consequences for the 42 per cent of children deemed 'phonic failures', which included systematic exclusion from artistic and creative aspects of the National Curriculum and 'subjects that are going to be helping them to be holistic learners'. By failing the phonics check, the education regime classified these young children as unsuccessful 'Others', as inadequate learners who must be 'punished and disciplined' and whose phonics learning must be governed ever more rigorously. Regarding this form of disciplinary power, Dahlberg et al. (2013) note that 'it often achieves its effects by the subject embodying disciplinary power and through doing so, governing him or herself' (p. 13). So, the physical exclusion of the Othered pupils from arts and creative subjects confirms and solidifies their unsuccessful learner identities to the children themselves, their families and to their teachers. In this way the phonics check operates as a highly productive technology of performance producing and then governing specific 'learner identities' (Bradbury, 2012).

In this educational regime, 5- and 6-year olds' poor PSC performance is viewed as a manifestation of their inability to adequately self-govern themselves and acquire an appropriate self-regulating learner identity which would enable them to perform to the expected norm. Additionally, such highly visible and public exclusion legitimates and verifies the 'successful' learner identities of those children who have shown the necessary self-regulation and self-governing abilities to pass the test. In this way the phonics test operates as a disciplinary technology that distributes, classifies and ranks children based upon crude and simplistic data, making them available as subjects for further regulation by the school. So, the 'failures' are prescribed additional curative 'treatments' such as increased phonics time, surveillance and inspection until the 'remedy' works and they become 'normalized'. At the same time, the successful self-governing learners who passed the test are further encouraged to build upon their competencies through creative, playful and enjoyable arts subjects. The 'failures' are excluded from such creative opportunities until their self-governing abilities are manifested through passing the test. However, as Reay and William (1999) suggest, negative learner identities become internalized by young children who quickly learn to associate themselves with being either 'good' or 'bad' learners. Long-term well-being and success at school are supported by young children acquiring positive learning dispositions in the early years (Whitbread & Bingham, 2012). The effects of the phonics check in labelling as 'failures' high percentages of young children not only from particular socio-economic, ethnic, birth date and gendered groups but also many deemed by their teachers to be 'good' readers would appear to be detrimental to such long-term learning dispositions.

Governing the teacher

Assessment regimes of truth discipline and govern not only young children but also their teachers (Roberts-Holmes, 2014). Within increasingly punitive education systems of governmentality, managed through processes such as Performance Related Pay and OFSTED inspection, teachers' professional knowledge and judgement about early literacy is negated and replaced by centrally governed and prescribed methods and outcomes (Bradbury, 2013). Thus, the compulsory national PSC brings both children and teachers within the same 'pervasive and effective system of surveillance and control' (Moss, 2014, p. 42) in which the 'malicious minutiae' (Foucault, 1979, 226) of percentages leads to a 'datafication of pedagogy' (Roberts-Holmes, 2014) where teachers' work is increasingly constrained by performativity demands.

As a result, teachers' locally based, complex, subtle and professional judgements about children's (literacy) learning becomes reduced to simplistic, crude sets of 'normalized' data, and any notion of children's holistic learning is replaced by statistics. These statistics are represented in particular modalities to reinforce the disciplinary regime they are generated by, as illustrated in Figure 6.2, which, apart from illustrating issues around the pass mark as discussed earlier, is designed to draw attention to a year-on-year improvement in test scores. Within this disciplinary and representational regime, teachers must internalize, self-regulate and self-govern their pedagogy in order to successfully produce the required data. In this way, the crude statistical measures and calculative apparatus of the phonics check discipline, regulate and govern head teachers' motivations and teachers' pedagogy since they are 'terrorized' by the need to ensure their pupils achieve nationally determined pass marks (Ball, 2013).

From the perspective of the head teacher featured in this case study, 'the grownup world of OFSTED' is crucial because the school itself is enmeshed within England's disciplinary inspectorial system. The most recent OFSTED training documents mention 'phonics' more than 150 times but 'comprehension' less than twenty times (OFSTED, 2011; see also Ellis & Moss, 2014) – paying far less attention to whether children understand what they are reading than to whether they can decode. OFSTED plays a powerful role in governing the English education system and uses data to discipline and punish schools judged to be unsatisfactory (Ozga, 2013). Based upon crude data calculations, OFSTED has the power to close down schools if they are deemed to be 'failing', whilst 'outstanding' schools are only inspected once every five years. In response to this system, the head teacher noted 'get the data right and you buy five years of freedom' (also see Roberts-Holmes, 2014). Within this penalizing context, the pressure to achieve the correct phonics data cannot be overstated, and nor can its detrimental effects upon teachers' professionalism and sense of self-worth.

The neoliberalist imperatives, strictures and demands manifested through the Government White Paper (DfE, 2010), and OFSTED's and the school's performativity regimes mean that teachers are heavily burdened with the responsibility to perform (Ball & Olmedo, 2013, p. 89). Noting the changes to the literacy assessment of young children, including the phonics check, one of the early years teachers in the school featured in this chapter stated her concerns about how the PSC was having a trickle-down impact on very young children:

> 'All these changes are killing me! … I'm constantly stressed out and feel like I'm fighting against myself sometimes. I want the children to do well but I feel like I don't know what I'm doing now! I know how young children learn at this age but people further up the school are constantly saying "oh why haven't you done this" and it's all the pressures and you start questioning yourself'.
>
> (Early Years Teacher, North London Primary School)

The school's constantly changing demands and expectations left this experienced early years teacher feeling exhausted, frustrated and confused. In order to help prepare the 4- and 5-year-old children for the PSC at age 5/6, this teacher felt obliged to engage with the assessment regime despite not agreeing with it. Regarding such ontological confusion Ball and Olmedo (2013, p. 90) note that:

> 'Teachers are no longer encouraged to have a rationale for practice, account of themselves in terms of a relationship to the meaningfulness of *what they do*, but are required to produce measurable and 'improving' outputs and performances, what is important is *what works*'.

The 'what works' discourse for this particular teacher was particularly acute as many of the children in her class had English as an additional language and although able to sound the words out phonetically and 'succeed', they did not understand the words themselves. However, if this teacher did not adhere to the head teacher's demands to teach systematic synthetic phonics every day to these young children, she would be deemed 'irresponsible'.

Concluding thoughts and 'Care of the Self'

This chapter has argued that the UK Government's Education White Paper (DfE, 2010) was explicitly framed within a 'regime of truth' centred upon an international neoliberal context of increased competition, performativity and accountability. Performativity within the White Paper was 'presented as the new common sense, as something logical and desirable' (Ball & Olmedo, 2013, p. 89) to prevent any further 'decline' of the English education system relative to other countries. This chapter has focussed upon one aspect of the White Paper that called for an urgent intensification and focus upon early years literacy and in particular upon the promotion of systematic synthetic phonics. To ensure the self-regulating adherence of all schools, the PSC was introduced as part of the system of accountability and discipline. Yet the check is riddled with incoherence and ineptness, which are manifested through its multimodal design, application and evaluation.

Throughout the chapter, we have maintained that the multimodal design and implementation of the PSC was representative of a 'highly prescriptive system of accountability' (Ball, 2013, p. 173) in which the public reporting and display of phonics check data set up divisive, competitive and disciplinary practices between OFSTED, schools, head teachers, teachers and children. In the case study cited, the school's pedagogical governance of these data was manifested through the public inclusion of some children into holistic arts lessons, whilst Others, who 'failed' the test, were excluded from their entitlement to a holistic curriculum. The exiled Others were subjected to increased governance, surveillance and inspection since their failure became a threat to the performance and reputation of the school. Indeed, if the school's self-governing techniques, as expressed by the head teacher, did not remedy the children's 'failure', then the entire school became vulnerable to OFSTED's further disciplinary governance (for further discussion see Ellis & Moss, 2014).

However, even within the disciplinary context of the English performativity regime, there were instances of teacher agency and resistance to the imposed phonics check, albeit in the early years prior to Year 1 (Roberts-Holmes, 2014). So, for example, the nursery teacher in this primary school stated that he 'did the phonics, but then tucked it away to get on with the *real business* of being with the children'. Like the Year 1 teacher, this early years teacher felt that 'the real business' of teaching involved child-centred learning principles and values, and in his reception classroom he was more able to resist the imposed demands of performativity. Through processes of reflexivity, dialogue and political action, this teacher had begun to be governed differently, and had created liberatory pedagogical spaces by engaging in 'care of the self' (Foucault, 1988). As Foucault's later work suggests 'people … are freer than they think' (Martin et al., 1988, pp. 10–11), when they practise everyday resistance to everyday power. Central to 'care of the self' is that critical educators apply professional ethics to education, and create new spaces within oppressive disciplinary regimes (see Peters, 2003).

For early literacy, what might these pedagogical spaces look like? This of course depends on teachers' professional judgement and responsive planning for the children in their classrooms, but there is a wealth of practice and research-based evidence to suggest that whilst teaching phonics is important, it is only one aspect of the highly complex process of literacy learning. Students attend to literacy in the classroom if it has a purpose, if it relates to their social and cultural worlds (Street, 1984) and if they have a clear sense of how it can be used. Literacy learning is creative and intertwined in children's personal experiences and lives. It is an interactive and collaborative process, where children enjoy many different kinds of texts including books, magazines and popular media (Maybin, 2013), and a multimodal experience where young children develop their knowledge and participate fully in society through oral, written, printed and digital media (Marsh, 2011; Flewitt, 2013).

What does this broader vision of literacy offer for the future of young children's classroom-based learning and for teacher autonomy in the face of reductive assessment regimes? On a wider collective scale, the English National Union of Teachers (NUT, 2014) has called for 'an alliance of forces to oppose and boycott the phonics check'. Instead of a meaningless phonics test or similar assessment technology that drives out other, more complex and democratic forms of literacy assessment, teachers' professional judgments need to be trusted. So, for example, child-centred assessments might include 'pedagogical documentation' (Moss, 2014) and multimodal critical literacies. We suggest such assessments are essential to challenge dominant discourses and to construct counter-discourses that are more closely aligned with teachers' pedagogical principles and values.

Appendix A

Scoring criteria from assessment framework for the development of the Year 1 phonics screening check (DfE, 2012a)

5. Scoring

The phonics screen check should be scored by the teacher as they work through the check. For each word, the teacher will record whether the child read the word correctly or not bearing in mind the following points:

Children may sound out phonemes before blending but do not have to. If a child sounds out the phonemes but does not blend the word, they must not be prompted to do so.

Children may elongate phonemes as long as they are blended to form the word. However, if children leave gaps between phonemes and do not blend them, this must be scored as incorrect.

Alternative pronunciations must be considered when deciding whether a response is correct. For real words, inappropriate grapheme-phoneme correspondences should not be marked correct (for example, reading 'blow' to rhyme with 'cow' would be incorrect). However, alternative pronunciations of graphemes will be allowed in pseudo-words.

A child's accent should be taken into account when deciding whether a response is acceptable. There should be no bias in favour of children with a particular accent.

Any pronunciation difficulties for a child should be taken into account when deciding whether a response is acceptable (for example, a child who is unable to form the 'th' sound and instead says 'fw' should have this scored correct).

If a child makes an incorrect attempt and then corrects themselves, this should be marked as correct as the child has shown the ability to decode. However, children should not be prompted to 'have another go'. If a child makes several attempts at a word, the final attempt should be scored, even if this is incorrect and a previous attempt had been correct.

The teacher should not indicate whether a child has decoded a word correctly or incorrectly during the administration of the screening check but may offer encouragement or support to ensure they remain focussed on the task.

Children should be given as long as necessary to respond to a word, although in most cases, 10 seconds should be sufficient. The teacher should decide when it is appropriate to tell the child to move onto the next word, taking care not to try to move the child on if they are still trying to decode the word.

Further information will be provided to schools in the Check Administrators Guide and training materials in April 2012.

DfE (2012, p. 21)

Notes

1 Association fallacy is an inductive, informal form of logic often based on hasty and simplistic generalizations, such as 'All cats have four legs. My dog has four legs. Therefore my dog is a cat'.

2 OFSTED is the Office for Standards in Education, Children's Services and Skills, England's powerful inspection system. See: http://www.ofsted.gov.uk/

References

Ball, S. (2013). *The Education Debate: Politics and Policy in the 21st Century*. Bristol: Policy Press.

Ball, S., & Olmedo, A. (2013). Care of the self, resistance and subjectivity under neoliberal governmentalities. *Critical Studies in Education, 54*(1), 85–96.

Bezemer, J., & Kress, G. (2008). Writing in multimodal texts: A social semiotic account of designs for learning. *Written Communication, 25*(2), 166–195.

Bradbury, A. (2012). Education policy and the 'ideal learner': Producing recognisable learner-subjects through early years assessment. *British Journal of Sociology of Education, 34*(1), 1–19.

———. (2013). *Understanding Early Years Inequality: Policy, Assessment and Young Children's Identities*. London: Routledge.

Clark, M. (2006). The Rose Report in Context: What will be its impact on the teaching of reading? *Education Journal*, (97), 27–29.

———. (2013a). Research evidence on the first phonics check for all Year 1 children in England: Is it accurate and is it necessary? *Education Journal*, (168), 12–15.

———. (2013b). The phonics check for Year 1 children in England: Unresolved issues of its value and validity after two years. *Education Journal*, (177), 13–15.

Coldwell, M., Shipton, L., Stevens, A., Stiell, B., Willis, B., & Wolstenholme, C. (2011). *Process Evaluation of the Year 1 Phonics Screening Check Pilot*. London: DfE.

Dahlberg, G., Moss, P., & Pence, A. (2013). *Beyond Quality in Early Childhood Education and Care: Languages of Evaluation* (3rd edition). Oxfordshire: Routledge.

Department for Education (DfE) (2010). *The Importance of Teaching: The Schools White Paper 2010*. London: The Stationery Office Limited. Available at: https://www.gov.uk/government/uploads/system/uploads/attachment_data/file/175429/CM-7980.pdf (accessed 15.04.2014).

———. (2012a). *Assessment Framework for the Development of the Year 1 Phonics Screening Check*. London: DfE Standards and Testing Agency. Available at: www.education.gov.uk/publications (accessed 15 April 2014).

———. (2012b). *Statistical First Release: Phonics Screening Check and National Curriculum Assessments at Key Stage 1 in England, 2011/2012*.

London: DfE. Available at: https://www.gov.uk/government/uploads/system/uploads/attachment_data/file/219208/main_20text_20_20sfr21-2012.pdf (accessed 2 May 2014).

Department for Education and Skills (DfES) (2006). *Independent Review of the Teaching of Early Reading. Final Report, Jim Rose*. London: DfES Publications.

Ellis, S., & Moss, G. (2014). Ethics, education policy and research: The phonics question reconsidered. *British Educational Research Journal, 40*(2), 241–260.

Flewitt, R. S. (2012). Multimodal perspectives on early childhood literacies. In J. Larson & J. Marsh (Eds), *The SAGE Handbook of Early Childhood Literacy* (2nd edition). London: Sage, 295–309.

———. (2013). *Early Literacy: A broader vision*. TACTYC Occasional Paper 3. Available at: http://tactyc.org.uk/occasional-paper/occasional-paper3.pdf (accessed 02 May 2014).

Foucault, M. (1979). *Discipline and Punish: The Birth of the Prison*. London: Penguin Books.

———. (1980). *Power/Knowledge: Selected Interviews and Other Writings 1972–1977*. Hemel Hempstead: Harvester Press.

———. (1988). Technologies of the self. In L. H. Martin, H. Gutman & P. H. Hutton (Eds), *Technologies of the Self: A Seminar with Michel Foucault*. Massachusetts: University of Massachusetts Press, 16–49.

Halliday, M. A. K. (1984). *An Introduction to Functional Grammar*. London: Edward Arnold.

Kress, G. (2014). What Is Mode? In C. Jewitt (Ed.), *Handbook of Multimodal Analysis* (2nd edition) (pp. 60–75). London: Sage.

Kress, G., & van Leeuwen, T. (2001). *Multimodal Discourse: The Modes and Media of Communication*. London: Routledge.

Marsh, J. (2011). Young children's literacy practices in a virtual world: Establishing an online interaction order. *Reading Research Quarterly, 46*(2), 101–118.

Martin, L.H., Gutman, H. & Hutton, P.H. (1988). *Technologies of the Self: A Seminar with Michel Foucault*. Massachusetts: University of Massachusetts Press.

Maybin, J. (2013). What counts as reading? PIRLS, EastEnders and The Man on the Flying Trapeze. *Literacy*, 47 (2), 59–66.

Moss, P. (2014). *Transformative Change and Real Utopias in Early Childhood Education*. London: Routledge.

National Union of Teachers (NUT) (2014). Teachers may boycott tests for four-year-olds, the *Guardian* Newspaper. Available at: http://www.theguardian.com/education/2014/apr/21/teachers-may-boycott-tests-four-year-olds-nut (accessed 2 May 2014).

OFSTED (2011). Getting them reading early. Distance learning materials for inspecting reading within the new framework: Guidance and training for inspectors (October 2011; Revised and updated July 2014 Version 4). Available online at: http://www.ofsted.gov.uk/resources/getting-them-reading-early (accessed 3 January 2015).

Organisation for Economic Cooperation and Development (OECD) (2006). *Starting Strong II: Early Childhood Education and Care*. Paris: OECD Publishing.

Ozga, J. (2013). Accountability as a policy technology: Accounting for education performance in Europe. *International Review of Administrative Sciences, 79*, 292–309.

Peters, M. (2003). Truth-telling as an educational practice of the self: Foucault, Parrhesia and the ethics of subjectivity. *Oxford Review of Education, 29*(2), 207–224.

Reay, D., & William, D. (1999). 'I'll be a nothing': Structure, agency and the construction of identity through assessment. *British Educational Research Journal, 25*(3), 343–354.

Roberts-Holmes, G. (2014). The 'datafication' of early years pedagogy: 'If the teaching is good, the data should be good and if there's bad teaching, there is bad data'. *Journal of Education Policy*, doi: 10.1080/02680939.2014.924561

Street, B. (1984). *Literacy in Theory and Practice* Cambridge: Cambridge University Press.

Torgerson, C. J., Brooks, G., & Hall, J. (2006). *A Systematic Review of the Research Literature on the Use of Phonics in the Teaching of Reading and Spelling*. Research Report RR711 DfES. Available at: www.dfes.go.uk/research (accessed 02 May 2014).

Townley, L., & Gotts, D. (2013). *Topic Note: 2012 Phonics Screening Check Research Report*. Slough: NFER.

United Kingdom Literacy Association (UKLA) (2012). *UKLA Analysis of Schools' response to the Year 1 Phonics Screening Check* Available at: http://www.teachers.org.uk/files/y1psc-survey-october-2012.pdf (accessed 21 May 2014).

United Nations Educational, Scientific and Cultural Organization (UNESCO) (2013). Literacy Policy. Available at: www.unesco.org/new/en/education/themes/educationbuilding-blocks/literacy/ (accessed 17 May 2014).

Whitebread, D., & Bingham, S. (2012). *School Readiness: A critical review of perspectives and evidence*. TACTYC Occasional Paper No 2. Available at: http://tactyc.org.uk/occasional-paper/occasional-paper2.pdf (accessed 2 May 2014).

Wyse, D., & Goswami, U. (2008). Synthetic phonics and the teaching of reading, *British Educational Research Journal, 34*(6), 691–710.

7

Critical and Multimodal Literacy Curricula

Peggy Albers, Jerome C. Harste and Vivian Maria Vasquez

With the rapid integration and use of new technologies – especially in light of how communication happens across geographical and interdisciplinary spaces – we undertake the task of describing how critical multimodality has changed the nature of how messages are communicated, and to what extent design operates in these messages to position viewers to consume, engage in and with, and to evaluate messages. Foucault's concepts of docility and disciplinary techniques help us position and understand how discursive practices in schools emerge. That is, local, state and national mandates regarding curriculum often outline a set of specific outcomes and means to those outcomes. In this configuration, educators are often positioned to become docile bodies and may be asked to implement scripted curricula, with mandated and standardized assessments, to achieve these outcomes. Such normalizing practices, we argue, diminish projects that include the arts and digital technologies and thus reduce creativity, innovation and exploration from literacy curricula. However, within such restrictive spaces, educators can and do implement alternative ways to teaching content.

This chapter addresses how we have intentionally designed literacy curriculum to include the arts and digital technologies to support critical literacy practices in elementary, middle and secondary classrooms. Critical multimodality details how modes operate as ensembles in texts in terms of their design, framing and visible discourses (Albers, 2011) as well as the importance of understanding how modes have particular role in how and what meaning is created and conveyed (Kress, 2003). As such, critical multimodality provides space for teachers to explore the significance of visual modes of communication, and interrogate perspectives expressed through these modes (Janks, 2000; Vasquez et al., 2010). Along with this approach to communicating visually is the need to engage teachers and students alike in critical attention to how selection/choice matters when they integrate image, sound and text to convey messages. We end the chapter with implications for practice across grade levels.

Situating docility and governmentality

Foucault used the term 'relationships of power' to present the multiple and varying ways in which humans interact – 'love relationship, an institution or economic relationship', and to remind us that 'power is always present' in these relationships (Foucault, 1988, p. 11). Governmentality was a term used by Foucault to mean 'a conduct of a conduct', complex relations that aimed to shape, guide or affect the conduct of a person, including governing the self and issues of self-control (Gros, 2011). For example, we might presume that power exists in educational relationships – and it does – and the activities within this relationship guide, shape and/or affect behaviour of those involved. However, Foucault might suggest that how power manifests itself does not rest solely with the educator but within a set of relations of power within which an educator operates and makes decisions, and the activities that shape or guide these behaviours. In 1992, Allan Luke brought forward the concept of pedagogy as inscription, of body writing and mapping. That is, knowledge around which bodies are disciplined (Foucault, 1995) emerges from techniques of power and regimes of normalization. Disciplinary power is 'enacted in a multiplicity of texts' (Luke, 1992, p. 110) that have material effects on people in everyday sites, such as schools, in such a way as to control a way of being, living and thinking. For Foucault, the body is the site of social production and that as bodies, 'the body is invested with relations of power … power exercised on the body … rather than possessed' (1995, p. 26). Bodies are subjugated to certain forms of disciplinary power including surveillance, a technique that disciplines the practices of a body to maintain the power of that who is doing the surveillance. Success, Foucault might argue, depends on the docility of a body and relations of power that act on it. That is, the more a body is disciplined through various techniques (e.g. threat to one's teaching position, salary reduction and student test scores and transfer to another grade level), the more obedient the body becomes, and the more the power the influencer has to exert or 'exercise' the body (Foucault, 1995, p. 26). The influencer desires this obedience with minimal challenge. The desired result is to control and increase the usefulness of bodies (e.g. increase ability of teachers to design instruction to fit standards with accompanying high-stake tests, while decreasing their ability to resist).

Within a Foucauldian perspective, then, although schools have become sites where teachers' bodies have become more obedient – docile – to educational mandates and less resistant to speak back (Luke, 1992; Janks & Vasquez, 2010), we suggest that within relationships of power emerge resistance. For us, the arts and multimodality offer ways through which a body's – an educator's – 'conduct to a conduct' involves an imaginative approach towards relations of power. It is here that we now turn.

Releasing the imagination: Art to change the world

Across history, artists have re-imagined the world and have shifted behaviours, thinking and activity. As in our previous writings (Vasquez et al., 2010), we argue that curriculum is too verbocentric, and that when the arts and multimodality are a central part of curriculum, people, as Maxine Greene wrote in her extraordinary book, *Releasing the Imagination* (1995), begin to see the world in new ways, and position themselves to make changes in the world as well as local classroom sites. Positioning people as participants in imaginative disciplinary techniques can create spaces for them to work against while within the larger set of disciplinary practices that intend to make bodies docile.

We see critical multimodality (Albers, 2011) as a powerful frame through which to explore the sociological, psychological, cultural and political discourses that underpin everyday texts (e.g. posters, billboards, statues and graffiti) and, because of our work in classrooms, texts that learners create. Critical multimodality understands how modes operate within texts as well as examines messages conveyed through the modal choices of the text-maker. Informed by social semiotics (Hodge & Kress, 1988), critical multimodality is guided by several important tenets. First, all communication is multimodal, and meaning is *framed*, *designed* and *produced* through modes (Jewitt & Kress, 2003; Albers & Harste, 2013). Modes are organized sets of semiotic resources for meaning-making (e.g. visual, aural, linguistic, musical and spatial). The more the resources used in the everyday social life of people, the more the patterns and regularities of such resources one can discern. Meanings are designed and framed through modal choices. That is, central to this tenet is how people make use of the resources that are available to them at a particular moment to create their representation, and how elements of a visual composition operate together, are spaced, connect (or not) with each other, 'move' on the canvas and so on. Production of meaning refers to both the creation and organization of the representation and the actual product or text (e.g. mug, dance, blueprint, painting, drama and webpage) as well as the technical skills (skills of the hand, eye, ear and body) used when working with media in creating the text. Meanings are produced, interpreted, remixed and conveyed through a range of representational and communicational resources, language being only one (Kress & van Leeuwen, 2001). Second, modal affordance, another associated concept, positions modes as having particular role in how and what meaning is created and conveyed. The affordance of a mode is material, physical and environmental (Kress, 2003). That is, there are particular ways in which modes operate according to their material properties and in social contexts. Visual modes (image and film), for example, carry information that sound modes (speech and music) cannot and have particular logics. Speech has a particular logic, one of sequence; one word follows another and its affordances carry both possibilities and constraints. Third, all modes are partial and carry different degrees of meaning, ensembles that vary in their contribution to the overall meaning. No mode is alone in carrying a message; others may take on lesser roles, but roles nonetheless. Last, and integral to critical multimodality, all modes are ideological and carry the assumptions and beliefs of the designer/ producer of the text or message; particular choices are made in the design of the message as well as the modes that will carry the intended message.

JR: Art to turn the world inside out

To illustrate critical multimodality in practice, we highlight the work of JR, a Parisian artist who was awarded the 2011 TED (Technology, Entertainment, Design) prize for his photographic installations. Although one of the most recognized photographer-artists in contemporary art, JR remains nearly anonymous. He sees the aim of his work 'to use art to turn the world inside out'; 'It's about breaking down barriers' (Day, 2010). His art interest started as a teenager in graffiti on outside walls, but when he found a camera in the Paris subway, he combined the two modes and became a 'photograffeur', an artist who *produced* enlarged photographs and pasted them on outside walls, often without permission. He *designs* art projects that are culturally, politically, psychologically and socially present in some of the most challenging areas of the world. *Portraits of a Generation* captured in photograph young people from the housing projects around Paris. *Face2Face* was a photographic installation in which he took photographic portraits of Palestinians and Israelis doing the same job, enlarged them to building size and posted them face-to-face in highly trafficked areas on walls throughout Israel and the West Bank (http://www.jr-art.net/projects/face-2-

face). By *framing* his work as side-by-side portraits, JR positioned viewers to notice that familiar facial responses (e.g. smiles and wrinkles) show familiar emotions. The design of this installation enabled viewers to see people as humans; only when viewers know that one man is a Palestinian and one an Israeli do their politics change the viewing.

We use the example of JR not only to illustrate the aspects of critical multimodality but also to present JR's work in Foucault's relations of power – illegal appropriation of outside wall space to post and juxtapose pictures of people who in certain parts of the world would rarely, if never, be placed together or be made visible in such public light. Disciplinary practices that tend to hide or ignore poverty as critical factors in education and social conditions are shifted because of how JR uses his art to make visible the very relations of power that keep populations docile and 'useful' citizens. From a critical multimodal perspective, JR's work presents art as a communication system that has the potential to disrupt notions that art is just for galleries or for decoration.

We have argued elsewhere (Albers et al., 2011) that text-makers as well as viewers must go beyond a superficial response to text. Current practices and talk around multimodal texts often limit discussions to aesthetic judgements about image: 'That's a nice picture', or educators say, when learners are asked to create a visual image, 'Don't worry about the art; I'm not good at art either'. Phrases such as these are disciplined techniques that over time position learners as docile bodies that in later grades withdraw from representing meaning visually and learn to understand that art is for those who have talent. As such, over time and across grades, learners are systematically disciplined into understanding art as an outside themselves and that art is not for transformation of ideas or concepts, but to accompany a written or spoken text. Yet, educators can imagine and desire to talk about multimodal texts in more complex and substantive ways. As shown in our work and others (Albers et al., 2011; Serafini, 2012; Harste & Albers, 2013), collectively, we demonstrate how educators can develop an informed and critical eye towards talking with students about how modes operate in their texts and re-imagine how discussion can and is organized around the complex meanings that underpin multimodal texts.

We suggest that visual representations within curricula are far more critical and generative and as such critical multimodality provides space for analysis and interrogation of the messages conveyed as well as the choices made by the designer/producer of the text. Furthermore, a framework for creating curriculum with critical multimodality in mind provides space for educators to disrupt disciplinary techniques aimed to encourage docility and open up engagements that work against normalizing practices and expectations that serve national mandates and standards, standards that reflect the experiences of the few rather than the many. For example, teachers were asked to read

A Street Called Home, a picture book based on the tapestries and poetry by Aminah Brenda Lynn Robinson (1997) of the everyday people who lived on her street, people virtually invisible by others outside this community. Teachers studied this picture book and then were asked to study their own community/ street and frame, design and produce a text about an 'invisible' person in their community – a person who gets passed by others without attention. These portraits were shared with others and posted for larger and critical discussions of social marginalization because of one's job, dress, home and so on.

In this next section, we present engagements that have encouraged teachers and students, both, to disrupt normalized understandings of language through art and to see the potential of art to shift, to transform and to break down barriers and turn the spaces in their world inside out.

Making curriculum critical and visible

As critical educators who work with literacy and language arts teachers, we see critical literacy as essential to today's literacy learning, especially with regard to multimodal texts. Taking on a critical stance addresses Foucault's concept of docility and positions learners to question commonplace assumptions about knowledge, to interrogate multiple perspectives, to focus on the sociopolitical and to take social action (Lewison et al., 2002). According to Harste (2003), to be truly literate for the twenty-first century, children need to do more than superficially respond to stories; they need to understand how language works, question the cultural story being told and decide how to act on their new awareness. Over the years we have worked with teachers and students, we have designed and developed a number of engagements that have become central to literacy curriculum. Vivian (Vasquez, 2004) has worked with young children to help them analyse and develop a language of critique of everyday texts (e.g. advertisements, cereal boxes, billboards and posters). Together, they study texts to uncover hidden messages of consumerism that is an essential part of critical literacy curricula as well as a way to participate more fully in the world. Jerry and Peggy have worked extensively with teachers and teacher educators, across art forms, to transmediate their understanding of literacy through painting and clay, respectively. They have studied the role of art as a way to open up imaginative and critical conversations with teachers and students on social issues (Harste & Albers, 2013). Collectively, we see the arts as opening up spaces where literacy is negotiated, challenged and experienced. The arts 'open our eyes, they stir our flesh' (Greene, 1995, p. 143) and teach us to see (Berger, 1972). Across our work, we have designed and articulated curriculum that involves teachers in a range of engagements that encourage them to understand language and power (Janks, 2010).

As educators we need to become aware of our own complicity and freedom and actively take stances to counter decisions that mitigate against the intellectual and professional nature of our work, including our efforts to create a critically literate citizenry for the twenty-first century. Said differently, our social practices – including how we prepare literacy professionals – must change. As a profession we need to become much more astute about the politics that undergird educational decision-making; decision-making that affects the in and out of school lives we are wanting our students to live and the people we wish them to become.

The Jacob Lawrence workshop and gallery walk

Harlem Renaissance painter, Jacob Lawrence used art to call attention to the African American experience in America. As a point of departure, in past workshops, we have invited teachers to create art that pays attention to some social issue about which they are passionate. After showing the videotape *Jacob Lawrence: The Glory of Expression* (Freeman, 1999), which highlights the artistic, social and political statements Lawrence made through his tempera painting, we invite teachers to design, frame and produce a painting – in the spirit of Lawrence's art – a visual statement of a social issue about which they are passionate. For example, one teacher painted an image of a teacher figure working within the confines of standardized behaviour. This image illustrates the exercised physical and academic control over students and the teacher. Those who are not disciplined are punished and physically removed from those who are disciplined. The image reflects the relationship between literacy and power, as it embodies a struggle for control.

The workshop culminates in a 'Gallery Walk' in which teachers move around to celebrate and talk about issues represented through art, and which are particularly important to them. These artful conversational spaces create opportunities for the teachers to talk about their issues differently and in so doing to see themselves differently. The Jacob Lawrence experience and Gallery Walk work to provide space for teachers to make their stance visible to a broader audience and engage in different critical conversations.

Multimodal responses through
children's literature: Sketch to stretch

Over the years we have amassed a huge array of children's books that address what we have come to call 'risky texts', which we define as texts that raise important social issues about which we need to break the silence. While painting is one way to invite students to look at a social issue from the other side, so too is drawing. We often ask students, working in groups of three or four to 'sketch what a story meant to them'. This strategy called 'Sketch to Stretch' (Harste, Short & Burke, 1988) more often than not is generative. Student groups share by holding up their sketch, allowing other groups to hypothesize what this group of artists thought the story meant, and then turning the discussion back to the artists who have the last word. By highlighting art and discouraging written text, students often capture aesthetic and emotional dimensions of the topic under discussion that orally would have been missed. In order for this or any strategy that is designed to cause readers to think deeply, it is important to begin with a piece of children's literature that is worthy of an in-depth discussion (see Harste et al. (2000) and Leland et al. (2013) for the titles of children's and adolescent book that deal with difficult social issues). Figure 7.1 is a sketch created by Chang, a Chinese student in one of Vivian's classes, after reading *When the Emperor Was Divine* (Otsuka, 2003).

The book is about the travails of a Japanese American family living in an internment camp during World War II. The story details three years in the family's life spent in cramped, impersonal and filthy lodgings at three different camps. The prose is written in a deceptively tranquil manner that keeps in check any sort of anger or rage over the deplorable circumstances of the family's interned life, including the destruction of their home and their family. Having recently come from China, Chang explained that the book brought to mind a story written by a famous Chinese writer Lu Xun. She

Figure 7.1 *Sketch to Stretch by Chang, inspired by* When the Emperor Was Divine

said, his story entitled *Medicine*, which was written in 1919, centres on a young boy who has tuberculosis (Lu, 2003). His family, desperate to find a cure, resorts to an old Chinese remedy, which is to have him ingest a mantou (steamed bun) covered in the blood of a person with a good soul. As the story goes, the boy dies in spite of eating the mantou which leads people to suspect the reason was the blood used came from someone who was killed unjustly, due to his radical ideas which the government found to be threatening.

Chang's sketch depicts people as ducks because she said these people were like ducks stretching their heads forward totally unaware of the unfair conditions in which they were forced to live, and seemingly unaware of the injustice of executing an innocent person. Chang noted, 'This is very much like the situation of the oppressed [Japanese people]. They don't know their status and even support the oppressors sometimes.'

Through sharing the image of the execution in her sketch in conjunction with her explanation of having read *Where the Emperor Was Divine* written in the United States in 2003, through the lens of *Medicine*, written in China in 1919, Chang expands the realm of opportunity for her classmates to come to some new understandings, views and narratives in relation to the book and in relation to their own experiences. As Barbara Kamler (2001) has argued, while it is important to make connections with participants around local issues, it is equally important that discussion not stop there but rather explore the global systems of meaning that are operating, which keep this issue in place.

Simple design, complex stories

In this engagement, teachers were positioned to consider their own lives and the critical events that shaped them. In one of our summer institutes, we invited Canadian author, Ryan Kerr, to share with teachers his book entitled *On growin' up:... a guide* (2011). He describes the book as a project that helped him to consider, embrace and share more of who he is. Through simple construction paper cut-outs, Ryan tells his story of growing up gay and coming out to the world.

After discussing this book with Ryan, teachers were invited to make their own multi-page booklet using construction paper cutouts to tell their story. To stimulate their thinking about what story they might tell, we began by having participants think about a time when school (or some other institution – be it family, friends or even the church) failed them. For the most part, people who become teachers have found the institution of schooling supportive, hence their interest in taking on the title 'teacher'. This engagement, in a sense, is meant to disrupt and invite teachers to think about times in their life when things did not go like they thought it should, experiences which may help them empathize with the students who find schooling difficult and whom they are trying to reach. Surprisingly, many times teachers themselves have stories when school, the very institution they are working for and advocating, failed them.

In another engagement simply called 'Secret Messages', teachers were asked to think about a secret they wished to share, use a range of media to convey this secret and place this secret in a brown paper bag. Secrets were taken out of the paper bag, unbeknownst to anyone whose secret was whose, and were hung up on a clothesline in the classroom to be shared with others. The Secret Messages opened up spaces for teachers to share the ideas about an issue, and to be candid about how these messages were relatable to others' experiences as well. One teacher's image represented a secret in which this teacher gave an 'A' on a test and offers insights into the control and the disciplinary practices that are exercised on educators: 'I gave a student an A because I didn't want to deal with the parents.' The relations of powers between and among student, teacher, parents and educational system (that requires grades) came to light in this art engagement.

Art as social action

I passed a little gallery and in the moment of passing saw a painting that had more power to stop me than I had power to walk on – Winterson (1995, p. 3)

Winterson's statement reminds us three of the power of the arts – centralized in literacy curricula – to stop us. Make us take a second and third look at teachers' and students' meanings produced in our classrooms. Figure 7.2 is just such an image that stopped us, an image created by a teacher after watching a YouTube video called *The Power of Words* (https://www.youtube.com/watch?v=CNhYbJbqg-Y).

This is a video story of a blind man sitting outside on a city sidewalk with a tin cup and a sign that says 'I'm Blind. Please help.' People pass by without much notice, and he receives a few coins. A woman comes along, rewrites the sign to read 'It's a beautiful day and I can't see it.' People read the sign, stop and begin to give coins and bills to the blind man. The blind man asks, 'What did you do to my sign?' She responds, 'I wrote a saying, but different words.' We find this teacher's image particularly significant as it reflects resistance to docility and positions all of us as change agents, change that comes from resistance to the very disciplinary techniques that work to control teachers and teaching.

Figure 7.2 *Teacher's multimodal response to The Power of Words*

The work that we have done across the years in literacy, curriculum and the arts enables us to understand that traditional print-based curricula, which often shape the way in which literacy is taught, experienced and learned, discipline the teaching body rather than enable its resistance. This is clearly seen through the nearly overwhelming adoption in the United States of the Common Core State Standards, standards that emphasize argumentation and written language over imagination and creativity – a word that does not appear anywhere in the standards. Larson (2013) argues, '...given our history with standardization, we can assume that the "common" means this mythical American "norm" that is centered on white, middle-class values and practices' (p. x). Within a Foucauldian perspective, normalization is a key technique of disciplinary power and non-conformity results in punishment. Florida, USA, for example, is attempting to tie teachers' salaries to test scores (http://www.politifact.com/florida/statements/2013/sep/25/charlie-crist/charlie-crist-florida-teachers-risk-having-pay-aff/). If their students score low on standardized tests, teachers' salaries are impacted negatively. Such legislation has created a 'crisis', and the market is poised and ready to respond with available and purchased materials. Success depends on teachers becoming docile bodies by acquiescing to the disciplinary powers that expect a normative curriculum.

However, resistance, as we have highlighted in the engagements above, can be cultivated, especially by those who work with and in the arts. Educators can position students to design multimodal texts with the intent to transform viewers' responses to social issues, to read and engage with art to learn, to advocate for others through art and to encourage social action through the art. Nearly eighteen years ago, Jerry and Vivian developed and continue to teach a master's programme in critical literacy for Mt. Saint Vincent University (satellite campus in Toronto) where teachers learn to read and respond critically to all types of texts. That this programme continues to be robust yearly in enrolment (nearly eighty students) expresses educators' desire to resist mandates that confine their pedagogy and practices. In California, USA, McLane High School art teachers, Marc Patterson and Mark Marhenke, engage their students in studying social issues in their community as part of their everyday art curriculum to support their students' literacy. In collaboration with the Fresno Art Museum, McLane High School students exhibited a show entitled *Whispers from the Street*, a focus on homelessness (http://fresnoalliance.com/wordpress/?p=3253). The exhibit was so powerful that art teachers and students were invited to show the work generated for this project at the White House in May 2014 (https://www.facebook.com/ mclaneseaproject/posts/686951864695315).

As Jerry has argued, teachers cannot do for students what they themselves have not done (Harste, 2003), teachers with whom we work share their insights and transformation with their students by having them design, frame and produce multimodal representations with the intention to evoke social awareness and illustrate the relations of power that exist in school spaces. Just as our teachers participate in critical analysis of multimodal texts, including advertisements, everyday texts (e.g. cereal boxes, candy wrappers and menus), children's literature and news articles, these teachers design similar engagements for their students.

Conclusion

As educators, we must understand that curriculum that invites critical multimodality contributes to more complex literacy practices, practices that prompt learners to make us see differently and to move us into thinking that is divergent rather than convergent. To us, this is a move away from docility and one towards a set of disciplinary practices that position educators as 'human resources' (Robinson, 2013) with a capacity to design thoughtful, imaginative and creative curriculum that prepares educators and their students for working democratically in the world. As such, educators who create critical curricula with multimodality and the arts in mind resist docility in which they shape, guide and affect behaviour of those involved.

Critical and multimodal curricula must be understood not only within the context of today's and future classrooms but also beyond. To prepare children to participate democratically in the world, they must have knowledge of how modes operate in a range of texts (e.g. advertisements, YouTube videos, lyrics and dance) and how texts act upon us that influence how we think, act and believe (Janks, 2010; Shannon, 2011).

We argue that creating curricula that centralize critical engagement with a range of visual and media texts opens up far more generative and imaginative discussions. Imagine what might happen if students themselves were encouraged to frame, design and create a parody of Psy's Gangnam style (https://www.youtube.com/watch?v=CH1XGdu-hzQ)? The conversations around the text would be more complex in terms of not only what the multimodal text meant but also about how and why it was made. This may lead into conversations about who is represented? How are they represented? Who is left out? What is missing when certain groups are left out? These conversations would generate a whole new set of questions that would drive future learning and position educators and students to reflect critically on the messages they create and convey.

Also, imagine if a different set of relationships were put into place, ones in which policy makers took on perspectives that recognized the significance of multimedia in the interpretation, construction and production of texts. How would, for example, the Common Core State Standards in the United States look if social issues like homelessness were viewed through the arts, as shown in *Whispers in the Street*, and were valued alongside print-based texts that focus on argumentation and opinion? What discussions around texts and complexity could happen when art, story, presentation and enquiry are taken into consideration? What would happen if policy makers re-examined the ways in which they themselves should be held accountable for providing the type of support teachers need to prepare students for a world that is highly interactive, immediate and global? Clear, thoughtful and critically reflective pedagogy, as we suggest through the arts, can lead to resistance and a release of imagination and, thus, a release from that which encourages docility. We see the arts as a way for teachers, embedded in relations of power – and perhaps at times reproduce them – to resist through direct participation in engagements that promote critical awareness of these relations of power.

References

Albers, P. (2011). Double exposure: A critical study of preservice teachers' multimodal public service announcements. *Multimodal Communication, 1*(1), 47–64.

Albers, P., Harste, J. C., & Vasquez, V. (2011). Making trouble and interrupting certainty: Teachers' critical and visual responses to children's literature.

In P. J. Dunston, L. B. Gambrell, S. K. Fullerton, V. R. Gillis, K. Headley & P. M. Stecker (Eds), *60th Yearbook of the Literacy Research Association* (pp. 68–83). Oak Creek: LRA.

Albers, P., Vasquez, V., & Harste, J. C. (2011). Making visual analysis critical. In D. Lapp & D. Fisher (2011). *The Handbook of Research on Teaching the English Language Arts* (3rd edition) (pp. 195–201). New York: Routledge.

Berger, J. (1972). *Ways of Seeing*. New York: Penguin.

Day, E. (2010). *The street art of JR*. Retrieved from http://www.theguardian.com/artanddesign/2010/mar/07/street-art-jr-photography

Foucault, M. (1988). The ethic of care for the self as a practice of freedom (interview with Michel Foucault). In J. Bernauer & J. Rasmussen (Eds), *The Final Foucault* (pp. 1–20). Cambridge: MIT Press.

———. (1995). *Discipline & Punish: The Birth of the Prison*. Westminster: Vintage.

Freeman, L. (Producer) (1999). *Jacob Lawrence: The Glory of Expression* [DVD]. Available from L & S Video, Inc.

Greene, M. (1995). *Releasing the Imagination*. San Francisco: Jossey-Bass Publishers.

Gros, F. (Ed.) (2011). *Michel Foucault: The Courage of Truth* (Trans. G. Bruchell) London: Palgrave Macmillan.

Harste, J. C. (2003). What do we mean by literacy now? *Voices from the Middle, 10*(3), 8–12.

Harste, J. C., & Albers, P. (2013). 'i'mriskin' it': Teachers take on consumerism. *Journal of Adolescent and Adult Literacy, 56*(6), 1–10.

Harste, J., Breau, A., Leland, C., Lewison, M., Ociepka, A., & Vasquez, V. (2000). Supporting critical conversations in classrooms. In K. M. Pierce (Ed.), *Adventuring with Books* (12th edition, pp. 506–554). Urbana: National Council of Teachers of English.

Harste, J. C., Short, K., & Burke, C. (1988). *Creating Classrooms for Authors*. Portsmouth: Heinemann Publishers.

Hodge, R., & Kress, G. (1988). *Social Semiotics*. Cambridge: Polity Press.

Janks, H. (2000). Domination, access, diversity and design: A synthesis for critical literacy education. *Educational Review, 52*(1), 15–30.

———. (2010). *Literacy and Power*. New York: Routledge.

Janks, H., & Vasquez, V. (2010). Editorial: Critical literacy revisited: Writing as critique. *English Teaching: Practice and Critique, 10*(1), 1–6.

Jewitt, C., & Kress, G. (2003). *Multimodal Literacy*. New York: Peter Lang Publishing, Inc.

Kamler, B. (2001). *Relocating the Personal: A Critical Writing Pedagogy*. Albany: State University of New York Press.

Kerr, R. (2011). *On Growin' Up ... A Guide*. Toronto: Ryan Kerr.

Kress, G. (2003). *Literacy in the New Media Age*. New York: Routledge.

Kress, G., & van Leeuwen, T. (2001). *Multimodal Discourse: The Modes and Media of Contemporary Communication*. London: Edward Arnold.

Larson, J. (2013). Operationalizing the neoliberal common good. In P. Shannon (Ed.), *Closer Readings of the Common Core* (pp. ix–xv). Portsmouth: Heinemann.

Leland, C., Lewison, M., & Harste, J. (2013). *Teaching Children's Literature: It's Critical!* New York: Routledge.

Lewison, M., Seely Flint, A., & Van Sluys, K. (2002). Taking on critical literacy: The journey of newcomers and novices. *Language Arts, 79*(5), 382–392.

Lu, X. (2003). *Selected Stories*. New York: W.W. Norton & Company.

Luke, A. (1992). The body literate: Discourse and inscription in early literacy training. *Linguistics and Education, 4*, 107–129.

Otsuka, J. (2003). *When the Emperor Was Divine*. Norwell: Anchor Press.

Robinson, A. B. L. (1997). *A Street Called Home*. New York: Harcourt Children's Books.

Robinson, K. (2013). *Finding Your Element: How to Discover Your Talents and Passions and Transform Your Life*. New York: Viking Adult.

Serafini, F. (2012). Reading multimodal texts in the 21st century. *Research in the Schools, 19*(1), 26–32.

Shannon, P. (2011). *Reading Wide Awake: Politics, Pedagogies, and Possibilities*. New York: Teachers College Press.

Vasquez, V. (2004). *Negotiating Critical Literacies with Young Children*. New York: Routledge.

Vasquez, V., Albers, P., & Harste, J. C. (2010). From the personal to the worldwide web: Moving teachers into positions of critical interrogation. In B. Baker (Ed.), *The New Literacies: Multiple Perspectives on Research and Practice* (pp. 265–284). New York: Guildford Press.

Winterson, J. (1995). *Art [Objects]: Essays on Ecstasy and Effrontery*. New York: Alfred A. Knopf.

Websites

Artventure (2014). In *Facebook* [Fan page]. Retrieved. January, 2015, from http://www.facebook.com/specificpage.

Purplefeather (2010). *The power of words* [Video File]. Retrieved from https://www.youtube.com/watch?v=Hzgzim5m7oU

Psy (2012). *Gangnam style*. Retrieved from https://www.youtube.com/watch?v=CH1XGdu-hzQ)?

Teachers risk having pay affected. Retrieved from http://www.politifact.com/florida/statements/2013/sep/25/charlie-crist/charlie-crist-florida-teachers-risk-having-pay-aff/.

8

Governing through Implicit and Explicit Assessment Acts: Multimodality in Mathematics Classrooms

Lisa Björklund Boistrup

In this chapter the overall context is mathematics education as a semiotic practice. The chapter focuses on a key notion in classroom work in relation to all students' possibilities to gain some kind of mathematical literacy: assessments taking place in day-to-day interactions between teachers and students. Assessment is here understood as something always present in teaching and learning, incorporating feedback as well as tests. The students display knowing through communicative resources such as speech, symbols, gestures and the like. The teacher captures student's displayed knowing and, in some way, he or she also assesses it. This assessment is shown to the student through feedback of various kinds. The assessment can be explicit, for example marks and/or comments on a test. What is foregrounded in this chapter is mainly the implicit feedback and assessments part of most of the interactions that take place on a daily basis in the classroom.

I argue in this text that teachers' interactions may differ from each other in such a way that students experience qualitatively different feedback from their teachers (see also Watson, 2000). These differences occur not only between classrooms but also between students in the same classroom with the same teacher. Moreover, it is argued that a consequence of such differences is that the affordances for students' engagement and learning differ.

Assessment as multimodal interactions

As a theoretical perspective in this chapter, social semiotics with a multimodal approach is adopted. From this perspective, assessment of knowing and learning is an instance of interactions, a matter of acts taking place between teacher and student or between student and student. The interest lies in students' demonstrated learning by means of a variety of communicative (semiotic) resources such as speech, pictures, symbols and the like (Kress, 2009; Selander & Kress, 2010).

In all communication, meanings are made through different semiotic resources that are co-present in communicational 'ensembles' (Kress & Van Leeuwen, 2001). Kress (2009) emphasizes the importance of understanding multimodal communication in order to fully understand a phenomenon like assessment (see also Björklund Boistrup & Selander, 2009; Pettersson & Björklund Boistrup, 2010). What communicative resources that are 'chosen' as means for communication are not arbitrary (Kress, 1993), but reflect both the interests of the person communicating as well as the communicative act in an interpersonal sense.

Drawing on earlier studies (e.g. Tunstall & Gipps, 1996; Torrance & Pryor, 1998; Morgan, 2000), I make the assumption that through assessments such as the ones in day-to-day teacher–student interactions, students are invited, or not, into a subject domain. Included here is what kind of engagement (agency) they are offered by the teacher's feedback.

Governmentality, institutions and assessment discourses

Foucault's (2008) concept of governmentality is used in this chapter. He describes the term as something that first appeared in the fifteenth century. Foucault displays a broad understanding of governmentality when he conceptualizes it as a wholeness constituted by the institutions, procedures and tactics that allows for the execution of power with the people as the target. Foucault also includes the tendency of steering – governing – that is common in society. Hence, in this chapter, governing is not solely addressed as in what the government does, but also other institutions, and their processes, within the school system. Decision levels that may affect teaching practices, including assessments, are the government. They are responsible for steering documents and official agencies such as the national agency of education.

Included amongst relevant other institutions affecting teaching practice are market-based institutions such as textbook editors.

A concept also adopted in this chapter is discourse (Foucault, 1993, 2003). Discourse, following Foucault, is conceptualized as a broad notion that incorporates not only all statements but also the rules that affect the formation of possible statements in the discourse. Consequently, a discourse is more than the entirety of what is communicated and the way it is communicated. It is also present in what is not communicated, or what is communicated through gestures, attitudes, presentations, patterns of actions and the rooms and furniture. For the people who are part of a discursive practice, like teachers and students, the rules of the discourses affect what actions it is possible to take (Foucault, 1993, 2003). For example, there are certain things that are 'allowed' to be communicated, and certain ways to communicate them. Often these limitations are not noticed by the people in the discursive practice. It is easier to perceive when a person breaks the rules of a discourse. In one classroom, different assessment discourses may be possible to construe (Björklund Boistrup, 2010, 2013). An inspiration for adopting discourse as something smaller than entire disciplines is Walkerdine (1988) who construed a 'testing discourse' where the teacher posed questions to which she already knew the answer.

The findings described in the chapter derive from research in classrooms in Sweden with students from 7 to 16 years old. In a previous research project, I construed four assessment discourses from five mathematics classrooms in grade 4 (10 year olds) (Björklund Boistrup, 2010, 2013). I paid attention to what kind of feedback was taking place, what the feedback was about and what role different communicative resources played in the assessments. The four discourses are as follows:

1. Do it quick and do it right

2. Anything goes

3. Openness with mathematics

4. Reasoning takes time

As the names of the assessment discourses imply, there are differences between them. They will be elaborated in this chapter when it is described how students and teachers are governed according to these discourses within the institution of school. As will be shown, the discourses hold qualitative differences in how students are invited, or not, to engage in and learn mathematics.

Governing through assessment from the view of the mathematics classroom

The data for this chapter derive from two research projects. One is a case study, previously mentioned, where five mathematics classrooms were visited with an interest in assessment and feedback between teacher and students (Björklund Boistrup, 2010). A basis for this chapter is also subsequent research when the discourses were adopted as analytical tools in action research performed by researchers and teachers in collaboration (Björklund Boistrup & Samuelsson, in preparation). In the analysis made for this chapter, I have also integrated the concept of governmentality.

The data used in the analysis for this chapter consist of videos and audios from mathematics classrooms. Each teacher and her communications with her students have been filmed with a handheld camera. Written material has additionally been collected where teachers' feedback, as well as decisions made on other levels than the classroom level, may be present. The transcripts from the films are made multimodally and the software videograph was used for transcriptions. In total, forty-seven mathematics lessons were filmed.

Greta and her students: A first encounter

One of the classrooms in this chapter is the teacher Greta (T) (pseudonym) who has introduced her class of nine-graders (15-years-olds) to working in pairs. The class is currently working on first grade functions, for example $y = x + 4$, and this time they are expected to draw graphs of four different functions in the same coordinate system (see Excerpt 8.1).

The students are asked to discuss the properties of the functions and their relations to the graphs and to take notes. The aim of the lesson is for the students to have opportunities not only to learn about functions but also to practice to communicate orally in mathematics. The reason for the teacher to address this was mainly that communication in mathematics is one of the abilities stated in the national syllabus in Sweden. When Greta (T) discusses with her students during their group work, different patterns of assessment acts in the form of feedback are possible to identify. In fact, I found it possible to construe different assessment discourses between different groups of students, which will be described below. The previously mentioned four assessment discourses frame the following account. Each discourse is described through analysis of data with specific emphasis on multimodal aspects such as the roles of different communicative resources

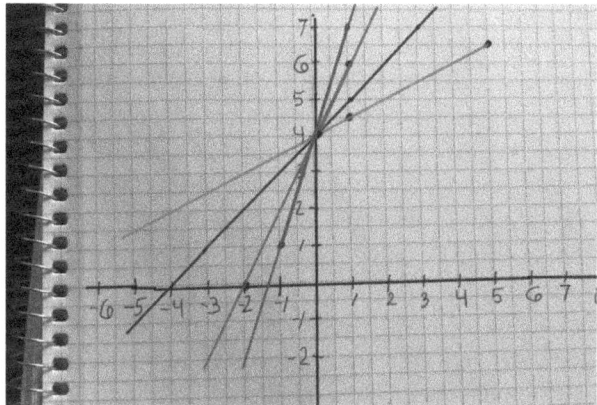

Excerpt 8.1. *Picture of one pair's work on functions and their graphs as they are shown in the end of their work. The functions here are y = x + 4; y = 2x + 4; y = 3x + 4; y = 0,5x + 4*

for students' learning of mathematics. For each discourse, governmentality will be discussed in the form of governing taking place in teacher–student interactions.

Description and example of discourse 1 'Do it quick and do it right'

The first discourse, 'Do it quick and do it right', has similarities to a traditional discourse of mathematics education described in the literature where the main 'rule' is that the work should be done quickly and what is counted is whether an answer is right or not (Björklund Boistrup & Selander, 2009). A similar assessment discourse is described in Broadfoot and Pollard (2000).

In discourse 1, 'Do it quick and do it right', the teacher's feedback focuses on procedures with limited mathematical content. Feedback in this discourse typically focuses on whether an answer is mathematically correct or not, instead of why and how the answer may be counted as mathematically relevant. Another typical feedback focus concerns how many items from the textbook the student has accomplished. The affordances for students to be invited to learn mathematics are limited since they are not really invited to engage in any aspect of mathematics through the feedback. Looking at the discourse from a multimodal approach, it may be possible to construe in writings when a teacher's feedback on a test is focused on the number of correct answers, for example when a teacher writes 11/21 (11 points out of 21). The teacher's red pen often has a role in maintaining this discourse since the marking of students' work is done in red without a specific focus on mathematics processes. Here it is important to keep in mind that the items on the test may well be mathematically rich and also inviting to the students. What is analysed here is mainly the subsequent feedback. In speech, teacher's feedback where this discourse is construed can be really short, along with body movements, and describe whether the student's work is correct or not or whether the student is doing the 'right' thing.

I now return to Greta (T) and her interaction with two students, Gry (S) and Gabriel (S), who are sitting at a table. Greta (T) starts the interaction by asking both students about their work. Here, it is mainly Gabriel (S) who answers. After just a minute, Greta (T) shifts her focus to address Gry (S) and she turns her body away from Gabriel (S) and towards Gry (S) (Excerpt 8.2). Both Greta (T) and Gry (S) are mainly looking at the papers on the table.

In Excerpt 8.2 Greta (T) interacts with Gry (S) and this goes on for a few more minutes. Greta (T) only looks at Gry (S) and she also uses the pronoun 'du', which in Swedish means you as in a single person. She addresses Gry (S) like this despite that Gabriel (S) is sitting close, following their interaction. The only topic during this interaction is methods in mathematics, in this case how to draw a graph from an equation and the need for Gry (S) to have at least one more coordinate in order to draw the line.

Governing students according to 'Do it quick and do it right'

To handle functions and their graphs, which is the focus in the interaction in the previous section, is clearly a focus on mathematical methods. In this respect the feedback could be construed as part of discourse 3, which is described below. However, in relation to how the students are invited to communicate in mathematics, which was the other aim with the lesson, the most significant discourse is regarded to be number 1 'Do it right and do it quick'. Greta (T) speaks only with Gry (S) and in Excerpt 8.2 a pattern is clear. Greta (T) poses questions to Gry (S) and Gry (S) tries to answer. Greta (T) is not silent in order to give herself some time for reflection. There is no feedback concerning the students' mathematical communication with each other. Greta's (T) body is turned only towards Gry (S), and what is important is Gry's (S) individual understanding of mathematics and not the group's common work and communication. I would argue here that feedback, such as in this interaction, governs students. In this case, Greta's (T) feedback directs students' individual work towards methods in mathematics, but not towards student-to-student communication in mathematics.

Time	Speech	Body	Gaze
28:15	Greta (T): *Here you've got one* [silence 1 sec] *coordinate. How can you proceed now?* Här har du en koordinat. Hur ska du göra nu då?*	Greta (T) is standing behind Gry (S) and leans over her work.	Greta (T) nods towards paper where one coordinate is marked in the system.
28:19	[silence 5 sec] Gry (S): *I don't know.* Jag vet inte.		
28:25	Greta (T): *What do you need to know, in order to be able to draw a line?* Vad behöver du veta för att kunna dra en linje?	Greta (T) draws a figurative line with her finger.	Greta (T) looks at paper and Gry (S)
28:27	[silence 4 sec] Gry (S): *Well, a value?*[giggles] Äh, värde?		Gry (S) looks in Greta's (T) direction.
28:35	Greta (T): *Can you put the ruler there now and draw the line?* Kan du lägga linjalen där och dra linjen nu?	Greta (T): walks around to Gry's (S) other side. Body more upright.	
28:38	[silence 2 sec] Gry (S): *What? Like this? Or how do you mean?* Vadå? Så här, eller hur menar du?	Gry (S) puts ruler on paper.	Greta (T) looks at Gry (S). Gry (S) looks at Greta (T) and on paper again.
28:41	Greta (T): *How do you know its direction now?* [high] Hur vet du hur den ska gå?		Greta (T) smiles.

Excerpt 8.2 *Greta (T) interacts with Gry (S).* *Speech in Swedish

Description and example of discourse 2 'Anything goes'

The second discourse, 'Anything goes', is more of the opposite to the first discourse and, as demonstrated below, is a discourse where students' performances, which can be regarded as mathematically inappropriate, are left unchallenged.

There is not much articulated feedback in the discourse 'Anything goes' apart from approval. There is a presence of open questions, but challenges are not common. Infrequently there are critical discussions about students' solutions, and wrong answers can also be left unchallenged. The students are invited by the teacher to use whatever semiotic resources they want, without any considerations by the teacher or the students on what resources have most affordances for their learning at that specific occasion. Often in this discourse the teacher is the most active agent. There seems to be a high possibility for the student to also take active agency since there is so much 'positive' approval going on. In fact, this is arguably not the case. Because the teacher values the students' performance so often, the teacher, at the same time, takes the role as the main agent, as 'the one that is evaluating'. Sometimes the teacher takes a more passive role in the discourse. He or she then does not interfere with students' reasoning even though something wrong is demonstrated. The affordances for students' learning in this discourse are low.

The discourse 'Anything goes' can be illustrated through a situation from a classroom with grade 4 students (10-year-olds). Angelica (S) and Ali (S) are working on problems dealing with patterns. The students are first asked to draw the next two subsequent figures of the pattern. They are also asked to tell the number of small squares for each figure. For the first five figures of the pattern shown in Excerpt 8.3, the number of small squares are 1, 4, 9, 16 and 25. The sequence referred to here is taken from the second of three lessons when the students are working on these particular problems. Angelica (S) and Ali (S) are working together, and they have solved the first items in the pattern.

When solving the items, Ali (S) and Angelica (S) have drawn the first eight figures of the pattern on their working papers. They discuss the item with Anna (T): 'Imagine that you have drawn ten figures. How many squares

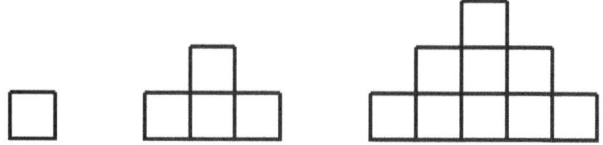

Excerpt 8.3 *Transcript from written material. First figures of the pattern.*

would the tenth figure then contain?'[1] Anna (T) asks how they found the answer to this question. Ali (S) looks at the calculator and says that they have 64. Anna (T) asks if that refers to the eighth figure which they have already drawn, and Ali(S) confirms that. Ali (S) then counts the squares one by one along the two upper edges of the eighth triangle, which add up to 17. He calculates 64 + 17 = 81 on the calculator. He then counts the squares in the next layer in the same way, and they add up to 19. Ali (S) adds 19 to the 81 on the calculator and says that this makes a hundred. Anna (T) accepts this answer and then poses questions to check that she has correctly understood their course of action. Anna (T), still looking at them and their work, calls their attention to the next question: 'How many squares would the fifteenth figure contain?'[2] It becomes clear that Angelica (S) and Ali (S) missed this item. Anna (T) repeats the question, and the students talk about how to solve it (Excerpt 8.4).

Time	Speech	Gestures	Body and gaze
16:37			Ali (S) looks at Anna (T). Angelica (S) looks down.
16:38	Ali (S): *It is just to count three more layers.* Angelica (S): *Yes* [sighs]. Ali (S): *Five more layers.*	Ali (S) points at figure at his paper and moves fingers. Stops pointing.	Ali (S) looks at his worksheet. Ali (S) looks at T. Angelica (S) looks at worksheets and at Ali (S). Ali's mouth is downturned and forehead is wrinkled.
	Ali (S): Det är bara att räkna upp tre lager till. Angelica (S): Ja. Ali (S): Fem lager till.		
16:44	Anna (T): *Five more layers, yes.*		T looks at Ali (S).
	Fem lager till ja.		
16:46	Angelica (S): *Yes* [sighs]. Ali (S): *Wow.*		Ali (S) shakes his head. Angelica (S) looks at Ali (S).
	Angelica (S): Ja. Ali (S): Wow.		

Excerpt 8.4 *Transcript from video material.*

At 16:38 in Excerpt 8.4, Angelica (S) and Ali (S) state that they then have to start counting five new layers. Ali's (S) mouth is downturned and forehead is wrinkled and Angelica (S) sighs. I read in this reaction that the students thought the situation annoying. Still they commence to work and then start drawing new layers on top of the figure they already drew. Anna (T) stands by their desks without saying anything for a while and then leaves.

Governing students according to 'Anything goes'

I read the governing in the interaction between Anna (T) and her two students here to signal that 'anything goes'. There is not much articulated feedback or feed forward in the sequence and Anna (T) seems to communicate acceptance of everything the students suggest without either recognising the suggestions as valid or recognising them as not accurate or fruitful. In neither of the two questions posed by the textbook are the students expected to actually draw the figures. The task is to imagine drawing them, and then through reasoning find the number of squares in the figure. The focus in this teacher–student interaction is on finding the correct answer, regardless of whether the method is really troublesome or not.

There is not much discussion focused on Angelica's (S) and Ali's (S) solutions and the students are governed towards a practice with little reflection on the quality of methods chosen. All semiotic resources seem welcomed by the teacher without hesitation, which could also signal that 'anything goes'. Here the calculator, which is not mentioned in the instructions, is also present. Angelica (S) and Ali (S) solve the problem by drawing, even though this was not part of the instructions for this particular task. They are hereby not invited to realize the number sequence in the pattern where it is possible to obtain the number of small squares through a multiplication of the number of the figure by itself. There are constraints for students' learning because of the lack of focus on mathematics processes in the assessment acts related to feedback. Also, the absence of planning and decision-making with regards to multimodal aspects is a reason why I regard this to be construed as 'Anything goes'. Here I refer to the fact that the students were drawing when they, in fact, would have learned more about patterns if this was not an option.

Description and example of discourse 3 'Openness with mathematics'

The third discourse, 'Openness with mathematics', has more of an open focus on mathematical processes. In this discourse the feedback goes in both directions, from teacher to student and vice versa. Occasionally, goals for the learning are present. Quite often the questions posed are open. The teacher and student often show interest in mathematical processes, and there is also an awareness of students' alternative interpretations of tasks. Sometimes the student is challenged with respect to her/his continued learning. The focus is mostly on mathematical processes and sometimes on the student's own reflection of her/his own learning. 'Wrong' answers are here used as starting points for discussions, and it is always clear what can be considered mathematically correct. Various kinds of feedback from teacher to student are often communicated through questions. Different semiotic resources are acknowledged and at times the teacher promotes, whilst at other times restricts, the use of semiotic resources dependent upon the meaning-making and learning process demonstrated by the student(s). This seems to be in order to serve the continuing learning process. The teacher and students communicate in longer utterances, but not more than a few utterances each time. In this discourse, there are considered to be affordances for students' active agency and learning of mathematics.

In the lesson with Greta (T), which we have encountered earlier in the chapter, this discourse was possible to construe from an interaction with two students, Gil (S) and Greg (S), who similarly like Gry (S) and Gabriel (S) struggled with drawing graphs from the equations. Early in this work, Greta (S) comes by and shows them how to do this. Here she sits down between the two students and her instructions are directed towards both students, which is displayed through her gaze directed towards both students.

Later during the lesson, Greta (T) approaches Gil (S) and Greg (S) again, who want to check that they have drawn their graphs correctly. Both students describe through speech and gestures to Greta (T) about their work. Greta (T) looks at their first four graphs and concurs with the students that they are correctly drawn. She then, through questions, directs the students' focus to a graph drawn in the next coordinate system. Gil (S) starts to explain about the drawing, but Greg (S) comments that there is something wrong with this graph. The two students start to discuss the drawing. Greta (T) is mainly silent while looking and listening to both students and their communication.

Sometimes she poses questions to either of the students and these questions seem to help the students to articulate their strategies to each other. In the end it is clear to the students what to do with the graph and how to proceed and Greta (T) leaves.

Governing students according to 'Openness with mathematics'

My analysis here is that Greta's (T) feedback governs student-to-student communication on functions. As is described for the discourse 'Openness with mathematics', Greta (T) provides feedback through questions. Her questions focus not only on how to draw graphs from equations but also help students to communicate with each other on mathematics. In this way her assessment acts govern the students towards a joint communication in mathematics. When she silently listens to them, I regard this as also a form of feedback displaying her interest, which governs the students' communication in mathematics. This interaction, which is just a few minutes in length, focuses primarily on basic notions in mathematics and communication. There are no silences in the interaction, and the pace is rather fast. Looking at the interaction from a multimodal perspective, it is clear in the interaction that Greta (T) captures the students' displayed mathematics learning through various communicative resources: figures, speech and gestures. She herself chooses to be mostly silent, whereas she addresses the incorrect graph through a gesture. In this way, she provides space in the multimodal ensemble for the students' oral communication, which was a topic of the lesson.

Description and example of discourse 4 'Reasoning takes time'

Finally, the fourth discourse, 'Reasoning takes time', takes the characteristics of 'Openness with mathematics' one step further with a slower pace and an emphasis on mathematics processes, such as reasoning/arguing, enquiring/ problem solving, and defining/describing.

In this discourse assessments take place in both directions between teacher and student. There are often instances of recognition of the students' demonstrated knowing, which are sometimes in relation to stated goals, and the questions posed are mostly open ones. At times feedback as interest and engagement are communicated by the teacher to the student and vice versa. The students are often challenged towards new learning with the focus mainly on mathematical processes and the students' reflections on her/his own learning. Here, most emphasis is on the processes enquiring/problem solving, reasoning/arguing, defining/describing and, occasionally, constructing/creating. Different communicative resources are acknowledged, and the use of semiotic resources can also be promoted or restricted when serving a certain process. In this discourse, silences in teacher–student interactions are common, and the possibility (for both teacher and student) to be silent serves the mathematics focus. Various kinds of feedback from teacher to student are often communicated, sometimes through open questions. Both the teacher and the student can be active for longer periods of time. In this discourse as well, the affordances for students to take active agency are high. The possibility to be quiet and think for a while promotes this potential agency. Similarly, the affordances for students' learning of mathematics are high and include a wide range of mathematics processes.

The following sequence where Eddie (S), Enzo (S) and Eric (S) are working on a task exemplifies the discourse of 'Reasoning takes time'. The teacher Erika (S) has presented the students in grade 4 (10-year-olds) with five different solutions to the same task (376 − 149 =). They are told that the objectives for this assignment are cooperation and subtraction. They should find the suitable solution in groups as well as determine what can be regarded as mathematically wrong with the other four. The five solutions are shown in Excerpt 8.5.

1. $370 − 150 = 220$ 2. $380 − 150 = 230$ 3. $300 − 100 = 200$
   $220 + 6 − 1 = 225$ $230 − 4 + 1 = 227$ $200 − 30 − 3 = 167$

4. $300 − 100 = 200$ 5. $376 − 100 = 276 − 40 = 236 − 9 = 227$
   $70 − 40 = 30$
   $6 − 9 = 3$
   $200 + 30 + 3 = 233$

Excerpt 8.5 *Transcript from written material. Assignment presented to students. Five different solutions to one task. Which one is correct?*

After Erika's (T) instructions at the beginning of the lesson, the groups start working. Erika (T) stands for several minutes in front of the class observing the students' work. Eddie (S), Enzo (S) and Eric (S) discuss the solutions. After a while, Enzo (S) raises his hand and calls for attention. Erika (T) arrives and Enzo (S) poses a question about there being two solutions with the same, and mathematically correct, answer: solutions 2 and 5. Erika (S) leans over their desks, looking at their work, and posing questions to the three students about the purpose of the task (that only one solution is correct). She also asks how they have reasoned so far. Part of the communication is shown in Excerpt 8.6.

Time	Speech	Gestures	Body and gaze
15:05	Erika (T): *What is your thinking then?*		Erika (T) looks at the worksheets.
	Hur tänker ni då?		
15:07	Enzo (S): Look.		Eric (S) looks at 376 – 149
	Kolla		
15:08	Eric (S): Well, that's two hundred twenty-seven. [Enzo (S): And that is] That one can't be right.	Eric (S) points at 376 – 149. Enzo (S) points at solution 4. Eric (S) points at solution 2.	Enzo (S) looks at solution 4. Eric (S) looks at solution 2. Enzo (S) looks at solution 2.
	Eric (S): Det där blir ju två hundra tjugosju. [Enzo (S): Och det där är] Det där kan inte bli det där.		
15:11	(*silence 2 s*) Eric (S): You take plus four when it should be minus four.		
	Du tar fyra när det ska vara minus fyra.		
15:16	(*silence 3 s*) Enzo (S): No, minus four, that's six plus one, that's also the same. (*silence 3 s*)	Enzo (S) points at solution 2. Enz stops pointing.	Students look at worksheet. Enz looks at Bx. Enz looks down.
	Nej, minus fyra, det blir sex plus ett, det blir också samma.		

Excerpt 8.6 *Transcript from video material. Speech in brackets, [], signals simultaneous speech.*

As shown in Excerpt 8.6, there are substantial pauses in the interaction. Sometimes these silences are followed by reasoning from one of the students. Subsequently, there are also silences followed by and during Erika's (T) utterances. After a while, the students' reasoning becomes more intense with a sustained focus on the mathematics involved in the task. Here, the students communicate their ideas for several seconds each. In one instance, Erika (T) points at solution 5 and asks whether they have done a calculation in that way before in class. The students answer no, and then there is a short discussion about solution 2. Before leaving, Erika (T) tells them that they get a few minutes more to think and also advises them to write down what is wrong with the ones that they know are definitely wrong. After Erika (T) has left them, the students' reasoning about solutions continues.

Governing students according to 'Reasoning takes time'

Looking at this example from the perspective of governmentality, a consideration is that Erika (S) is governing both herself and the students according to 'Reasoning takes time'. She takes the time to reflect when she stands in the front of the classroom looking at the students' group work. A consequence seems to be that she then is prepared when she approaches the three students in the example, and, hence, her feedback focuses on mathematical processes like problem solving, communication and describing mathematics. Looking at the interaction with an interest in multimodality, I also read that she pays attention to the students' communication by ways of their speech and writing. Through this kind of feedback the students are governed by her towards engaging in mathematical processes. An essential notion of the multimodal ensemble that constitutes the interaction is silence as a communicative resource. Both Erika (T) and the students are frequently silent, which is a substantially different kind of practice than 'Do it quick and do it right', and makes room for deeper mathematical discussions. Erika (S), in the end, is also governing in terms of multimodality and communicative resources when she tells them to write down their reasoning.

Discussion

In this chapter I have addressed the semiotic practice of the subject domain of mathematics education. Mathematical literacy is a broad notion, and what has been in focus here is how students may be invited into oral communication in mathematics through assessment practices of day-to-day classroom interaction between teachers and students.

I argue that we can never discuss teaching practices as a matter of teachers doing 'good' or not. No classroom is isolated, and they are all strongly affected by governings through decisions made by authorities – decisions that teachers have to follow. In this text the main focus has been on looking at governmentality and assessments from the perspective of teacher–student interactions within the classroom. Hereby, there are essential notions that I have not addressed. One is how dialogue pedagogy, as part of governmentality, may be analysed as a technique, which shapes active, self-regulating, responsible individuals (Fejes, 2008), which in a way assigns the individuals with most of the responsibility. A closely related theme is addressed by Murphy (this book). As I see it, it is important to critically discuss what today is called 'educational assessment'. These assessment programmes have, as Murphy puts it, 'become political tools with the potential to be inscriptive rather than descriptive, and to regulate rather than open up possibilities for learning' (pp. 26). Although both these themes are important, they were beyond the scope of this chapter.

The discourses presented in this chapter, with the connections between assessment acts, focuses in the mathematics classroom and roles of semiotic resources, offer teachers, students *and* decision-makers the means to grasp essential aspects of assessment practices in mathematics classrooms. There is positive power in an increased awareness of discourses like these. For teachers, the discourses can be a starting point for identifying how various assessment discourse practices take place in the classroom. In such an activity, the implicitness of assessment practices is made more explicit. One example here is how the discourse 'Do it quick and do it right' is possible to construe in the classroom, and possibly contrary to the teacher's original plan. The reason for this can be institutional governings, for example, through a strong tradition within mathematics teaching and/or through demands from municipalities, where a dominant discourse such as 'Do it quick and do it right' can be construed. The discourses in this chapter can be a starting point for discussions about assessment practices and what kind of governings they hold among teachers and school heads and among people responsible on the municipal and national levels.

Acknowledgements

I thank the teachers and their students with whom I have participated in the projects from which this chapter is written, especially the teachers Åsa Broomée, Ingalill Jonsson, Lotta Lagerlund and Sussie Olovsson. I also thank Rachel Heydon and Sharon Murphy for insightful comments on an earlier version of the text. Finally, I thank the municipalities of Linköping and Norrköping, Linköping University and Stockholm University for funding my research on classroom assessment in mathematics.

Notes

1 Original excerpt in Swedish: Tänk dig att du har ritat tio figurer. Hur många kvadrater hade den tionde figuren då innehållit?

2 Original excerpt in Swedish: Hur många kvadrater hade den femtonde figuren innehållit då?

References

Björklund Boistrup, L. (2010). *Assessment discourses in mathematics education: A multimodal social semiotic study*. Ph.D. thesis, Stockholm University, Stockholm.

———. (2013). *Bedömning i matematik pågår! För elevers engagemang och lärande*. Stockholm: Liber. [Ongoing assessment in mathematics! For students' engagement and learning].

Björklund Boistrup, L., & Samuelsson, J. (Submitted) Power-relations in particpatory action research in mathematics education.

Björklund Boistrup, L., & Selander, S. (2009). Coordinating multimodal social semiotics and an institutional perspective in studying assessment actions in mathematics classrooms. In V. Durand-Guerrier, S. Soury-Lavergne & F. Arzarello (Eds), *Proceedings of CERME 6, Sixth Conference of European Research in Mathematics Education* (pp. 1565–1574). Lyon: Institut national de recherche pédagogique.

Broadfoot, P. M., & Pollard, A. (2000). The changing discourse of assessment policy. In A. Filer (Ed.), *Assessment: Social Practice and Social Product* (pp. 11–26). London: Routledge/Falmer.

Fejes, A. (2008). To be one's own confessor: Educational guidance and governmentality. *British Journal of Sociology of Education, 29*(6), 653–664.

Foucault, M. (1993). *Diskursen ordning* [The order of the discourse]. Stockholm: Brutus Östlings Bokförlag Symposium.

———. (2003). *Övervakning och straff* [Discipline and punish]. Lund:Arkiv förlag.

———. (2008). Regementalitet [Governmentality]. In T. Götselius & U. Olsson (Eds), *Diskursernas kamp* [The battle between discourses] (pp. 183–204). Stockholm: Brutus Östlings Bokförlag Symposium.

Kress, G. (1993). Against arbitrariness: The social production of the sign as a foundational issue in critical discourse analysis. *Discourse and Society, 4*(2), 169–191.

———. (2009). Assessment in the perspective of a social semiotic theory of multimodal teaching and learning. In C. M. Wyatt-Smith & J. Cummings (Eds), *Educational Assessment in the 21st Century* (pp. 19–41). London: Springer.

Kress, G., & Van Leeuwen, T. (2001). *Multimodal Discourse: The Modes and Media of Contemporary Communication.* London: Arnold.

Morgan, C. (2000). Better assessment in mathematics education? A social perspective. In J. Boaler (Ed.), *Multiple Perspectives on Mathematics Teaching and Learning* (pp. 225–242). Westport: Ablex Publishing.

Murphy, S. (2015). Beyond governmentality: The responsible exercise of freedom in pursuit of literacy assessment. In Mary Hamilton, Rachel Heydon, Kathryn Hibbert, Roz Stooke (Eds), *Negotiating Spaces for Literacy Learning* (pp. 25–42). London: Bloomsbury.

Pettersson, A., & Björklund Boistrup, L. (2010). National assessment in Swedish compulsory schools. In B. Sriraman, C. Bergsten, S. Goodchild, G. Palsdottir, B. Dahl Søndergaard & L. Haapsalo (Eds), *The Sourcebook on Nordic Research in Mathematics Education* (pp. 373–385). Charlotte: Information Age Publishing.

Selander, S., & Kress, G. (2010). *Design för lärande: Ett multimodalt perspektiv.* [Design for learning: A multimodal perspective]. Stockholm: Norstedts.

Torrance, H., & Pryor J. (1998). *Investigating Formative Assessment: Teaching, Learning and Assessment in the Classroom.* Buckingham: Open University Press.

Tunstall, P., & Gipps, C. (1996). Teacher feedback to young children in formative assessment: A typology. *British Educational Research Journal, 22*(4), 389–404.

Walkerdine, V. (1988). *The Mastery of Reason. Cognitive Development and the Production of Rationality.* London: Routledge.

Watson, A. (2000). Mathematics teachers acting as informal assessors: Practices, problems and recommendations. *Educational Studies in Mathematics, 41*(1), 69–91.

9

The Secret of 'Will' in New Times: Assessment Affordances of a Cloud Curriculum

Kathryn Hibbert

One of the outcomes of a 'knowledge economy' and its corresponding surveillance mechanisms is the competitive anxiety it spawns amongst governments intent on seeing their schools outperform the others on international testing regimes. The challenge is figuring out how to integrate accountability without systematically dismantling the very essence of teaching and learning. Teachers largely enact the culture they live, and they have been living in a culture in which 'teacher proof' materials proliferate, and curricular prescriptions abound (Lofty, 2006). The literature on *Governmentality* offers us one way to talk about this phenomenon. Yet, within governmentality, teachers have both the privilege and the responsibility to practice freedom. How might we break away from reductionist modes of assessment and capture learning in situ? How might experiences from interdisciplinary educational settings inform thinking about what we do in schools? How might changing the way teachers and students interact with one another (space, resources and form) translate teaching and learning? Actor network theory (ANT) helps explain how participation in activities or networks mobilizes practices in particular ways. In this chapter, I explore the notion of freedom in the context of a nascent 'cloud curriculum' for teaching Shakespeare, leveraging multimodal affordances made visible through the efforts of New Literacy scholars.

Why Shakespeare?

At the time of writing of this chapter, many, including myself, were marking the 450th birth anniversary of playwright William Shakespeare. Given the growing concern that students and teachers hold regarding the relevance of Shakespeare in today's curriculum, I was intrigued by a news report that featured 100 Syrian children performing an adaptation of *King Lear* in the Zaatari Refugee camp in Jordan:

> ...many of the children...have never read or seen any of Shakespeare's work. But they are no strangers...to the tragedy of the human condition. And this particular play – a story of exile, a ruler losing grip with reality, a land divided by rival groups, a tale of human cruelty – seems especially relevant. (Zakaria, 2014, n.p.)

Outside of the constructs of formal schooling, it would seem, Shakespeare's ability to help us imagine 'other ways of living...other sets of values and beliefs...and other ways of defining oneself' (Gibson, 1993, p. 14) resonate in powerful ways.

In North America, disenchantment with the Bard mimics much of the discourse about education today; an inability to see how learning about Shakespeare, in this case, was going to prepare students for employment (Lighthill, 2011). Utilitarian conceptions of education have dominated North American educational reforms in recent decades, ostensibly designed to equip students with the necessary skills to be productive employees (Rose, 1999). However, in 1996, literacy scholars, collectively known as the New London Group (NLG), argued persuasively that the 'role of schools has fundamentally shifted' and called upon teachers to prepare students for a *civic pluralism* that would allow them to 'participate fully in public, community and economic life' (p. 60). Acknowledging the multiplicity of cultures, languages and texts in our society, the NLG argued that states, schools and pedagogies 'must be strong as neutral arbiters of difference' to create 'a new civility in which differences are used as a productive resources and in which differences are the norm' (p. 69). In this context, education is conceptualized as 'design', linking

> ...powerfully to the sort of *creative intelligence* the best practitioners need in order to be able, continually to redesign their activities in the very act of practice...learning and productivity are the results of the designs (the structures) of complex systems of people, environments, technology, beliefs and texts. (my emphasis, p. 73)

Artist Friedensreich Hundertwasser lamented, 'our real illiteracy is our inability to create'.[1] How has this happened? Nikolas Rose (1999), a sociologist who has studied the ways in which scientific development has altered conceptions of identity and governance suggests that as expertise (in this case, literacy expertise) has been 'rendered governable', it has 'changed the expertise itself' (p. 153). Rose also suggests that 'empirically identifiable differences in ways of thinking and acting' can offer a 'means of problematization … and solution' (p. 173). Multimodality, with its interdependence on a multiplicity of modes to make meaning, expands our human capacity to create, represent and communicate knowledge and understanding in multiple ways, thereby expanding our capacity 'to [re]invent [ourselves], individually and collectively, as new kinds of political actors' (p. 179).

I place my enquiry within an educational context in Ontario, Canada that has, coincidental to the work of the NLG, significantly increased the standardization of curriculum, assessment, reporting to parents and 'teacher 'training'. To do this, I first explore notions of 'governmentality' with a view to better understand the past and current state, but also as a means of thinking through resistance and freedom that may take us into a new future.

Act 1: Government, governance and the production of *governmentality*

In the thirty years since I entered the teaching profession, I have observed that as more and varied forms of literacy, curricular, and pedagogic practices were enabled through an array of texts, language and contexts, a parallel movement was taking place in Ontario's[2] schools to define, standardize, prescribe, measure and report on learning. In those same thirty years, philosophers (e.g. Foucault) and sociologists (e.g. Rose, Dean) were writing about issues of surveillance, power and control as a means of exploring the mechanisms of legitimization or rationalization. As Foucault (1982) described it, they were exploring the 'different modes by which … human beings are made subjects' (p. 777). The concept of *governmentality* offered a way of noticing or attending to the production, assemblage and movement of knowledge within the context of differentiated power relations that several scholars have grappled with (e.g. Miller & Rose, 1990; 2008; Dean, 1999).

Government, Dean (1999) defines as

> … any more or less calculated and rational activity, undertaken by a multiplicity of authorities and agencies, employing a variety of techniques and forms of knowledge, that seeks to shape conduct by working through our desires, aspirations, interests and beliefs, *for definite but shifting ends and with a diverse set of relatively unpredictable consequences, effects and outcomes.* (my emphasis, p. 11)

Governance, 'can be good or bad', but tends to be viewed more positively when it appears to facilitate 'non-state mechanisms of regulation, to reduce the size of the political apparatus and civil service' (Rose, 1999, p. 16). However, when used to manage 'social and economic affairs' (p. 16), governance translates ideologies into regulation: what Michael Apple (2000) calls 'official knowledge', legitimized for public institutions of education. In Ontario, educational regulations are set out in the Education Act,[3] and governance of the province's teachers is directed by the 'Ontario College of Teachers' (OCT). The OCT 'licenses, governs and regulates Ontario's teaching profession in the public interest', including setting 'ethical standards and standards of practice' (www.oct.ca). These standards set the parameters of professionalism, articulating expectations for knowledge, skills and values in addition to the ethical standards of care, trust, respect and integrity. The College issues 'professional advisories' to 'identify and clarify' responsibilities enabling members to govern their own conduct. In other words, they set the conditions within which teachers practice professional autonomy.

Governmentality, however,

> … is a matter not of the representation of individual mind or consciousness, but of the bodies of knowledge, belief and opinion *in which we are immersed*…the idea of mentalities of government then, emphasizes the way in which the thought involved in practices of government is collective and relatively taken for granted. (Dean, 1999, p. 16)

An increased focus on accountability with its accompanying standardization of curriculum, policies, measures and reporting introduced a professional tension for teachers, directing their attention in no small measure to the textual audit regimes, a move that 'does not always, if ever…promote learning' (Fenwick, forthcoming). Compliance with regulations can constrain a teacher's ability to enact professional autonomy.

Finding freedom in governance

According to some, the 'creation of freedom' is central to good governance (Rose et al., 2009, p.12). Practicing freedom in an audit culture requires first understanding 'how we are governed in the present' (p. 26). To escape the 'fixed subject positions allotted by workplaces', we must also understand our 'own role in producing these subjects' (Fenwick, 2007, p. 22). Subjectivity is constituted *in relation*, where 'individuals (or collectives) constitute themselves by making the world an object of reflection and action, and build *experience* in this interaction' (Olesen, 2006, p. 58). Importantly, Fenwick and Somerville (2007) draw our attention to the idea that 'the constitution of subjectivity [takes place] within the gaze of others' (p. 254). Whose gaze is aimed at teachers and with what effect? Does the need for recognition and belonging in the profession of teaching encourage teachers to 'attach themselves to a particular gaze' (p. 254) as we have observed in previous literacy studies? (Hibbert et al., 2007).

As a new teacher, I was also a curriculum writer and developer. One consequence of the standardization movement since then was a repositioning of teachers from curriculum designers to knowledge *receivers* (Belenky et al., 1997). Although arguably teachers retain the freedom to exercise their professionalism in terms of enacting curricula in ways that respond to the needs of their learners, subtle changes in the ways teachers talked about their work reveal the [perhaps unintended?] implications of this regulatory move: curriculum was *delivered*, *covered* or *implemented* and 'training' largely replaced professional development (Hibbert, 2004). Of even greater concern was language that signalled an alignment to one of the many commercial literacy programmes (e.g. 'I am a Four Blocks® teacher') that proliferated in response to the competitive international zeal to be the 'best' (Hibbert, 2004; Hibbert & Iannacci, 2005).

The role of assessment in 'governed mentality'

Driving the 'governed' mentality most significantly was the implementation of standardized provincial assessment (Education, Quality and Accountability Office – or EQAO) and reporting systems. Regardless of what a year's worth of in-classroom assessment yielded, it paled in comparison to the public attention paid to the relative scant information gathered and reported in the Grade 3, 6 and 9 EQAO assessments. Media published school-by-school rankings of results in literacy and numeracy, and right wing organizations like the Frasier Institute used them to talk in very narrow terms about 'quality'. Despite cautions issued by EQAO itself not to decontextualize the results from the local information (e.g. board, school and classroom assessments), that is precisely and predictably what happened. Boards of Education across the province responded with a focus on 'data' and results in ways that obscured meaningful dialogue about authentic, situated teaching and learning.

Tom Billington (2012), a psychologist in the United Kingdom (where OFSTED, the Office for Standards in Education, inspects and regulates services for children), argues that such practices reflect society's inability to grapple with the significant variability we encounter in the learners we teach – especially in a context preoccupied with 'norms' and accountability. He wondered if the focus has been too heavily on meeting the needs of government than of children – especially those that fall outside of the normative structures that have been created and imposed – exhausting 'our capacities for authenticity' (p. 3). Measurement, he says,

> ... helps to control the complexity of government for it is through measurement that children's lives can be reduced to the smallest number of characteristics in the shortest time available. Indeed, the measurement of children can operate in ways which deny individuals any identity whatsoever. (p. 26)

Teachers' professional identities within this context are also at risk. Dean's claim that our 'understanding of ourselves is linked to the ways in which we are governed' (2010, p. 14) was borne out in a study that traced the colonization of teachers' knowledge through Ministry training (Hibbert et al., 2007).

Processes of confrontation

A central theme of Shakespeare's plays concerns 'exile', which can be experienced as a loss of language or identity;

> The language I have learned these forty years,
> My native English, now I must forego:
> And now my tongue's use is to me no more
> Than an unstringed viol or a harp,
> Or like a cunning instrument cased up,
> Or, being open, put into his hands
> That knows no touch to tune the harmony. (Richard II, 1.3)

Shakespeare also teaches us that life affords all sorts of opportunities for reunion, restoration and rebirth. Ball and Olmedo (2013) calls it an act of *self-care* when teachers begin to question 'the *how(s) of power* inside and around him or her, the *how(s)* of his or her beliefs and practices' (p. 86). Examining our professional experiences with an eye to confronting and understanding our past affords a means to create an alternative future. This requires us to be honest about those parts of ourselves that have been adopted and/or co-opted: 'that piece of the oppressor that is planted deep within each of us' (Lorde, 1984, p. 123). To exercise freedom, teachers need to first become reacquainted with their own professional knowledge and power.

The labour of becoming[4]

The *Cult of Efficiency* Stein (2001) argues, with its systems of centralized decision making and monitoring, has produced a de-professionalized and disconnected cadre of 'workers'. It may have had the unintended effect of 'immobilizing' people, separating them from their own ability to make decisions, judgments and take action based on what they know, in favour of abdicating this critical professional discernment to disembodied tools and instruments. An inability to act renders us unable to participate in creating our own future:

> **Estragon**: (*anxious*) And we?
> **Vladimir**: I beg your pardon?
> **Estragon**: I said, And we?
> **Vladimir**: I don't understand.
> **Estragon**: Where do we come in?
> **Vladimir**: Come in?
> **Estragon**: Take your time.
> **Vladimir**: Come in? On our hands and knees.
> **Estragon**: As bad as that?
> **Vladimir**: Your Worship wishes to assert his prerogatives?
> **Estragon**: We've no rights anymore?
> (*laugh of Vladimir, stifled as before, less the smile*)
> **Vladimir**: You'd make me laugh if it wasn't prohibited.
> **Estragon**: We've lost our rights?
> **Vladimir**: (*distinctly*). We got rid of them.
> (*Silence. They remain motionless, arms dangling, heads sunk, sagging at the knees*).
> **Estragon**: (*feebly*). We're not tied? (*Pause*). We're not –
> Beckett, S. (1953). *Waiting for Godot*, Act 1.

Like Vladimir and Estragon, we 'are living in an age of anxiety' in education (Barrs, 2000, p. 287). But we're not tied.

Act 2: Multiliteracies theories: Introduction or re-acquaintance?

The sociomateriality of multiliteracies is not new. Several scholars (e.g. The New London Group, 1996; Selber, 2004; Kist, 2005; Cope & Kalantzis, 2009) have written about the *multiple* literacies of the past. However, as Eisenstein

(1979) articulates in her book, *The Printing Press as an Agent of Change*, the ability to publish and distribute multiple copies of print text all but obliterated attention to anything other than print, especially in light of its contribution to increasing literacy on a mass scale. History will judge whether or not we are in the midst of a similar transition today given the proliferation of digital information, 'apps' and increasing ways for the general population to access, document, share and create. 'New multimodal configurations' and 'genres of knowledge' are emerging with technology expanding opportunities for considering how knowledge is assembled, produced and disseminated (Jewitt, 2008). Multimodality 'deals with all the means we have for making meanings – the modes of representation – and considers their specific way of configuring the world' (Kress, 2004). In particular, 'meanings always relate to specific societies and their cultures, and to the meanings of the members of those cultures' (n.p.).

In the education community, much attention has been focused on understanding the affordances of the new tools for teaching and learning (Jenkins, 2006). As those affordances have been explored and applied in classrooms, enthusiasm for their pedagogical potential has grown. So too has teacher frustration with the privileged, reductionist forms of 'linguistic assessments', inadequate as an authentic reflection of student achievement or as a relevant source of information contributing to pedagogical decision-making. Scholars and practitioners have thus turned their attention to how they might capture and document their students' achievement in multimodal ways (e.g. Towndrow et al., 2013), raise the semiotic awareness of teachers (Ott, forthcoming) and how new forms of participation mediate our evolving subjectivities and cultural practices (Hibbert, 2013).

ANT forwards the notion that by translating the setting (and the materiality), we translate knowledge. In multimodality,

the processes of making texts and reading texts are both processes of design; and both are in important sense inversions of the social and semiotic arrangements of the era of the dominance of the constellation of writing and book. It has now been overtaken by the new constellation of image and screen ... In the multimodal landscape of communication, choice and therefore design become central issues. If I have a number of ways of expressing and shaping my message, then the questions that confront me are: which mode is best, most apt, for the content/meaning I wish to communicate? Which mode most appeals to the audience whom I intend to address? Which mode most corresponds to my own interest at this point in shaping the message for communication? Which medium is preferred by my audience? Or by me? How am I positioning myself if I choose this medium or this mode rather than those others?

All of these call for choices to be made, resting on my assessment of the environment in which communication takes place, in all its complexity … (Kress, 2004, n.p.)

The teacher and the learner engaged in multimodal learning are making increasingly sophisticated sets of decisions about their work – increasing the autonomy of both in the process. It is the culmination of this thinking that led to the conceptualization of a 'cloud curriculum'.

Act 3: 'The cloud curriculum'

In 2010, I met with Andrew Lester,[5] an enthusiastic marketing and media executive so enchanted by award winning, internationally recognized teacher and author Lois Burdett[6] that he reorganized his professional life to bring her work teaching Shakespeare to children to life in the virtual world. To ensure the design and development was pedagogically sound and relevant to twenty-first century learners, he invited me to collaborate on the curriculum project (Figure 9.1).[7]

As Lois and I reminisced about our teaching experiences, it became clear that we shared a fundamental desire to see each student for the unique individual s/he was and find ways to nurture their intellect and passion for learning. Having experienced both the drudgery of 'controlled vocabulary' texts and dreary – if not insulting – 'teacher training', we agreed that *both*

Figure 9.1 *Sample from A Midsummer Nights' Dream in the 'cloud curriculum'*

teachers and students need to engage with rich literature, powerful, timeless ideas and important themes. As Lois exclaimed when reviewing letters that her young students wrote after studying Shakespeare: 'You can't write that way unless your soul is touched' (Burdett, personal communication, 2013). Our challenge was to conceptualize how to take this dynamic energy into a multimodal curricular project. We began with a few key assumptions:

1. Learning is fluid and educators and students are diverse.

2. Curriculum is intended to be dynamic, evolving and responsive to learners and teachers: guided by state expectations for grade levels – but not shackled by them.

3. Educators and students are most engaged when their own *creative intelligence* is activated.

As a project team, we wanted to find ways of engaging *with* our students in flexible ways with multiple texts, and examine their growth over time in situ. We wanted to provide exemplary but modifiable models that would stimulate the creativity, thinking and growth of others while allowing a tailoring to individual needs and contexts. Lois' original work resonated strongly with teachers as evidenced by the thousands of letters she has received from teachers around the world. However, we wanted to honour the *situatedness* of learning by recognizing that we cannot simply transfer knowledge and wisdom; rather, we must create spaces for teachers and students to engage with the resources gathered and produced in the service of creating their own knowledge. Changing the ways in which teachers and students interact with one another (space, resources and form) and leveraging the affordances of digital technology to support multimodality led us to conceptualize the project in the form of a ***cloud curriculum***, building upon the notion of cloud computing.

Briefly, this means that the curriculum would be hosted on a network. In the cloud, the initial curriculum resources developed would be flexible enough for teachers to manipulate materials to respond to the unique needs of their students. For example, if selected vocabulary is needed to be expanded, reduced or translated, teachers could access and modify the resources to suit their students. Importantly, the cloud builds in a dynamic feedback loop that allows all participants (teachers, students and developers) an opportunity to view the effectiveness of the resources, how they are used and modified. Opportunities for participants to share back into the community stimulate a process of continual improvement and engage them in a co-production of knowledge.

The 'Secret of Will'

Burdett's approach to teaching and enthusiastic achievement of her students caught the attention of many, including Director and documentary filmmaker Conrad Beaubien. In 2002, Beaubien's award-winning film *The Secret of Will* documented and assembled a series of multimodal artefacts of literacy learning. There were interviews with Burdett, samples of student work, clips of student dramatic and musical performances – both on the thrust stage at the internationally renowned theatre in Stratford, or in the school gymnasium, where their performance was famously attended by cast from the professional company. Clips and interviews of children captured at the age of 7 were augmented with reflective interviews from the same children at about the age of 15. Much of the discussion in the film focused on the language and, in particular, writing. However, the filmmaker was able to capture so much more: the integration of living curriculum in the garden they planted, the gesture, intonation and expressions from both the children and their delighted audiences and the enthusiasm for what they were learning and had learned. In *Literacies*, Kalantzis and Cope (2012) call on educators to help their students learn 'to see the world from multiple points of view, not assum[e] that things are exactly what the texts say they are' (p. 167), an approach that Burdett used in her teaching. Following is an excerpt, transcribed from interviews included in the documentary (Table 9.1):

Table 9.1 Transcribed excerpt from Beaubien, C. (2002). The Secret of Will.

Burdett: *It was the whole process that was important, not just the answer but the whole process of learning. Shakespeare is not an end in itself, but a means to an end. After they learn about Shakespeare the person, they become involved in the actual play.*

(Teenage Ellen): *Ms. Burdett would read us things from the actual books and then she would read us a revised version.*

(Teenage Katie) *She would read these books and then explain how the words fit into the context.*

(Teenage Anika): *and then we'd act it out. She'd pick people from the class to come up and tell she would tell us what lines to say. And then she's say all right, now these are the characters, and I want you to go and write a diary entry or a letter from this person to this person about what they would say after what just happened. – and it made a big difference. Because when we went to go write then, because we had actually just been those characters.*

(Continued)

Table 9.1 Transcribed excerpt from Beaubien, C. (2002). The Secret of Will.

> **(Teenage Laura)**: *We all have crystal clear knowledge of what happens in the story which is kind of cool because we were only in grade 2 or 3.*
>
> **(Child Laura)**: *In MacBeth, he taught us you don't have to listen to someone – like Lady MacBeth – Lady MacBeth kind a forced him into it. You don't have to listen – just because she's your wife, and just because you don't want to disappoint her – You should listen to your own mind..*
>
> **(Teenage Morgan)**: *I've read constantly since I was in grade 2; we were read to so much and we wrote so much that it's just something that you want to do.*
>
> **(Child Morgan)**: *False face must hide what false heart doth know. And I like that, because he has to sort of lie a bit. He lies to people and he doesn't show what he really thinks on his face. He hides it, but his heart really knows what he's thinking.*
>
> **(Teenage Morgan)**: *We had that language, we had all those big words and we knew what they meant and we could talk in Shakespearean ways and that's just the way we thought all the time, and some people just don't have that vocabulary that we had at 7 years old.*
>
> **(Child Morgan)**: *The witches told him that he would, and so he went and he killed Duncan and then he kept on getting eviler and more and more – if you go up – way up to the top of evilness you cannot come down. It's very, very hard.*
>
> **(Teenage Anika)**: *When I look at the group of people who have been in her class – we are the people who in a class will volunteer to read our work out loud to class and we love to write poetry. We love to think outside the box – so I think all of us came away with that. We can do anything, and it doesn't matter what other people think.*

Literacy assessment in 'new times': From what is–to what is possible

Multimodality offers us a way to assess, evaluate, document and report learning that makes current forms obsolete. After conducting a series of pan-Canadian interviews – nearly a decade ago – into the misalignment of teaching and testing, researchers concluded that 'Ministry of Education personnel were wrestling with these issues and were at various stages of innovation with their responses' (Asselin et al., 2005, p. 821). A *decade* later, students continue to largely complete 'paper and pencil' provincial assessments. The 'constraining influence' this has on what happens (or doesn't) in schools (Kalantzis et al., 2010; Unsworth, 2014, p. 40) cannot be underestimated. For example, Kremer and Sanders (2012) point out that Shakespeare didn't simply create scripts, 'he wrote *plays* – live productions to be acted out in front of audiences with costumes and sets and music and make-up, intonations and accents' (p. 57). With our 'epistemological commitment' (Kress, 2003) to print however, the significant attention is paid to the 'script' with much less attention on the textual vibrancy of the play. It is an example of how the cultural materials of a dominant group or interest operationalize their structural power while reducing the richness of the literacy event itself.

The affordances of multimodal literacy have drawn my attention to a different kind of power: the power of texts to move us – emotionally, spiritually – to help us connect with others or ourselves, to help us make meaning and to help us continue to see our students and their learning in new ways. Peggy Albers reflected that 'drama encouraged [her] to think across systems of communications – language, art, drama, music – to design, develop, and direct a single production … [her] students also thought across these communication systems in order to interpret and become their characters' (2006, p. 76). Like Shay (2008), I am interested in the social practices that acknowledge 'the multiple contexts which constitute assessments' in these new times (p. 528). What might it look like? How can it reflect the freedom and autonomy teachers seek so that they may participate more fully in their lives? How might we capture and document learning to reflect such multiplicity?

In my professional educational work, I engage in interdisciplinary research and practice. In my work with medical imaging, for example, I have observed that diagnostic images taken of patients are referred to as 'studies'. When I enquired about this, my radiology colleagues told me that the image is intended to represent an entire process, and that physicians use it to look for changes that have occurred since the previous sample in addition to comparing what they see to images that are considered 'normal'. Deviation from the norm in this case could signal a need for specific types of intervention, or could provide insights into anatomy and pathology previously unknown. Both come from studying the images (static and dynamic), making comparisons, putting what they see into context with what they know about a patient's history and current complaints. What would happen if we thought about our assessment practices as 'studies' contextualized in our students' lives?

Leveraging the cloud

Teachers have long performed practices which have recently been coined 'pedagogical documentation'.[8] Documenting student learning is an important part of responsive teaching, and helps teachers to 'see the child, over and over again' (Lindgren, 2012, p. 333). Importantly, pedagogical documentation allows the teacher to attend to both the *content* of their student's knowledge and the *process* of their learning. Documentation occurs not only to create a record to compare with curricular expectations but also the artefacts (images, audio, video and samples of work) become the 'texts' at the centre of a recursive dialogue that can occur between teacher and learner, reflectively by teachers, between parents and their children or teachers and parents (and their children).

A 'cloud curriculum' offers a persuasive model of a dynamic and participatory multimodal space that allows flexible and participatory teaching and learning – while creating an 'audit trail' that serves the pedagogical documentation process. It reconnects students and teachers with learning how to express their own ideas rather than just accurately reproducing the ideas of others. Opportunities for feedback are possible that go beyond the teacher, the current classroom and the home. With a focus on both content and process, educators can not only pay close attention to how and what students are learning but they can also make the learning process visible to them (and others) along the way so that they can build on strengths, add to their repertoire of strategies and remediate any weaknesses. Students are enabled to develop fluencies in modes that are deeply embedded in their culture – and increasingly in the workplace they will enter. The web is ideally suited to inspire, document and share the knowledge of learners (Kalantzis & Cope, 2012). It can afford us the opportunity to use artefacts of student learning as 'studies'.

In the face of increasing pressure for education to serve employability, Fareed Zakaria[9] reminds us that a liberal education

> … makes you a good citizen. The word liberal comes from the Latin *liber*, which means 'free'. At its essence, a liberal education is an education to free the mind from dogma, from controls, from constraints. It is an exercise in freedom.

Too much time and attention have been paid to the 'operationalization of competence (and in particular the development of assessment tools), and not enough has been paid to the fact that there are some dramatically different paradigms or "discourses" about what competence actually *is*' (Hodges & Lingard, 2013, pp. 10–11). In order to move towards a more integrated understanding of this concept, Pink (2009) argues that it is necessary that we move beyond the 'performance' mindset of the past, in favour of 'mastery' mindsets of our future. Educators with a 'performance' mindset encourage learners to meet standards in order to 'perform' competency, whereas educators with a 'mastery' mindset create the conditions in which students are challenged to seek mastery. The process they engage in, whether at work, at school or at home, aligns with the deep human need we all have to lead our own lives, and to learn and create through autonomy, mastery and purpose (Pink, 2009).

Notes

1 Hundertwasser, F. Quote attributed to the artist, written on the wall of the Kunsthaus Museum, Vienna Austria.

2 In the Canada, education is a provincial responsibility and therefore varies somewhat from province to province. I am using my experience in the province of Ontario as an example.

3 Education Act: http://www.e-laws.gov.on.ca/html/statutes/english/elaws_statutes_90e02_e.htm

4 Venn, C., & Terranova, T. (2009). Introduction. Thinking after Michel Foucault. *Theory, Culture & Society, 26*(6), 1–11.

5 QWILL Media

6 See: '*Shakespeare Can be Fun*'. http://www.fireflybooks.com/Shakespeare

7 *Note*: There is no financial arrangement

8 The term is often attributed to Loris Malaguzzi, founding director of Reggio Emilia preschools; however the practice has been an important part of teaching for many decades. The concern is that this practice has been co-opted in ways that serve accountability needs more so than learning needs.

9 Commencement Keynote Address, Sarah Lawrence College: http://www.slc.edu/news-events/events/commencement/fareed-zakaria-keynote.html

References

Albers, P. (2006). Imagining possibilities in multimodal curriculum design. *English Education, 38*(2), 75–101.

Apple, M. (2000). *Official Knowledge: Democratic Education in a Conservative Age*. New York: Routledge.

Asselin, M., Early, M., & Filepenko, M. (2005). Accountability, assessment, and the literacies of information and communication technologies. *Canadian Journal of Education, 28*(4), 802–923.

Ball, S. J., & Olmedo, A. (2013). Care of the self, resistance and subjectivity under neoliberal governmentalities. *Critical Studies in Education, 54*(1), 85–96.

Barrs, M. (2000). Gendered literacy. *Language Arts, 77*(4), 287–293.

Beaubien, C. (2002). *The Secret of Will: One Grade 2 Class + William Shakespeare = A Journey of a Lifetime*. Toronto: Twelfth Night Films.

Belenky, M. F., Bond, L. A., & Weinstock, J. S. (1997). Otherness. In M. F. Belenky, L. A. Bond & J. S. Weinstock (Eds), *A Tradition that Has No Name: Nurturing the Development of People, Families and Communities* (pp. 3–66). New York: Basic Books.

Billington, T. (2012). *Separating, Losing and Excluding Children*. London: Routledge Falmer.

Burdett, L. (2013). Personal communication.

Cope, B., & Kalantzis, M. (2009). Multiliteracies: New literacies, new learning. *Pedagogies: An International Journal*, 4,164–195.

Dean, M. (1999). *Governmentality. Power and Rule in Modern Society.* London: Sage.

———. (2010). *Governmentality. Power and Rule in Modern Society* (2nd edition). London: Sage.

Eisenstein, E. L. (1979). *The Printing Press as an Agent of Change: Communications and Cultural Transformations in Early-Modern Europe.* Cambridge: Cambridge University Press.

Fenwick, T. (2007). Escaping/becoming subjects: Learning to work the boundaries in boundaryless work. In S. Billet, T. Fenwick & M. Somerville (Eds), *Work, Learning and Subjectivity.* New York: Springer.

Fenwick, T., & Somerville, M. (2007). Approaching subjectivity in work: Perspectives, environments, issues. In S. Billet, T. Fenwick & M. Somerville (Eds), *Work, Learning and Subjectivity.* New York: Springer.

Foucault, M. (1982). The subject and power. *Critical Inquiry, 9*(4), 777–795.

Gibson, R. (1993) Why teach Shakespeare? *The Newsletter of the Shakespeare and Schools Project* (Autumn), 15.

Hibbert, K. (2004). *Examining 'enunciative space' in an online community of practice.* Doctoral dissertation, Faculty of Graduate Studies, University of Western Ontario, London.

———. (2013). Finding wisdom in practice. The genesis of the Salty Chip, a Canadian multiliteracies collaborative. *Language and Literacy, 15*(1), 23–38.

Hibbert, K., & Iannacci, L. (2005). From dissemination to discernment: The commodification of literacy instruction and the fostering of 'good teacher consumerism'. *Reading Teacher, 58*(8), 2–13.

Hibbert, K., Heydon, R., & Rich, S. (2007). Beacons of light, rays, or sun catchers? A case study of the positioning of literacy teachers and their knowledge in neoliberal times. *Teaching and Teacher Education: An International Journal of Research and Studies, 24*(2), 303–315.

Hodges, B., & Lingard, L. (2013). *The Question of Competence: Reconsidering Medical Education in the Twenty-First Century.* Ithaca: Cornell University Press.

Jenkins, H. (2006). *Confronting the Challenges of Participatory Culture: Media Education for the 21st Century.* Chicago: The John D. and Catherine T. MacArthur Foundation.

Jewitt, C. (2008). *Challenge Outline: New Literacies, New Democracies.* London: London Knowledge Lab, Institute of Education. Retrieved from http://www. beyondcurrenthorizons.org.uk/wp-content/uploads/bch_challenge_paper_ democracies_carey_jewitt.pdf

Kalantzis, M., & Cope, B. (2012). *Literacies.* London: Cambridge University Press.

Kalantzis, M., Cope, B., & Harvey, A. (2010). Assessing multiliteracies and the new basics. *Assessment in Education: Principles, Policy & Practice, 10*(1), 15–26.

Kist, W. (2005). *New Literacies in Action: Teaching and Learning in Multiple Media.* New York: Teachers College Press.

Kremer, N., & Sanders, H. S. (2012). Shakespeare in 3D: Bringing the Bard to life through new (old media). *Voices from the Middle, 19*(4), 57–63.

Kress, G.R. (2003). *Literacy in the New Media Age.* London: RoutledgeFalmer.

Kress, G. (2004). *Reading images. Multimodality, representation and new media.* Retrieved from http://www.knowledgepresentation.org/BuildingTheFuture/Kress2/Kress2.html

Lighthill, B. (2011). 'Shakespeare' – an endangered species? *English in Education,45*(1), 36–51.

Lindgren, A. (2012). Ethical issues in pedagogical documentation: Representations of children through digital technology. *International Journal of Early Childhood, 44,* 327–340.

Lofty, J. S. (2006). *Quiet Wisdom: Teachers in the United States and England Talk About Standards.* New York: Peter Lang.

Lorde, A. (1984). *Sister Outsider: Essays and Speeches.* New York: Ten Speed Press.

 Miller, P., & Rose, N. (1990). Governing economic life. *Economy and Society, 19*(1), 1–31.

———. (2008). *Governing the Present: Administering Economic, Social and Personal Life.* Cambridge: Polity Press.

Olesen, H. S. (2006). Learning and experience. In S. Billet, T. Fenwick & M. Somerville (Eds), *Work, Subjectivity and Learning.* New York: Springer, 53–67.

Ott, M. (in preparation). Assessment narratives: The affordances of video inquiry for formative assessment of multiliteracies.

Pink, D. (2010). *Drive: The Surprising Truth about What Motivates Us.* New York: Riverhead Books.

Rose, N. (1999). *Powers of Freedom: Reframing Political Thought.* Cambridge: Cambridge University Press.

Rose, N., O'Malley, P., & Valverde, M. (2009). *Governmentality.* Legal Studies Research Paper No. 09.94. The University of Sydney, Sydney Law School. Retrieved from http://ssrn.com/abstract=1474131

Selber, S. (2004). *Multiliteracies for a Digital Age.* Urbana: Conference on College Composition and Communication National Council for Teachers of English.

Shay, S. (2008). Beyond social constructivist perspectives on assessment: The centering of knowledge. *Teaching in Higher Education, 13*(5), 595–605.

Stein, J. G. (2001). *The Cult of Efficiency.* Toronto: House of Anansi Press.

The New London Group. (1996). A pedagogy of multiliteracies: Designing social futures. *Harvard Educational Review, 66*(1), 60–92.

Towndrow, P. A., Nelson, M. E., & Yusuf, W. F. B. M. (2013). Squaring literacy assessment with multimodal design: An analytic case for semiotic awareness. *Journal of Literacy Research, 45*(4), 327–355.

Unsworth, L. (2014). Multimodal reading comprehension: Curriculum expectations and large-scale literacy testing practices. *Pedagogies: An International Journal, 9*(1), 26–44.

Zakaria, F. (2014). *Why Shakespeare fits with Syria tragedy.* GPS TV. Retrieved from http://globalpublicsquare.blogs.cnn.com/2014/04/08/why-shakespeare-fits-with-syria-tragedy/

10

Myth-Making and Meaning-Making: The School and Indigenous Children

David Rose

Introduction

The themes of this book bring together two fields of study that seem only distantly related at first sight, a sociological study of governance in education and the semiotic study of communicative modalities. But the breadth of these themes gives me an opportunity to tie together two perspectives on schools and Indigenous children, which I hope the reader will find illuminating and useful. One perspective is on the governance of the colonizing modern European culture over what happens to Indigenous children in school (beyond the formal role of government); the other is on the realization of the colonizing culture in the modalities of teaching and learning that Indigenous children are subjected to in school. However, the chapter is not merely a complaint, it contains two parts: the first part is an analysis of these factors and effects, using a framework from social theory, the second is a procedure for overcoming them, developed and proven in a long-term action research programme.

The background to the chapter starts from my own long-term commitment to education for Indigenous people, from the Pitjantjatjara homelands in central Australia (Rose, 1999, 2011a) to metropolitan universities (Rose et al., 2004, 2008). My experience working with a generation of Pitjantjatjara children who had completed primary school but remained almost entirely illiterate, and addicted to petrol sniffing, led me to ask why their schooling had been so unsuccessful, and what role this may have played in their self-destructive activity. At the urging of their elders, it also led me to seek out how to teach literacy more effectively, culminating over the last 15 years, in the development of a teacher professional learning programme known as *Reading to Learn* (Rose 2015, in press a).

Reading to Learn began with an action research project, *Scaffolding Reading and Writing for Indigenous Children in School* (Rose et al., 1999), that worked with teachers to synthesize strategies for teaching reading and writing that had been developing in Australia over the previous decade (Rose & Martin, 2012). At the start of the project, no students tested in the Pitjantjatjara community primary schools were reading more than basal picture books by the end of primary school, and no Pitjantjatjara students tested in urban secondary schools were reading above junior primary levels. By the end of the project's first year, most of these students were reading at age appropriate levels, and independent evaluation showed average literacy growth at a rate normally expected over four years (McCrae et al., 2000). Since then, *Reading to Learn* has grown in scope as a classroom and professional learning programme for primary, secondary and tertiary teachers, and in scale across Australia, south and east Africa (Dell, 2011; Millin, 2011) and western Europe (Coffin et al., 2013). The results of up to four times typical literacy growth rates have been consistently replicated (Culican, 2006;Rose, 2011b;Rose & Martin, 2013). Central to the programme's effectiveness are, on one hand, an analysis of governmental factors in education systems that constrain effective teaching for disadvantaged students, and on the other hand, a design of multimodal strategies to enhance literacy learning for all students.

Governmentality and Indigenous education

Although 'Western culture' is often opposed to 'Indigenous culture' as though they were polar contrasts, the opposition is highly misleading. To begin with, what aspects of each culture are being contrasted? One aspect that could reasonably be compared is social hierarchy. Whereas Indigenous communities tend to favour an ideology of 'egalitarian mutuality'(Maddock, 1972), the dominant organizing principle of modern Western societies remains social stratification. The colonizing culture is organized by socio-economic class, whether or not the political system is democratic. Colonized communities do not sit outside the class system, but are more or less integrated in it, often in the lowest economic stratum, with high unemployment, low education, poor health, high welfare dependency, incarceration and various other markers of social disadvantage.

For this reason, the problems that Indigenous children experience with school are not entirely different from the problems that many other children experience from economically disadvantaged groups. Poor education outcomes are frequently associated with families' lower socio-economic class positions; the poorer the family, the poorer their children's school outcomes are likely to be. Indigenous children's lack of school success is not just because they are Indigenous, but is widely associated with economic disadvantage in the modern societies they are part of. If we are serious about improving the education outcomes of Indigenous students, we have to start with an analysis of the school's role in reproducing socio-economic disadvantage. To this end I will draw on Basil Bernstein's (1990/2003, 2000) analysis of what he calls 'the pedagogic device'.

Like the societies they serve, Bernstein points out, education systems are also highly stratified. He analyses their organization in terms of the division of labour in exchange of knowledge. At one level is the production of knowledge, primarily by researchers and theorists in the upper echelons of academe. The second level he describes as the recontextualizing field, in which knowledge is transformed for pedagogic purposes. The third level he calls the field of reproduction, where recontextualized knowledge is exchanged between teachers and learners. Bernstein compares this hierarchy of pedagogic fields with religious hierarchies, from which it evolved in the early modern period, of prophets, priests and laity. Crucially, Bernstein draws two broad divisions in the recontextualizing field, a pedagogic recontextualizing field (PRF) including teacher education faculties and educational publishers, and an official recontextualizing field (ORF) that includes state education departments and boards of studies.

The official and pedagogic recontextualizing fields are often in conflict over what each considers appropriate pedagogies, curriculum contents and assessments. Bernstein suggests that these struggles are associated with conflicts between class fractions in the society served by the education system, primarily between fractions of the modern middle class, that have evolved over the past century in tandem with the evolution of schooling. Bernstein distinguishes between an 'old middle class', whose base is in economic production and in professions such as management, engineering, law, medicine, and a 'new middle class', whose base is in the production and exchange of symbolic commodities such as education and media. These groups have different economic interests, and tend to hold different positions over what constitutes valid curriculum and pedagogy. Where the old middle class tends to favour pedagogies in which teachers' authority, transmission of knowledge and criteria for assessment are explicit, the new middle class tends to prefer pedagogies in which learners appear to have more control, discovering knowledge for themselves at their own pace, achieving criteria unique to their own person. These types of pedagogy have long been characterized as 'traditional' and 'progressive', respectively. Bernstein contrasts them as 'visible' and 'invisible', since hierarchy, sequencing and criteria are explicit in the traditional mode, but masked in the progressive mode.

The progressivist movement swept Australian education faculties from the late 1970s, as 'whole language' literacy pedagogy, and more specifically 'process writing', in which children were expected to spontaneously develop literacy competences through 'immersion' in 'language-rich environments', and teachers were proscribed from intervening in and hence constraining children's creative development (Christie, 2004, 2010). These ideas are alive and well today in many parts of the world, with the term constructivist now generally used to refer to the approach. Alexander, in his revealing study of primary school pedagogy around the world, notes the following piece of progressive philosophy (2000, p. 548), prominently displayed on the classroom wall of one of his Michigan, USA schools.

Important issues to me –

Process orientation vs product orientation

Teaching students vs teaching programmes

Teacher as facilitator vs teacher as manager

Developing a set of strategies vs mastering a set of skills

Celebrating approximation vs celebrating perfection

Promoting independence in learning vs dependence on teacher

The ideological polarizing of process versus product and independent learning versus teaching of skills arguably advantaged children from literate middle-class families, who typically arrive at school with an average 1,000 hours experience of parent–child reading, in contrast with children who start with little or no such experience (Adams, 1990;Williams, 1995). For Indigenous children, whose family culture is often purely oral, with little or no home reading, and may also be non-English speaking, it has remained an ongoing calamity. All over Australia, Indigenous children right through primary school typically produced short texts of a few sentences, in response to the progressivist instruction to 'write from personal experience'. The texts were brief recounts or observations/comments, using only words they knew how to spell, and sentences they knew would not be corrected by the teacher, in the so-called 'editing' stage of process writing (Gray, 1990; Rose et al., 1999; Rose & Martin, 2012). Text 10.1 illustrates a common standard for many students in upper primary school, after four or five years of process writing.

Text 10.1 Example of process writing in upper primary

On the holiday
I went my dads for 3 week
weaksan we went to ante Jhinshous
forcrismus. I got Leogo and a humonic
I was vere happy to se her.
From BLak

It was not that children writing such texts lacked the resource of spoken English, but that they could not use this resource as a basis for learning to read and write, as whole language and process writing expected them to. Hence, a pedagogic movement that was ostensibly liberatory failed to provide many Indigenous children with the resources they needed to succeed in school, and proceed to further education. This has been a double tragedy for Indigenous people, as progessivism/constructivism took over in an era when they needed access to high-level education more than ever before. Until the 1970s in Australia, education for Indigenous children was often restricted, and the lives of Indigenous people were controlled under racist legislation. As the ideological climate shifted, authoritative pedagogic practices were often associated with authoritarian political regimes, and abandoned in favour of progressivist pedagogies. This kind of polarization continues today as constructivism is promoted in post-colonial contexts. Examples include the 'new literacies', advocates Street, who opposes teaching of technical literacies as 'simply imposing western conceptions of literacy onto other cultures' (1996, p. 2). In the South African context, Street associates literacy 'attached to formal education' with 'vested interests which depend upon the old views for their legitimacy' (1996, p. 2), smearing state literacy programmes by association with apartheid.

Bernstein's analysis helps to show why this kind of polarization is not helpful for Indigenous and other disadvantaged student groups, as the pedagogic conflict does not originate with their interests or needs. Whereas progressivism/constructivism has long been legitimated with values such as creativity, personal development, freedom of expression and learner-centred practice, in opposition to 'traditional' reproductive, teacher-centred rote-learning, at the bottom, is a struggle for control of education, between elite middle-class fractions.

The opposition between these fractions of the middle class is an opposition not over the distribution of power but over principles of social control. At economic and political levels the opposition is an opposition over the role of the State. (Bernstein, 1990/2003, p. 212)

This analysis sheds a different light on objections within the PRF to state-sponsored literacy assessments, as constraining freedom of expression in favour of 'objective and processable representations' (DeVault, 2008, p. 40). These testing regimes were certainly introduced by conservative governments, such as the UK Thatcher government in the 1980s, in response to perceived failures to improve education outcomes, and are clearly associated with the struggle between the state-controlled ORF and the university-based PRF. However, they have been continued and expanded by social democratic parties, such as the Rudd-Gillard Australian government of 2007–2013, that represent the interests of less privileged groups, alongside the old and new middle classes.

One such assessment regime, introduced by the Hawke-Keating Labor government in the 1990s, and continued by the conservative Howard government, was the Australian National Profiles for literacy and numeracy. These National Profiles were organized into eight assessment levels, and each level was considered to correspond with expected literacy growth over 1.5 school years. The enormous gap revealed by this and other assessments, between the literacy of Indigenous and other student groups, led to large-scale funding of education research programmes, of which *Scaffolding Reading and Writing for Indigenous Children* was one. Within the first year of this project, independent evaluators reported average improvements for junior secondary students at '2.5 Profile levels' (McCrae et al., 2000, p. 69). As this growth would normally be expected over four years, the project received national publicity, ultimately leading to the development of the *Reading to Learn* programme.

Hence, *Reading to Learn* did not emerge from a commitment to one ideology of pedagogic practice or another, but to the needs of Indigenous students and their communities. It has been taken up and expanded in Australia, Africa and Europe in response to the needs of other less advantaged student groups. How the programme meets these needs is illustrated below. However, in the course of the training, teachers are asked to track the literacy growth of students in the top, middle and bottom bands of their classes. The purpose of the assessment is for teachers to analyse how their practice is enhancing the skills of all the students in their classes, moderated against standards for each stage of school.

The assessment enables teachers to objectively identify the language resources that students are using in their writing. Fourteen criteria are scored from 0 to 3, giving a potential total score of 42. Criteria cover dimensions of social context, text organization, discourse patterns, grammar and graphic features. Teachers collect text samples from their students before starting the professional learning programme, and at the end. Figure 10.1 shows results for these 'pre-intervention' and 'post-intervention' writing samples, averaged

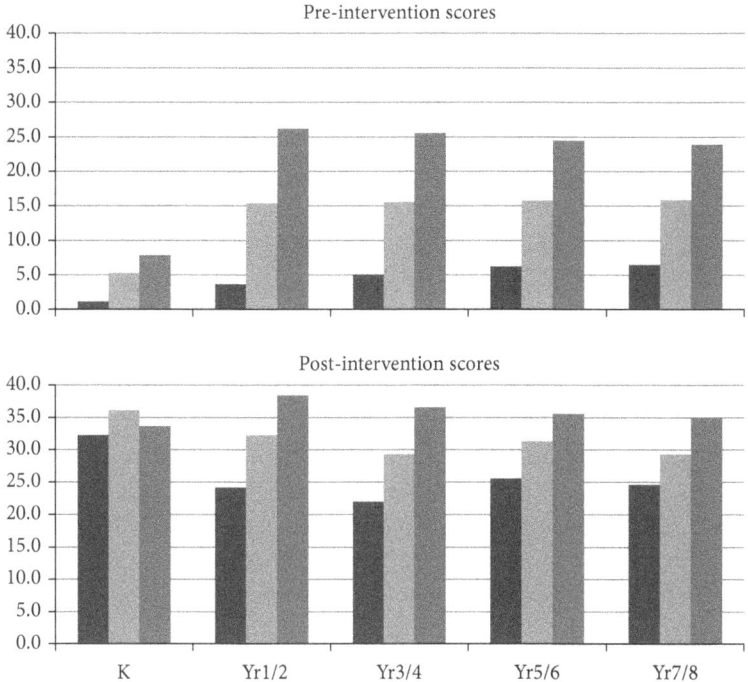

Figure 10.1 *Pre- and post-intervention scores show gap between student groups*

across assessments by 400 teachers in one training programme in 2010, representing at least 10,000 students. This programme included schools with up to 50 per cent enrolments of Indigenous students. Pre-intervention and post-intervention scores are for the same students, in the top, middle and bottom cohorts in each school stage.

The pre-intervention scores in Figure 10.1 show the mean differences in written language resources of high-, middle- and low-achieving students in each school stage. As this is a large sample across classes and schools, it may be read as approximating differences in the Australian and similar education systems as a whole. What is particularly interesting is that the gap between top and bottom groups is comparatively narrow at the start of school, labelled K for kindergarten, but that after a year or two (Yr 1–2) the gap has tripled, and remains steady through each following school stage. The top group in Yr 1–2 has clearly benefited from the literacy practices of their early years teachers, as their average results have shot up to the median standard for the school stage. These children are now reading and writing independently, and are likely to be actively engaged in learning from reading. The middle group has also obtained some benefit, but the bottom group appears to have received very little benefit from these literacy practices; their results are still near zero, and improve only slightly through each subsequent stage. The children who were failing at the start of primary school are still failing at the start of secondary, despite all the interventions prescribed by various literacy theories. These large-scale data confirm what teachers know intuitively, that the gap between the top and bottom students in their classes and schools will essentially be the same at the end of each year, and each student's school career, as it was at the start.

The pre-intervention scores also support the view introduced above, that problems that Indigenous children experience with school are similar to the problems that many other children experience. A key difference is that a much larger proportion of Indigenous students fall into the failing group, with serious consequences for their future lives, and for their whole communities. As such, the data also support the view presented in Gray (1990) and Rose (1999) – that the problems of Indigenous students cannot be addressed merely by a focus on cultural difference, but require significant changes in mainstream teaching practices. Central to this position is the recognition that teachers need more effective tools to enable all their students to succeed at similar levels, if the achievement gap in each classroom is to be narrowed.

The gap has clearly narrowed in the post-intervention scores in Figure 10.1. Each column shows results for the same teachers and students as the pre-intervention scores above. The post-intervention results are 6–8 months after the pre-intervention, and achieved while teachers were learning to use the strategies outlined above. Post-intervention scores show that average growth in Kindergarten is 70 per cent above pre-intervention scores, and the gap between low- and high-achieving groups is halved. All these children are now independently reading and writing, at an average high standard for Kindergarten, and are well prepared for the start of junior primary. In the other year levels, growth is 30–40 per cent above the pre-intervention scores, and the gap is reduced to 20–30 per cent. Students who normally remain in the failing range are now reading and writing at an acceptable average standard for their grade levels. However, the top groups have also accelerated to an average very high standard for their grade levels. These data are discussed in more detail in Rose (2011b; in press a, b) and Rose and Martin (2012, 2013).

In sum, relations between governmentality and Indigenous students' problems in school have been discussed here more broadly in terms of the interests of various groups in contemporary societies. Control measures such as state literacy assessments and national curricula are interpreted in terms of a struggle between the official and pedagogic recontextualizing fields, to influence practices in schools. While these measures may be experienced by agents in the PRF as constraining freedom of expression, they can also be used to serve the interests of groups whose needs have not yet been effectively met by progressivist theories and practices advocated in the PRF, particularly the needs of Indigenous students.

Modalities of teaching and learning literacy

In this section, I compare some current literacy practices of the school with the designed practices of *Reading to Learn*, in terms of semiotic modalities. Modalities of meaning have been a major focus of research in recent decades, as presented by the chapters in this book. However, classroom teaching and learning are particularly complex, as multiple semiotic dimensions are unfolding simultaneously, moment-by-moment, in a social context involving 20–30 or more learners, exchanging knowledge through various modalities in a great variety of activities.

One example is the common activity in the early years of school known as Shared Book Reading. In this activity, the teacher reads a picture book with the class, often in the form of a 'big book' mounted on an easel that all children can see. Typically, the teacher begins by talking through the pictures, using them to orient the children to the plot, settings and characters of the story before reading the words to them. This may be done interactively, by asking children what they can see in the pictures and what they know about their themes. In addition, other modalities may be used to orient children to the field, such as pictures, videos, toys, objects, activities. The teacher may read the text after or while discussing the pictures. A common practice is for the teacher to point at the words in the book as they are read aloud. Typically, a shared reading book may be read repeatedly, until the children are thoroughly familiar with the story, and can say many of its words along with the teacher as she reads.

Shared Book Reading shares many features with the practices of parent–child reading in literate middle-class families (Williams, 1995). The goal of both is to engage children in written modes of meaning, through a pleasurable social activity, in which the parent or teacher is the guide. Parent–child reading appears to have evolved as a middle-class cultural practice, alongside the evolution of schooling in the last century, and Shared Book Reading appears to have evolved in parallel. Although it is often discussed and advocated in the PRF, many of its features seem to be intuitively practised by teachers, as reading in the home is intuitively practised by carers. It can be highly effective in engaging children from all backgrounds in the pleasure of reading. I have often witnessed early years teachers engage Indigenous children in understanding, enjoying and saying the words in English picture books, although they may have no reading and little English at home.

To understand why it is effective, we can analyse its components using a functional model of language as text-in-context (Martin & Rose, 2007, 2008). In this model, language and its social contexts are complementary dimensions of the process of making meaning, in which language enacts relation between interactants, and construes their experience. Social relations and social activity are realized as unfolding patterns of discourse in texts, which are in turn realized as patterns of wordings, or grammar, which are in turn realized as patterns of sounds in speech and letters in writing. We can thus distinguish three levels to language: patterns of discourse, patterns of grammar and patterns of sounds or letters, together realizing patterns of social relations and activities. These three levels of language underpin common understandings of tasks in reading: recognizing written words and their letter patterns is widely known as 'decoding'; recognizing meanings of words in sentences is known as 'literal comprehension'; recognizing connections between meanings in discourse is often termed 'inferential comprehension'; and interpreting texts in terms of the readers' knowledge and values is often called 'interpretive comprehension'.

Shared Book Reading provides students with interpretive comprehension by relating their experience to images in the book, and other sources such as pictures, videos, toys, objects, activities. It provides inferential comprehension by talking through the sequence of the story, using the images for support. It provides literal comprehension by discussing the meanings of words as they are read in the context of the unfolding story. Crucially, these understandings are built through the modality of spoken interaction between teacher and learners; comprehending the story is interwoven in the social relations enacted between teacher and child. The only level of the reading task not directly addressed in Shared Book Reading or parent–child reading is decoding of written words.

The engagement with written ways of meaning afforded by Shared Book Reading should form a solid basis for children to develop as readers, and for many children it certainly appears to do so. But many Indigenous and other children do not go on to become independent readers, as the pre-intervention data in Figure 10.1 illustrate. The problem lies with the other literacy activities of the early years classrooms that are typically conducted with other texts, words, sounds and letter patterns. The lower level parts of language are dislocated from the meaningful, engaging activity of shared reading, and taught as discrete elements of the daily programme, which many children experience as disconnected segments.

Despite the dominant progressivist philosophy of early childhood education, many of these activities used for teaching beginning literacy have very old origins, involve a good deal of rote memorization, and operate with a rudimentary bricks-&-mortar model of language, in contrast to the social semiotic model outlined earlier. It is widely assumed that children must recognize the letters of the alphabet and the sounds they represent, before they can begin to read, so the alphabet system is practised by rote memorization. Children repeat the names of letters, as they are pointed to, often with pictures illustrating words that start with the sound represented by the letter ('a' is for apple), and practise writing the letters. This practice originated in the classical period. However, as the Roman alphabet does not cover the sounds of northern European languages such as English, children must also memorize systems of digraphs that represent these sounds, commonly known as phonics. This practice originated in the monasteries of medieval Europe. The next level in the bricks-&-mortar model is word recognition, widely taught using the 'sight word' or 'whole word' activity, in which children may have weekly lists of decontextualized words to memorize. The next level is to put these words into sentences, for which children are given basal picture books that build in levels, from a word or phrase on a page, to a sentence, to a paragraph and so on. The theory of language here is (a) componential, building larger bricks out of smaller bricks, and (b) representational, assuming that words represent concepts, that written words represent spoken words, and written letters represent spoken sounds.

Nevertheless, these practices often do work for learners who already have extensive experience and understanding of written ways of meaning. Children who start school with 1,000 hours of parent–child reading are clearly advantaged in this regard, and this may be a key factor in the evolution of this middle class cultural practice. However, children who do not have this experience often find it difficult to associate these decontextualized practices with meanings in texts, so that their reading skills develop more slowly. Thus, children who participate eagerly and intelligently in Shared Book Reading, and experience it as a meaningful communicative activity, can come to perceive reading individually as a meaningless activity of memorizing strings of words in a basal picture book. This helps to explain why otherwise intelligent children may still be unable to read more than basal picture books by the end of primary, and still be reading at junior primary levels in secondary school, as discussed for Pitjantjatjara students earlier (for more detailed discussion see Rose, 2010).

These problems are addressed in the *Reading to Learn* programme, by using the comprehension and engagement provided by Shared Book Reading as the starting point for a carefully designed sequence of multimodal activities. The representational theory is replaced by a realizational theory of meaning, in which social relations and experiences are realized by patterns of discourse, realized by wordings, realized by sounding and lettering. That is words make sense in the context of sentences, that make sense in the context of texts, and sounds and letters are alternative modes of realizing words.

Hence, beginning literacy activities start with sentences from a shared reading book that students are thoroughly familiar with, understand and can say each word in sequence. A sentence is written on a cardboard strip, and the teacher guides students to point at each written word as they say them aloud. In two or three repetitions, children are usually able to point and say the familiar words accurately. This activity is more effective for teaching one-for-one word recognition than the standard decontextualized 'sight/whole word' activity, as learners are supported by their grasp of meanings in context, along with the visual and manual modalities of pointing, enabling them to recognize the written words as equivalent expressions of the spoken words they already know.

Once children can point and say the words accurately, the teacher guides them to cut the sentence into groups of words expressing meaning segments such as who or what it is about, what they are doing, where and when, and then to cut up individual words. This manual activity is enhanced by learners mixing up the cards and re-arranging them, first into their original order, and then into alternative orders to make new sentences. This creative activity is known as Sentence Making.

Only after children have a thorough grasp of the patterns of wordings in the sentence are they guided to recognize and spell the patterns of letters that realize each of its words. In this step they are guided to cut up the words into their letter patterns, and to practise writing them on slates (small white or blackboards). Figure 10.2 shows guided word recognition and guided spelling activities with Pitjantjatjara teachers and students.

Once they can accurately spell each word, and form its letters, children are guided to write whole sentences using these words. These activities

Figure 10.2 *Guiding word recognition and guided spelling activities*

may be repeated with a series of sentences from a shared reading book, and then again with the next shared book. In this way, children's written language resources are built up in cycles that begin with engagement and comprehension of texts in context, followed by manipulation of wordings in sentences, further followed by practice with writing letter patterns in words, and writing patterns of words in sentences.

The goal for children is to ultimately use these resources to create texts of their own. This strategy of building up written resources through reading and guided practice contrasts with a more common approach that asks children to write from personal experience whether or not they have developed these resources. Texts 10.2 and 10.3 contrast results after a full year of standard early years literacy activities, with results for the same student after two months of the *Reading to Learn* strategies outlined earlier. In the 'pre' sample the child is only able to write a name and a few other words, which were illustrated with a simple stick figure. This child would fall in the bottom Yr 1–2 group in Figure 10.1. The post-sample is a coherent description of a topic the class has been studying. The accompanying illustration showed the seal, the hole in the ice and the terrible storms above.

Text 10.2 Outcome of standard literacy practices in the first year of school

John simon
He 10 sogd
and h and he
He is happy

Text 10.3 Outcome with same student after 2 months of Reading to Learn

The seal is on the ice
She had to got her baby some food.
They The seal want through a
hole in the ice. She dives down deep
to get some siqd for
the baby seal waiting. The
mummy and the baby
go in to the water. Wen terrible
storms come they stay all winter.

An effective professional learning programme

This brief outline of early years strategies is just one component of the *Reading to Learn* professional learning programme. On demand from teachers and schools, the programme has grown to meet the needs of early years, primary and secondary teachers, across subject areas. Other sets of strategies include *Preparing for Reading*, which enables all students in a class to follow challenging texts with comprehension; *Paragraph-by-paragraph reading*, in which dense texts may be read and key information identified; *Detailed Reading*, in which short passages are read and discussed in detail; *Joint Rewriting*, which guides students to appropriate the language resources of accomplished authors; and *Joint Construction*, which guides students to write whole texts successfully. These are all multimodal activities, involving spoken, written, visual and manual modalities, as written wordings are orally discussed, and students visually and manually identify wordings in texts using highlighters, and take turns to write on the board. Crucially, they are also whole class activities, in which the teacher guides all students to identify, comprehend, discuss and write meanings, step-by-step. The students are in control for each task, but the teacher is their authoritative guide (Christie, 2004). This practice addresses the fundamental problems that all teachers face: the wide range of 'learning abilities' in every classroom, and the low reading and writing skills of many students. Whereas classroom interactions in most classrooms typically involve just a few top students who consistently respond to teacher questions (Nutthal, 2005; Rose & Martin, 2013), the interactions in these *Reading to Learn* activities are carefully designed to engage every student in the classroom talk-around-text, by enabling them to successfully identify meanings in the texts being read, and propose wordings in the texts being written. Predictably, this practice has been criticized from progressivist/ constructivist positions as 'teacher-centred', but the aim of *Reading to Learn* is to democratize the classroom (Rose, 2005). The problem we see in current classrooms is not the power difference between teacher and students, but the hierarchy of success and failure between students.

Conclusion

Both learning to read and write and learning from reading are multimodal activities that children of the most privileged groups in our society are immersed in from the earliest age, so that their transitions from home to school, and from primary to secondary, and secondary to further education are relatively smooth and assured. The skills that teachers are given in their preservice training generally mesh with the needs of these groups of students, and ensure their successful progression. In contrast, the same training does not meet the needs of non-middle-class students as effectively, and often barely at all, especially for Indigenous students. Teachers are not trained to teach these students to read at the levels they should be reading for their ages and grades, nor how to write successfully for assessment. As a result, too many children remain in a low or failing range throughout their school careers, affording them few options for their lives to come.

The state, through the official recontextualizing field, attempts to pressure teachers to improve outcomes by imposing standardized assessment regimes and curricula. Indirectly, this puts pressure on the pedagogic recontextualizing field that may be experienced as constraining freedom and creativity. Bernstein contextualizes these conflicts in a struggle between fractions of the global middle class for control over the production, reproduction and changes in forms of consciousness that education affords. Literacy is at the heart of this struggle, as it is the primary modality through which the symbolic resources of modern culture are acquired. Reading and learning from reading are the means by which semiotic capital is exchanged and accumulated in the institutions of modernity. Families that lack this capital know this even more keenly than those who were born into it. Indigenous families and communities know it only too well, as so many were deliberately excluded from it in days gone by. Today there is no need for openly racist practices of exclusion, if teachers do not know how to teach their children to read and learn from reading. This is one form that the relationship between Indigenous peoples and the colonizing culture now takes. It cannot simply be blamed on the state restricting academic freedom, any more than it can be blamed on the cultural or linguistic differences of students. Surely, the primary responsibility for teachers' capacities to meet the needs of their most disadvantaged students must lie with those responsible for educating teachers.

References

Adams, M. J. (1990). *Beginning to Read: Thinking and Learning about Print: A Summary*. Urbana-Champaign: University of Illinois.

Alexander, R. (2000). *Culture & Pedagogy: International Comparisons in Primary Education*. Oxford: Blackwell.

Bernstein, B. (1990). *Class, Codes and Control 4: The Structuring of Pedagogic Discourse*. London: Routledge.

———. (2000). *Pedagogy, Symbolic Control and Identity: Theory, Research, Critique*. London: Taylor & Francis.

Christie, F. (2004). Authority and its role in the pedagogic relationship of schooling. In L. Young & C. Harrison (Eds), *Systemic Functional Linguistics and*

Critical Discourse Analysis. Studies in Social Change (pp. 173–201). London and New York: Continuum.

———. (2010). The 'Grammar Wars' in Australia. In T. Locke (Ed.), *Beyond the Grammar Wars: A Resource for Teachers and Students on Developing Language Knowledge in the English/Literacy Classroom* (pp. 55–72). New York: Routledge and Francis Taylor.

Coffin, C., Acevedo, C., & Lövstedt, A.-C. (2013). *Teacher Learning for European Literacy Education (TeL4ELE) Final Report*. Geneva: European Union, Retrieved from http://tel4ele.eu/

Culican, S. (2006). *Learning to Read: Reading to Learn, A Middle Years Literacy Intervention Research Project, Final Report 2003–4*. Melbourne: Catholic Education Office. Retrieved from http://www.readingtolearn.com.au

Dell, S. (2011). Reading revolution. *Mail & Guardian Online*. Retrieved from http://mg.co.za/article/2011-04-03-reading-revolution

DeVault, M. L. (2008). *People at Work: Life, Power, and Social Inclusion in the New Economy*. New York: New York University Press.

Gray, B. (1990). Natural language learning in Aboriginal classrooms: Reflections on teaching and learning. In C. Walton & W. Eggington (Eds), *Language: Maintenance, Power and Education in Australian Aboriginal Contexts* (pp. 105–139). Darwin: Northern Territory University Press.

Maddock, K. (1972). *The Australian Aborigines: A Portrait of Their Society*. Baltimore: Penguin.

Martin, J. R., & Rose, D. (2003). *Working with Discourse: Meaning Beyond the Clause* (2nd revised edition 2007). London: Continuum.

———. (2008). *Genre Relations: Mapping Culture*. London: Equinox.

McRae, D., Ainsworth, G., Cumming, J., Hughes, P., Mackay, T., Price, K., Rowland, M., Warhurst, J., Woods, D., & Zbar, V. (2000). *What Has Worked, and Will Again: The IESIP Strategic Results Project* (pp. 24–26). Canberra: Australian Curriculum Studies Association.

Millin, T. (2011). *Scaffolding Academic Literacy with Undergraduate Social Science Students at the University of KwaZulu-Natal Using the Reading to Learn Intervention Strategy: An Evaluative Study*. M.Sc. Dissertation, The University of Edinburgh Moray House School of Education, Edinburgh.

Nuthall, G. A. (2005). The cultural myths and realities of classroom teaching and learning: A personal journey. *Teachers College Record, 107*(5), 895–934.

Rose, D. (1999). Culture, competence and schooling: Approaches to literacy teaching in indigenous school education. In F. Christie (Ed.), *Pedagogy and the Shaping of Consciousness: Linguistic and Social Processes* (pp. 217–245). London: Cassell.

———. (2005). Democratising the classroom: A literacy pedagogy for the new generation. *Journal of Education, 37*, 127–164. Retrieved from http://www.readingtolearn.com.au

———. (2010). Meaning beyond the margins: Learning to interact with books. In J. Martin, S. Hood & S. Dreyfus (Eds), *Semiotic Margins: Reclaiming Meaning* (pp. 177–208). London: Continuum.

———. (2011a). Beating educational inequality with an integrated reading pedagogy. In F. Christie & A. Simpson (Eds), Lit*eracy and Social Responsibility: Multiple Perspectives*. London: Equinox.

————. (2011b). *Implementation and Outcomes of the Professional Learning Program, 2010: Report for Western NSW Region, Department of Education and Training*. Sydney: Reading to Learn. Retrieved from http://www.readingtolearn.com.au

————. (2015). *Reading to Learn: Accelerating Learning and Closing the Gap*. Sydney: Reading to Learn. Retrieved from http://www.readingtolearn.com.au

————. (in press a). New developments in genre-based literacy pedagogy. In C. A. MacArthur, S. Graham & J. Fitzgerald (Eds), *Handbook of Writing Research* (2nd edition, p. 30). New York: Guildford.

————. (in press b). Evaluating the task of language learning. In B. Miller, P. McCardle & V. Connelly (Eds), *Development of Writing Skills in Individuals with Learning Difficulties (Studies in Writing Series)*. Leiden: Brill.

Rose, D., Gray, B., & Cowey, W. (1999). Scaffolding reading and writing for indigenous children in school. In P. Wignell (Ed.), *Double Power: English Literacy and Indigenous Education* (pp. 23–60). Melbourne: National Language & Literacy Institute of Australia (NLLIA).

Rose, D., Lui-Chivizhe, L., McKnight, A., & Smith, A. (2004). Scaffolding academic reading and writing at the Koori Centre. *Australian Journal of Indigenous Education, 30th Anniversary Edition*, 41–49. Retrieved from http://www.atsis.uq.edu.au/ajie

Rose, D., & Martin, J.R. (2012). *Learning to Write, Reading to Learn: Genre, Knowledge and Pedagogy in the Sydney School*. London: Equinox.

————. (2013). Intervening in contexts of schooling. In J. Flowerdew (Ed.), *Discourse in Context: Contemporary Applied Linguistics Volume 3* (pp. 447–475). London: Continuum.

Rose, D., Rose, M., Farrington, S., & Page, S. (2008). Scaffolding literacy for indigenous health sciences students. *Journal of English for Academic Purposes, 7*(3), 166–180.

Street, B. (1996). Preface. In M. Prinsloo & M. Breier (Eds), *The Social Uses of Literacy: Theory and Practice in Contemporary South Africa* (pp. 1–9). Philadelphia: Benjamins.

Williams, G. (1995). Joint book-reading and literacy pedagogy: A socio-semantic examination volume 1. *CORE, 19*(3), Fiche 2 B01–Fiche 6 B01.

11

Digital Literacies and Higher Education

Richard Andrews

Introduction

I will approach the topic of this chapter, within the wider framework of multimodality and governmentality, by taking a path towards the centre of the issues in digital literacies and higher education. The theoretical landscape is one charted by studies in multimodality over the last twenty years (Kress & van Leeuwen, 1996/2006; Kress, 2009). Once we arrive there, I will aim to shed light on the nature of the issues facing higher education worldwide in relation to digital literacies and multimodality. These issues include the relationship between students and higher education institutions; and between the submission of assignments in different modes and media, on the one hand, and institutions' more conservative approach to assignment regulation and submission on the other.

First, within the theme of the book as a whole, what is the relation between higher education and governmentality? In the Western democratic/liberal tradition, universities are independent. Although their funding is partly derived from the state and they are almost wholly accountable to the state in terms of various measures of quality (research, teaching etc.), they fight hard to maintain academic, curricular and pedagogic freedom. Students, too, are used to academic freedom and the power to exercise critical judgment, but often find that the universities in which they register with are more conservative and slow-moving than their own quick-fire, digitally savvy approaches to learning. Because higher education institutions are largely independent and self-governing, they have become specialists in writing their own rules of governance, process and procedure. Their power, therefore, is exerted through the exercise of their policies and procedures, manifested in terms of reference for committees, detailed (but never entirely comprehensive) guidance as to how to deal with problems, regulations for the award of degrees and admissions processes – a model that they may have learned from governmental bureaucracy, but one which is more likely to be handed down from the monastic beginnings of universities and their dependence on independent regulation. A collection of this grey literature from the universities of the world would create a truly Borges-like library; it is also in a continual process of updating, revision and approval. It is not surprising that higher education institutions engage in such self-referential generation of material. As learning communities, they need to be self-regulated. Their very existence depends on retaining the power to award degrees and to undertake research in uncharted territories of knowledge and imagination. To retain these powers, they must have internal systems for regulation, but must also be seen to have such systems from an external perspective, and in relation to the law and with regard to external markets.

Power is exercised, ultimately, as far as students are concerned, by the award of academic qualifications. In order to achieve success in this game, students must abide by the rules, which usually involve attending a minimum number of lectures/seminars and subsequently (and crucially) submitting a number of 'assignments' that are graded and that are awarded credit. The accumulation of credit – except in the case of a singular award like the Ph.D. – reaches a point at which the degree, or certificate, or diploma is awarded. Key, therefore, to the success of the student is an understanding by students of the academic literacies and expectations that are involved as well as of the substance of their particular discipline or course of study.

Criteria

At a local level, power is exerted within higher education institutions, on students, via the *criteria* for success in essays, dissertations and other assignments. Although the criteria are for the guidance of lecturers marking students' work, students are made aware of these criteria through handbooks – and would be advised to play close attention to these criteria, as these are the most transparent ways in which their grades are assigned.

Key (generic) skills are built into such criteria, and are listed, for example as 'scholarly skills, critical analysis, methodological and research skills, communication'. These four generic skills could easily be applied to undergraduate or to doctoral level work. What is sometimes stated as missing from the criteria are skills in information and communication production and management, but what is often hidden in the actual criteria is the emphasis on argument and creativity. Let us deal with these three missing ingredients, as they are central to digital literacies and higher education, and to the exercise of power by the institution and the students. Later in the chapter, we will also look at the relationship between argumentation, digital literacies and multimodality.

Information, communication and technology (ICT) skills

If ICT skills are not explicitly referred to, then what are they? They change according to the available media. Currently, in 2014, students access digital information via a range of media: smartphones, tablets, laptops, University-supplied hardware (computer labs). They access online course material, library catalogues, e-books, e-journals and sometimes access course material through services like Mendeley (see www.mendeley.com). They do so to seek information, to undertake literature searches, to access digital archives and digitized course readings; and, at more advanced levels, to access data sets for review and/or secondary analysis. The availability of digital resources is increasingly influencing purchasing decisions, both by individual students and by libraries. The number of devices owned by students is multiplying (albeit with integration between the devices for the most savvy lecturers and students); peer recommendation is proving more of a factor; and the use of e-books is rising faster than the use of conventional books.

All the above is indicative of what it means to be a literate student in the twenty-first century. But literacy also includes making/producing, and these factors will be addressed later in the chapter in a discussion of the impact of digitization on the production of students' assignments.

Argumentation

Argumentation remains key to success in higher education. It has emerged more explicitly in criteria for success at undergraduate, master's and doctoral levels as an awareness of its centrality has increased. For example, criteria like 'is an integrated whole and presents a coherent argument', 'the exercise of independent critical power' and 'includes discussion of findings and how they advance the study of the subject… and in doing so demonstrates a deep and synoptic understanding of the field of study' (Institute of Education, University of London MPhil/Ph.D regulations) all point towards clear and highly competent argumentation. Argumentation could be mentioned in undergraduate or master's criteria ranging from 'poorly organised and unfocussed presentation of arguments' in a fail grade to 'exceptional clarity, focus and cogency in organisation and presentation of arguments and conclusions' in the top grade. The core constituent elements of argumentation are the ability to sequence a logical or quasi-logical set of propositions supported by evidence. There will be further discussion of argumentation in non-linear settings when digitization is considered later in the chapter.

Creativity

The term 'creative' often appears in undergraduate and master's criteria only in the case of the top grade, where phrases like 'creative and critical handling, presenting and inferring from data' are included along with 'high levels of creativity and independence of thought in the application of knowledge', with '*elements* of creativity' in the next grade down. The appropriation of creativity is interesting, as within an academic context for the submission of assignments, it appears to be assumed that creativity is closely related to criticality, independence and agility of thought. There is little on the creative conception and presentation of the project. Again, I will return to this issue in the consideration of the impact of digitization on composing practices in higher education.

Academic *literacies*?

Putting together what was discussed above in relation to 'ICT skills', and bearing in mind what students are asked to do, and the opportunities available to them in responding to those requirements, are the terms *literacy* and its pluralistic version, *literacies*, still fit for purpose? The move over the last thirty years or so to pluralize literacy and situate literate practices in social and political contexts (see Street, 1995; New London Group, 1996) has been useful in helping us to understand how any communicative act is grounded or 'situated' in its context(s). Essentially, the move is towards an understanding of communication as rhetoric: informed by context, taking into account power relations, but also admitting agency on the part of the rhetor or composer. The terms *literacy* or *literacies*, however, even their widest definitions, do not fully reflect the multimodal nature and potential of these communicative discourses within higher education (or any communicative act). Being literate cannot escape the core definition of being able to read and *write* to a particular level in specific contexts; it does not embrace the need to interpret various modes and their various combinations, and the possibilities of *composing* in a range of modes and media for academic purposes. The rest of the chapter explores these possibilities.

Digitization and multimodality

What do digitization and multimodality mean for higher education? Usually, in discussing these phenomena, it is helpful to distinguish between them, but in the case of this chapter, the overlap and common affordances have a direct bearing on academia. First, they allow more direct representation of observed and collected material or 'data'. Rather than transcribe an oral interview into written words, the actual oral interview itself can be represented in an essay, assignment or dissertation. This transduction from one mode to another, or rather, the lack of transduction and transcription in this case, is not only a labour-saving device: it actually presents the original material of interest in direct relationship to the reader, unmediated by the composer/writer. Commentary upon it will most probably be in writing.

Second, the 'most-probably-in-writing' default is not necessarily the only way in which critical commentary can take place. Commentary can take place through juxtaposition. Such juxtaposition can take place within single images, and between imagery and sound, sounds and words, words and gestures.

Third, assignments and dissertations themselves can be in multimodal and digital format. Three examples from higher education will suffice: one from an undergraduate final year dissertation, one from a master's dissertation proposal and one from a doctoral submission.

The undergraduate dissertation, 'What is the range of marks made on paper by a five-year old boy? How do these marks demonstrate a development in written literacy?' was inspired by a number of studies of emergent literacies at the four-to-five-year transition from home to school. The body of the 10,000 word assignment is an analysis of children's drawings collected over a period of time, showing how writing emerges from a visual base. The thirty-seven-page dissertation contains eleven figures, some in colour and some in black-and-white. It also contains an appendix of a further ninety examples of the child's drawings and mark-making over the period of collection. The photographs of the artwork were collected digitally; the text generated digitally; but in other respects, we could say this was a(n) (excellent) conventional academic format, with the main mode in the main body of the text being verbal, with selected images for illustration and discussion. The fact that the majority of the images (the bulk of the visual data set) were in an appendix is significant: it suggests the genre is primarily verbal, with images as ancillary to the written text. There are now many such examples of undergraduates, master's and doctoral assignments that incorporate images as well as verbal (written) text, not only in the arts, but also in the humanities, sciences and social science disciplines (Figures 11.1a and 11.1b).

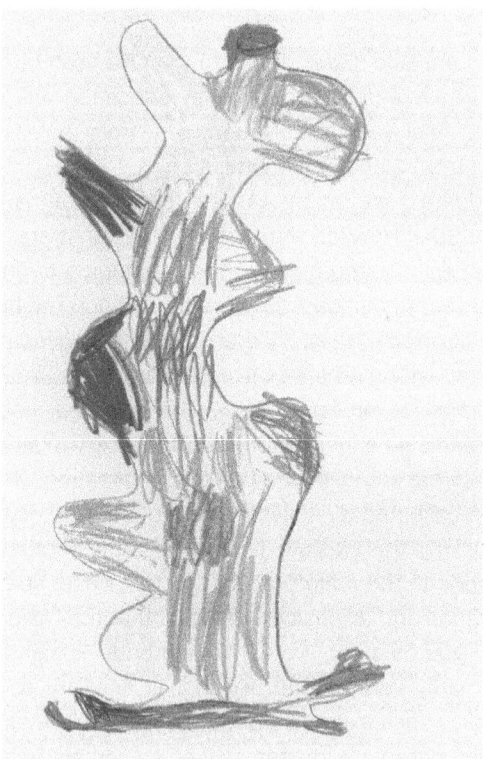

Figure 11.1a and b *Images from an undergraduate dissertation on early mark-making and emergent writing*

The proposal for a master's level dissertation (Crook, 2014) is innovative in the sense that its topic and mode of expression are closely aligned (and indeed necessarily aligned); and that, as a result, it challenges the conventions and guidance as provided in the programme handbook for the specific MA on which the student is registered. Taking into account in- and out-of-school activity, it began by asking a broad question: 'How do students engage with online, multimodal compositional practices?' bearing in mind students' current use of tablets and smartphones for composition. Noting that most studies in the field of multimodal composition have concentrated on the relationship between word and still image, it focuses elsewhere: on the relationship between image and sound, including voice. The main research question was therefore distilled to 'How do Year 7 [11–12 year old] students approach composition using photo-voice elements?' At the time of writing (composing) the present chapter, the research was still underway, but part of the supervisor's early responsibility was to make sure that the regulations and guidance of the MA programme allowed for a digital submission that would incorporate image and sound. Such clearing of the institutional pathway by the supervisor, on behalf of the student, required a 'flipping' of the convention. Normally, two hard copies of the dissertation would be required, accompanied by a digital pdf version. In the case of the dissertation on image and sound composition, the reverse is agreed: the digital version is the primary work to be assessed, accompanied by two hard copies (which will not communicate the full range of modes in the study). As in the next example, the conventional written/hard copy version becomes *an insurance element of submission* for both the student and the supervisor. This creates more work for the student, who not only has to attain high production standards in the digital submission, but has to attain the usual high (production) standards in the submission of two hard copies as well.

My third example is a submitted CD-ROM entitled 'Picturing voices, writing thickness: a multimodal approach to translating the Afro-Cuban tales of Lydia Cabrera'. The front page of the CD-ROM opens up as – literally – a photograph of a desktop: the desktop of the researcher on the project. Her post-it reveals her acknowledgements; a notebook is opened to reveal notes and sketches; folders open to reveal the collection of stories in Spanish and English; audio files open to reveal read-aloud versions of some of the stories. Another hot spot opens to reveal photographs from the collection, based in an archive collection in Miami – which, with all its filing cabinets, box files and folders, is printed on the CD-ROM itself. Critically – one could say, conventionally – the thesis itself is accessed via a computer screen in the desktop. This thesis defies convention in its marvellous combination of modes (words, sound, still image); its imaginative and digital archiving of the tales of Lydia Cabrera; its inventive and interactive interface with the reader; and its witty, delightful presentation. It was the result of hard work: such a production is doing more than a conventional writing and printing of a thesis and binding it (the binding usually done by paid experts). It involves composition at the highest levels by combining modes, using different media, unearthing and representing the work of Lydia Cabrera and commenting on it, and making it accessible to a wider range of readers/listeners.

Composition, rhetoric

These examples suggest that literacy/literacies, whether in the tight dictionary definition of being able to read and write, or in the wider definitions of communicative competence in a range of social situations, are being superseded by a more inclusive emphasis on composition, rhetoric and framing.

Composition more accurately describes the process of making in a multimodal and digital environment, in that whether one is working merely in one mode (e.g. the written word) or more, the act is one of *putting together* elements of semiotic systems in order to make meaning. For words, the compositional process is largely linear; for images, it is more spatial. When there is more than one mode in operation, the act of composition raises issues of contiguity, and the complementarity and/or tension that arises from such juxtaposition.

Rhetoric is the over-arching theoretical field that embraces framing (see later in the chapter) and composition. What distinguishes it from socially situated language theory is that it adds the dimension of power/politics; it is eclectic as far as verbal/written language is concerned, embracing not only different languages, but also different modes of communication. Its history in describing (and then prescribing) public discourse in emergent democracies in the classical period is well documented. Contemporary theories of rhetoric (see for example, Andrews, 2014) choose to move on from the classical tradition and situated rhetoric as the arts of discourse in contemporary communication.

One of composition and rhetoric's key heuristics is framing.

Framing as a methodological strategy in higher education

Framing as an active verb – to distinguish it from off-the-shelf *frames* in genre-as-text-type theory – is a key aspect of the art of composition. The regulations and guidance we have looked at earlier in this chapter in relation to master's assignment and dissertation submission, or doctoral thesis submission, are constraints and parameters set by institutions to regulate (and ultimately pass or fail) students' work. The student him- or herself can frame their work within these parameters, but still have a degree of freedom in the way that they interpret and make the frames. Framing is an act that both separates the created work from that outside it and provides a border that can be transgressed.

The act of framing – not frames themselves – is an important move in designing research; in the design of buildings and other cultural artefacts; in all the arts; and in the design and production of publications. Framing is not a theory in itself. Rather, it is a device or strategy that is informed by a number of theories.

Among these are contemporary rhetoric, deriving from the work of Roland Barthes, Jacques Derrida, Gérard Genette and others. In *Mythologies* (1976), for example,[1] Barthes examines a range of contemporary cultural activities and artefacts from the real world. Each phenomenon or activity is 'framed' as a sociologically informed construct, and then analysed. In his another work, he brings together photography and the verbal arts to emphasize pleasure and the aesthetic dimension. In *Seuils* (subtitle 'Thresholds of Interpretation') (1987), Genette discusses the literary framing of a work of fiction within what he calls its 'paratext', which includes aspects such as title and preface. Antecedents of framing in other fields are Gregory Bateson (1954) and Tversky and Kahneman (1986), from a psychological perspective, and Erving Goffman (1974) from a sociological point of view, each of whom – in their different ways – sees framing as central to understanding. Framing also plays a significant part in discourse theory, as in Deborah Tannen's edited book *Framing in Discourse* (1993), which grows from a tradition of sociolinguistics and conversation analysis; or in Andrews (2011).

Derrida (1979) is worth considering at greater length. He explores the philosophical notion of framing via consideration of paintings and draped human figures surrounding portals and windows in classical and neo-classical buildings. In particular, he is interested in the 'thickness' of these framing devices, and paradoxically, the membrane-like nature of the frame: 'the incomprehensibility of the border, at the border, appears not only at the inner limit, between the frame and the painting, the drapery and the body, the column and the building, but also at its outer limit' (1979, p. 24). This outer limit, that is what the outside edge of the frame signifies, is 'the entire historic, economic, and political field of inscription' (1979, p. 24).

No 'theory', no 'practice', no 'theoretical practice' can be effective here if it does not rest on the frame, the invisible limit of (between) the interiority of meaning (protected by the entire hermeneutic, semiotic, phenomenological, and formalist tradition) and (of) all the extrinsic empiricals which, blind and illiterate, dodge the question. (1979, p. 24)

The 'question' is the nature and function of the *parergon* – the liminal line between the *ergon* (the work itself) and the *milieu*. Part of the nature of the *parergon* is the fact that it is 'a form which has traditionally been determined not by distinguishing itself, but by disappearing, sinking in, obliterating itself, dissolving just as it expends its greatest energy' (1979, p. 26). Nevertheless, the frame draws attention to what is inside it, and asks the audience to bring aesthetic considerations of unity, balance, harmony and so on to their 'reading' or experience of what is inside the frame.

Distilling these various perspectives to a working methodological approach is not as problematic as it might at first appear. Indeed, the distillation might take the form of questions to be asked in the design and production of a research dissertation, a research project and its reports; in business communication; in the design of buildings; and in the making and analysis of art forms.

These questions would include:

> Who is 'speaking'? You, or a number of voices? In one voice or several?
>
> Who is your audience?
>
> What is the substance of your message? Does it have an argument, or is it a different kind of message?
>
> What are the genre conventions within which you are working? What expectations are there?
>
> Do you wish to subvert convention?
>
> In terms of framing your work, will you make the frame explicit? Will you transgress or break the frame?
>
> Within the frame, what modes will you use?
>
> What are the possibilities and tensions of contiguity between modes?
>
> What forms of articulation (joining) will you use throughout the work, if any?
>
> How will the audience navigate through your work?
>
> Is there any risk of misunderstanding or misreading because of a lack of recognition of the frames that are being used?
>
> What media will you use to convey the message?

To conclude by reverting to 'The Parergon', Derrida also suggests that 'a systematic, critical, and typological history of framing appears possible and necessary' (1979, p. 37). That history has begun in the field of the semiotics of literary and visual art, but has yet to be applied to digital, multimodal research environments in education and the social sciences. The implications for such a history of framing need also to be addressed by higher education.

Implications for higher education

What are the implications of framing and the changing nature of composition, from a rhetorical perspective, for students, supervisors and examiners in higher education? Electronic submission of assignments and dissertations is now commonplace, and as Malins and Gray (1999/2010) pointed out over fifteen years ago, digitization has opened up possibilities for the conception of new kinds of submission in the practice-based art and design departments. It is not only in art and design departments that such possibilities are evident: such scope is now available to all the disciplines. This means that students can go beyond the examples described earlier, where an undergraduate student included a large collection of still images in her dissertation, a master's student proposed to submit a dissertation on image and sound in a digital format or a doctoral student submitted her thesis via CD-ROM. Digitization now affords the possibility of sound links, moving image and even access to three-dimensional virtual worlds as part of the main body of the assignment.

There is thus a responsibility on lecturers, supervisors and tutors to understand and to be able to respond critically to such multimodal and digitized conceptions, drafts and final submissions. The principles of multimodal composition need, at the very least, to be understood, if not practised, by academics in positions of power. Markers, examiners and others concerned with gatekeeping the standards of academic production in our universities also need to recognize the paradigm within which students are working, and the forms and formats in which they present their work for assessment. It is likely that, if it is not already the case in some universities and departments, digital submission will become the norm; that paper versions of assignments will become optional rather than essential; and that responses (feedback, grades, moderation etc.) will have to be conducted electronically rather than in print.

Let us take the case of the submitted doctoral thesis as the 'largest' of the works likely to be received by an examiner. The inclination of many examiners, partly for generational reasons and partly because of the love of the printed book, is to request or print out for themselves a hard copy. Their reading is linear; it is predicated on searching for a sequential argument; it expects a written response. Digital and multimodal submissions, however, can require a different kind of reading. Rather than being confined to an appendix, the visual, spatial, aural and other non-verbal modes require different criticality and different modes of argumentation to be understood. Not least, sequentiality may not be explicit, evident or even relevant. In a submitted website, for example, the reader chooses where to enter and thus builds up his or her own argument as to the logic and rationale of the work. Still images are not read sequentially, but by a process of scanning, focusing on the top-middle of the image, and then making sense of the rest of the image in relation to those salient points (Kress & van Leeuwen, 1996/2006). The balance of modes is a crucial aspect of sensitive and critical reading. In a multimodal submission, which modes are dominant and at which points in the reading process? Is there complementarity and/or tension between the modes?

New forms of criticality and power

As suggested in previous writing (Andrews, 2007, forthcoming), criticality takes various forms in students' work. Briefly, and conventionally, these can include weighing up one source with another; opposition to received wisdom and published views; a 'vow of suspicion' (Ricoeur, 1970); drilling down at the points of dispute in a field; detachment; and the development (and defence) of one's own position. In a digital and multimodal environment, criticality can include all of these elements, plus awareness of the affordances of the different modes used; exploration of the tensions between different modes; justification and rationale-building for new forms of communication; meta-awareness of the hybrid genres in which you are working; bringing together of creativity and criticality, not only in the conception of the work itself, but also in the presentation.

Command of these critical dimensions, and their expression in multimodal form, gives the potential for powerful communication. As well as being submitted for assessment and examination in the university, students can publish their work online. While confined within the regulations and guidance of the university on the one hand, they can also speak to a wider audience. Research also has the potential to be less *post facto* and more upstream of practice and policy. Design in practice-based research can more readily be disseminated and further tested, not only in the arts but in other disciplines too. There is more chance that other students will read the finished work, as well as the drafts, of their peers. Data from *EthOS*, the British Library's digital service for the collection, storage and dissemination of digital versions of UK theses, suggest that readership can increase 100-fold. Blogs and other forms of interactive, dialogic online communication can provide a forum for discussions and debates on published works.

Conclusion

In the Introduction to this chapter, I suggested that students need to abide by the rules and guidance of the university in question in order to gain credit and success in the submission of assignment and dissertations for assessment. But it was also pointed out that universities were slow in updating their regulations and guidance, as well as highly protective (in some cases) of the verbal basis of argument, academic discourse and creativity. It follows that there are implications for students who wish to submit work that is innovative and that breaks the boundaries of what is expected.

Students are represented on key academic committees in most universities, often at the highest levels (e.g. Senates). Their views on academic practice are also expressed through feedback (not always as evident in response to dissertation supervision as to taught courses), through other quality assurance mechanisms and through surveys like England's National Student Survey. There is therefore an opportunity to not only comment on existing academic policies and practices, but also to suggest new practices. As digital and multimodal fluency become standard,[2] and as digital submission of coursework and dissertations becomes more widespread, it is likely that assessment practices and regulations will need to adapt. Students, therefore, are in an increasingly powerful position to influence, through the various channels of democratic expression in universities, the parameters within which their work is assessed, ensuring that these are kept up to date with the resources and forms of expression available to them. There will be battles to be fought through student representation on the acceptance of digital and multimodal submission, but these are worth fighting for.

Universities, for their part, need to see learning with new technologies and their own information and communication technologies and systems as closely related. There is an obligation on universities to review assessment guidelines, taking into account not only the channels and media through which work is submitted for assessment, but also the implications for modal mix and variation in individually submitted assignments. Universities can improve the conditions for learning by reviewing their assessment guidelines and making sure assessment is up to speed with multimodal production possibilities, even though a multimodally produced piece of work takes much more design dexterity than a seemingly monomodal written piece. Resistance on the part of universities is often the result of a too-close association between academic excellence on the one hand, and verbal dexterity on the other. While oral and written expressions will remain central to expressions in higher education, it must also acknowledge the proximity and juxtaposition of other modes. Crucially, too, argumentation must be seen as possible, if different, in different modes. The issue of implicit and explicit argumentation needs to be addressed, as although an argument may be evident from the juxtaposition of word against image, or sound against shape, an understanding of how images, sounds, movement and so on argue within their own terms, and without abstraction, is also important.

Ultimately, the skills that were evident and prized in a pre-multimodal world remain important. What we need to add to the mix is a dimension of critical awareness and practice of both how to read digital/multimodal texts, and how to create them (see OECD, 2000).[3] There are considerable implications here for lecturers, assessors and examiners in universities who are the gatekeepers of standards and practices, and yet who need to acknowledge the multimodal clamouring at the gates. One of the skills that has expanded is that of the management of 'information' and knowledge – and so the contemporary student and lecturer both need to devise new systems for the management of their own data, references, sources, drafts, completed work and other aspects of academic production. Such management will allow greater flexibility in the combination, transformation and presentation of new works – some of which will have value as artefacts well beyond the functional need to satisfy assessment criteria and academic regulations.

When the products of academic reflection and creativity manifest themselves in this way, with much closer access to the sometimes visceral, first-hand nature of experience and possibility, it is likely that readership will increase and some of the more formal types of framing in academic institutions will seem more permeable.

Acknowledgements

I am grateful to Jane Davison of Royal Holloway, University of London, for collaboration on the section on framing as a methodological strategy and permission to adapt a joint blog as part of a section in the present chapter – a collaboration that arose at a MODE seminar at the London Knowledge Lab in October 2013. The blog that resulted is posted at http://multimodalblog. wordpress.com/2013/10/15/framing-as-a-methodological-strategy/. I am also grateful to Katherine Crook, Anna-Marjatta Milsom and the unnamed undergraduate student, for permission to cite their work. Every effort has been made to seek copyright, and the author and publisher would be glad to hear from anyone with regard to reproduction of the images included in this chapter.

Notes

1 See also Barthes (1988) where he sets out the limitations of the 'old rhetoric'.

2 There are different degrees of take-up of digital and multimodal composition in and beyond academia. This is not so much a question of a digital divide, either generationally or geographically, but more of a question of spectra of digital access and use. Even as far back as 2000, OECD was defining five levels of literacy, the top two of which described 'higher-order information processing skills' and which most university students would be expected to attain (see OECD 2000, p. xi), thus demonstrating their fluency in multimodal composition as well as their ability to 'read' multimodally.

3 Building critical awareness will require a social and political understanding of power relations in relation to reading multimodal texts; and, along with the requisite technical skills, similar understanding in the making of multimodal texts.

References

Andrews, R. (2007). Argumentation, critical thinking and the postgraduate dissertation. *Educational Review, 59*(1), 1–18.

———. (2011). *Re-Framing Literacy*. New York: Routledge.

———. (2014). *A Theory of Contemporary Rhetoric*. New York: Routledge.

———. (forthcoming). Critical thinking and/or argumentation in higher education? In M. Davies & R. Barnett (Eds), *Critical Thinking in Higher Education*. Basingstoke: Palgrave Macmillan.

Barthes, R. (1976). *Mythologies*. London: Paladin.

———. (1988). The old rhetoric: An aide-memoire. In *The Semiotic Challenge* (pp. 11–94, trans. Howard, R.). Oxford: Blackwell.

Bateson, G. (1954). *A Theory of Play and Fantasy: Steps to an Ecology of Mind*. New York: Ballantine.

Crook, K. (2014). A proposal for a small-scale inquiry. MA in English Education, Institute of Education, University of London.

Derrida, J. (trans. Owens, C.) (1979). The Parergon. *October, 9*, 3–41 (Summer 1979).

Genette G. (1987). *Seuils*. Paris: Le Seuil. (Lewin J.E., trans. (1999)) *Paratexts: Thresholds of Interpretation*. Cambridge: Cambridge University Press.

Goffman, E. (1974). *Frame Analysis*. New York: Harper & Row.

Kress, G. (2009). *Multimodality: A Social Semiotic Approach to Contemporary Communication*. Abingdon: Routledge.

Kress, G., & van Leeuwen, T. (1996/2006). *Reading Images: The Grammar of Visual Design*. London: Routledge.

Malins, J., & Gray, C. (1999/2010). The digital thesis: Recent developments in practice-based Ph.D research in Art and Design. *Digital Creativity, 10*(1), 18–28. Retrieved from http://dx.doi.org/10.1076/digc.10.1.18.3195

New London Group. (1996). A pedagogy of multiliteracies: Designing social futures. *Harvard Educational Review, 66*(1), 60–93.

OECD. (2000). *Literacy in the Information Age: Final Report of the International Adult Literacy Survey*. Paris: Organisation for Economic Co-operation and Development and the Ministry of Industry.

Ricoeur, P. (1970). *Freud and Philosophy: An Essay on Interpretation*. New Haven: Yale University Press.

Street, B. V. (1995). *Social Literacies: Critical Approaches to Literacy in Development, Ethnography and Education*. London: Longman.

Tannen, D. (Ed.) (1993). *Framing in Discourse*. New York: Oxford University Press.

Tversky, A., & Kahneman, D. (1986). Rational choice and the framing of decisions. *Journal of Business, 59*, 251–278.

12

The Pecket Way: Negotiating Multimodal Learning Spaces in a User-run Community Education Project

Mary Hamilton

Introduction

This chapter addresses a rare example of a user-run programme, self-consciously designed as a literacy education project but uncompromisingly independent of externally imposed governance structures.

The chapter describes the reasons for and history of this commitment to self-governance, the challenges the project has faced during its twenty-year history and its achievements, including the most recent 'post-project' phase designed to maintain the visibility of this work for future education and learners through the creation of an oral history and archive.

It explains why and how multimodal forms of expression have been central to the process of self-governance and inclusion as part of recognizing individual differences. It describes how they have been used as a means of challenging disabling forms of communication and exclusive forms of literacy. Multimodality in this context includes careful attention to oral practices in relation to literacy, encouragement of forms of visual expression and records of events that include writing, alongside images, material artefacts and audio. Embodied forms of learning such as journey sticks and celebratory performances were central to 'The Pecket Way'. The material environment and artefacts collaboratively created by the project took on great symbolic significance as a focus for shared meanings and experience as well as day to day remembering and reassurance of the reality and stability of the project as a special, welcoming and celebratory space for learning. These material artefacts include the college building itself, decorative banners and posters, training and course materials, photos, food, logos and finally, the website as a virtual surviving surrogate for the college that now no longer exists as either a physical or a legal entity.

Data for this chapter are drawn from participant experiences across two years in the steering group for the Pecket Well archive project along with materials posted on the website and in the archive. Oral history interviews and documentary evidence from the Changing Faces project (Hamilton & Hillier, 2006) are also referred to.

The chapter takes a socio-material theoretical approach to this case, in order to explain the connection between multimodality and governance in its history and to extrapolate from it about other institutional environments that aim to offer convivial and care-full (Feeley, 2014) experiences of education. This example aims to illustrate the possibilities of, and challenges faced by, groups who set out to share the power of decision-making with the users of educational programmes, thereby reshaping the social relations of literacy production. The analysis will also consider how far the wider governance environment can account for the rise and demise of Pecket Well College, tracing connections outwards from the day-to-day organization and decision-making of the college.

Pecket Well was a user-run and managed collective based in the North of England that operated between 1992 and 2011. Members had met through an adult literacy education class but, along with the tutor, they left this class to search for a more satisfactory alternative (Nugent, 2013). They raised money to buy an old co-operative society building and refurbished it as a residential centre for adult basic education courses. During the lifetime of the collective it produced not only autobiographical writing but also many other documents, including training materials and course outlines, advocacy letters, minutes and management documents. The autobiographical writing started with individual experiences that offered a challenging commentary on established education, both in school, but more unusually in adult education. It discussed the institutional structures, the pedagogies and the teachers as it searched for a different kind of education and approach to language and literacy that offered an inclusive and democratic experience (see Flanagan et al., 1994; Hamilton et al. 2014). As an independent charity, it was funded by many sources during its lifetime and a core activity for members was fund-raising to pay for the college building and the courses themselves. As funding became increasingly hard to obtain, it became impossible to maintain the building and in 2010 it was sold and, like many other community projects of the time, the collective eventually dispersed.

When the physical building of Pecket Well College was lost, members set about creating a virtual and documentary 'home' for the Pecket Way of working in the form of an archive, website and oral history. From the website we can learn in detail about the processes Pecket Well College developed based on accounts from people involved and the artefacts that survive. These tell us about processes of learning, organizing courses, raising funds and managing the college, the range of people involved, why they were there, their hopes and fears for the college and the structures they created at different stages.

Why Pecket Well College needed to be created

Why were the people who formed the initial project dissatisfied with their education to date? Understanding this involves understanding how governmentality works in, as Foucault puts it, the organized practices (discourses, rationalities, and techniques) through which subjects are produced and controlled. First, the founding members of Pecket Well were angry about the disabling discourses around literacy that they had experienced. These presented non-readers and writers as not fully able to make decisions for themselves and thereby limited their access to resources and to their rights as citizens. Hamilton (2012) discusses this aspect of governmentality in relation to Charles Taylor's (2007) notion of modern social imaginaries which are hard to surface and overcome, in particular the ideal of a public space for rational debate and communication to which literacy is central. This is the first challenge.

The second, and related, dissatisfaction felt by the group was the individualism and broader lack of democracy within education and a desire to change the social relations within which learning takes place. This is problematic for learners at any age but it is a key issue for adults engaged in lifelong learning who are used to making autonomous decisions in other aspects of their lives.

In challenging these discourses and the institutional forms that hold them in place, members of Pecket Well were asking the questions that are core to this book about how literacies and curricula are produced across domains, whose interests they serve, how some forms of expression are more acceptable than others, how learners and educators are positioned within these literacies and how things could be organized differently.

Pecket Well founder members were not alone in raising these questions but travelled alongside a strand of literacy work that emerged from adult literacy in the United Kingdom in the 1970s and 1980s which saw itself as a counter-cultural movement, viewing adult literacy as a form of cultural and class politics, characterized by the ideals of participatory and popular pedagogies, shared authorship and voice (Mace 1979; Hamilton, 2014). This strand of work also made links with parallel movements of working class and popular writing and history (Mace, 1995; Woodin, 2005); primary school education (Barnes et al., 1969; Searle, 1986) and international popular education and development projects such as REFLECT (Archer & Cottingham, 1996) and (Freire, 1972; Horton, 2003; Gaventa, 2004; McCaffery et al., 2007; Rogers & Horrocks, 2010). Together these initiatives developed a distinctive set of practices and understandings about literacy that are now deeply undermined by contemporary neoliberal policies and practices.

At the time when Pecket was developing, the group attracted a number of important allies who shared these understandings, from funders and advocates to local councillors and other professionals such as architects, academics and lawyers. Of particular importance was the sustained vision and commitment of a professional adult literacy tutor as well as community development workers.

In this chapter I use socio-material theory to make the link between the aspects of governmentality discussed earlier and multiple forms of expression. Socio-material theory sees social reality in terms of complex flows rather than structures, of projects which form and unravel over time, depending on the power of the networks of 'actants' that are enrolled to their cause (Fenwick & Edwards, 2013). Allies from the sympathetic strands of literacy work described earlier were important to Pecket Well in establishing and growing their project. A further key way in which power can be consolidated is by drawing not only people but also material resources, representations and artefacts into the project. This suggests that multiple modes of expression, creating a range of literacy-related artefacts, can support and strengthen particular visions and projects. This, as we will see, complements pedagogical rationales for why multimodal methods in teaching and learning took an essential role in Pecket Well's project of creating a democratic and inclusive space for learning.

The Pecket Way: How to negotiate a space for democratic learning in literacy

Having surmounted the initial barriers to create an embryonic community, how is it possible to carve out a space for democratic learning?

Central to Pecket Well's ways of working was the careful attention given to democratic and inclusive ways of working with language and paying detailed attention to wider access issues (see Flanagan et al., 1994). The process of decision-making was often slow and contentious and methods of working were refined and meticulously documented throughout the history of the college. Over time, this became known within the college as 'the Pecket Way' and was crystallized as a set of rules that embodied the vision and values of the collective.

The idea was to model a democratic polity within the relationships and politics of the college using democratic principles and adapting these for an educational/learning domain. Although it was not made explicit in the college descriptions of its activities, the values underpinning this vision were very close to those promoted by the co-operative movement that began in the North of England in the nineteenth century and are strongly rooted in communities there (see Robertson 2010; Webster et al., 2012). These are described in the International Cooperative Alliance principles as 'self-help, self-responsibility, democracy, equality, equity and solidarity ... co-operative members believe in the ethical values of honesty, openness, social responsibility and caring for others' (International Cooperative Alliance (undated) Co-operative identity, values & principles http://ica.coop/en/whats-co-op/co-operative-identity-values-principles).

As applied to education, these values infuse the ethos, curriculum, pedagogy and governance of organizations (see Facer et al., 2012, p. 336) and give coherence to Pecket's distinctive approach. Pecket's central concern with language and literacy led to sensitivity to the ways in which language was used to empower or disempower people and prioritize the development of alternative ways of communicating. Many of the specific techniques that were used focus on communication processes. This is a particularly important contribution of the collective to knowledge about democratic and inclusive processes and was expressed in the rules in this way:

√ *Identify strengths in each person and find ways of building these into learning*

√*Recognize that everyone has skills and value them; cooperate and share strengths*

√*Give people the space to express themselves*

√*Support each other to become more confident, take risks and try new things*

√*Ask everyone to use plain language so even difficult ideas can be shared*

√*Train writing hands to learn to listen and write down exactly what they hear*

X *Avoid using the terms 'student' and 'tutor' but rather use 'member', 'worker', 'participant' or 'workshop leader' depending on the situation (language matters)*

X Don't use the term 'literacy' because of its connections with the word members hated which was 'illiteracy'. In particular avoid the word 'illiterate' which members felt was an insult and found very offensive

Pecket was inspired by an experience of residential learning on a university campus that some members had taken part in, organized by a national development project called *Write First Time* (see Shrapnel Gardener, undated). There were several adult residential colleges in the United Kingdom, but none for adult basic education (see Drews & Fieldhouse, 1996). There were many other precedents to draw on to create alternative forms of education, as already suggested: cooperative forms based on collaboration and reciprocity; popular and anti-colonial education movements (e.g. Deiand Kempf, 2006; Andriotti, 2008) which emphasize marginalized peoples' control of resources along with resistance to disabling discourses; Montessori and holistic educational approaches with children including the language experience approach that informed primary school teaching of literacy (Barnes et al., 1969; Searle, 1986); approaches such as arts-based education that value multiple forms of expression as a way of promoting creativity in learning (Flood et al., 2004; Hall & Thomson, 2007; Hibbens, 2014).

Pecket used a version of the 'language experience' approach to literacy learning in which the tutor becomes a 'writing hand' – a mediator and scribe rather than an expert transmitting knowledge of writing (Mace, 1995; Frost & Hoy, undated). Writing produced through this approach was shared through performances and reading events, and published in a variety of forms with the involvement of participants as editors and distributors. Once participants became familiar with these ways of working, they moved into designing curricula and running training events. In turn, these activities built confidence for participating in the management and decision-making processes of the college more generally and the same principles were used to demystify the processes of administration and decision-making. Accessible, illustrated newsletters and annual reports were produced that could be understood and shared by all.

This new way of approaching literacy involved reorganizing and blurring the roles of the teacher/learner as activities extended into the new spaces of public performances and reading events; editing and publishing and user-designed and user-run courses. As a charity, Pecket Well had a management group of directors that included user members of the college. It also had trustees who were key advocates for the organization, arguing for grant funding and making the college visible in a wider arena. Staffing was fluid across these different arenas. Professional expertise was not closely regulated and the roles of learner, teacher, manager, author and editor were shared. People who started out as students at the college could move on to be volunteers or accept paid roles and take on responsibilities within the management group as well.

This meant a great deal of attention had to be paid to transparency and inclusivity in the process of communication: making use of shared oral records and writing hands. One example involved the invention of the management wheel (see this on the website at http://pecket.org/journey-sticks/our-management-wheel/). This is explained in the Pecket oral history as follows:

> We wanted to keep our rule of everyone understanding our decision making process and needed to find a way of 'picturing' our new structure. Malcolm had a brainwave and thought of a wheel – our Pecket Management Wheel!
>
> After that review we held regular management training events and devised a system of training new Directors 'on the job' by having Trainee Directors in post for one year before becoming full Directors.

Further illustrations of multimodal communication are presented in the following section, all of which are available on the website at www.pecket.org.

Multimodal spaces and resources at Pecket Well

The examples described here, from the archive site, were among those seen as being especially significant to preserve in the virtual record. They were continuously talked about in the steering group discussions as people remembered, reconstructed and came to terms with their collective history. Some things that were most central to the experience of Pecket are difficult to represent in a digital archive – the wall-hanging, for example, has to be maintained and stored separately, and the building can only be evoked through the many images and references to it. The quotations are taken directly from the site.

Journey sticks

http://pecket.org/journey-sticks/

'At Pecket we used journey sticks to help us learn. People went for walks in the countryside collecting objects and a stick along the way: They came back to the college and attached their objects in order along the stick. Then they used the journeystick to remember and describe the walk to the whole group. Often these stories were written down by writing hands and recorded. Journeysticks got people out in the countryside and helped people to get used to each other and relax. Telling their stories helped with confidence and communication skills'.

Our wall hanging – symbol of our identity!

http://pecket.org/journey-sticks/pecket-wall-hanging-symbol-of-our-identity/

'At One World to Share our 2nd residential 5 day course held at Hazelwood Castle near Leeds we decided we wanted to run a wall hanging project and produce our own 'banner'. Financial support from Halifax Building Society and Yorkshire Arts made this possible. Leeds textile artist Vicky Mitchell came to our next residential course at Ilkley and started working with us on the design.

The design represents the idea of breaking down barriers and bringing people together. People shared many cups of tea, stories and ideas during its making. One section has a series of fabric 'hands' drawn from participants own hands – in and amongst is the shape of a foot. One participant Barbara had cerebral palsy and couldn't place her hand flat to draw around it. She found her own solution and placed her foot onto the fabric so someone could draw round it!

During the process of making it the wall hanging travelled to various community venues – a real collective effort.

Once our wall hanging was completed it had pride of place in the large workroom at Pecket Well College.

We also had postcards printed that helped us to publicize Pecket and our courses. The postcards were used to tell people about Pecket and encourage contact when they posted them back to us'.

Food, drink and 'thank you tokens':

http://pecket.org/wp-content/uploads/2013/07/Stones-residential-Ripponden-1986-album1.pdf

Sharing food and drink and giving thank you presents was a repeated part of Pecket events and underlined the key place of public celebration and acknowledgement of learning that is part of the Pecket Way. Bodies as well as minds and feelings have to be taken care of for successful learning to take place. The images on the website show cakes made in the shape of the characteristic 'wishing well' logo and iced with words 'Congratulations! We bought the College'.

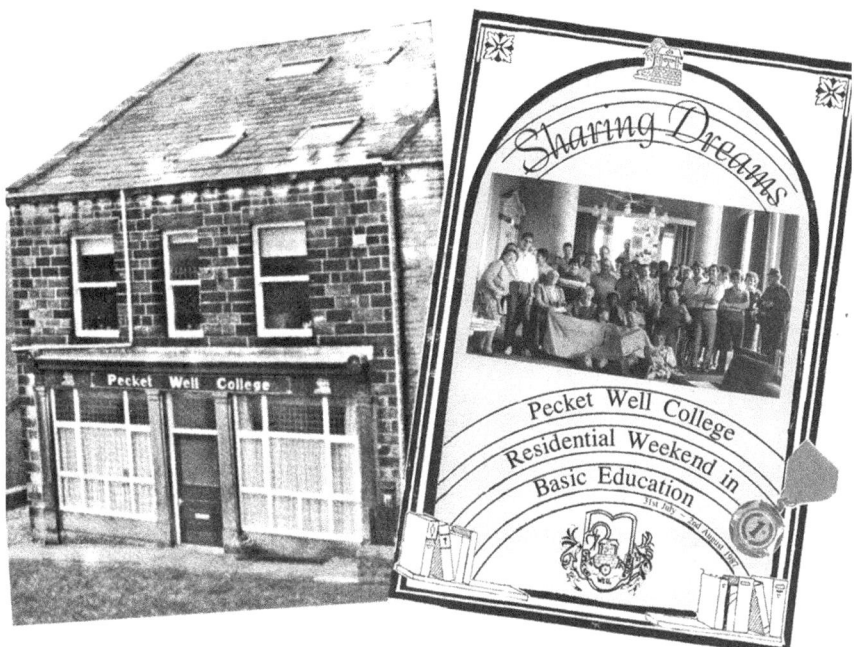

Figure 12.1 *Examples of Multimodal Resources at Pecket Well: The Pecket Well Building and Sharing Dreams*

The Pecket Well building

http://pecket.org/journey-sticks/opening-day-2/

The old co-operative society building (see Figure 12.1) on the edge of the Yorkshire village of Pecket Well was bought by the group and was created as a space to meet and learn in the way they chose. This gave the group independence from authorized education and meant they no longer had to rely on sympathetic gate-keepers. The disused building had to be renovated extensively to adapt it for residential use by a wide range of people.

The website holds a collage of photos from the college opening day which was a major publicity event advertising the courses and the fund-raising campaign and strengthening local links. Many creative ways of celebrating the opening included physically surrounding the building with people; the use of TV, radio and film media; tree planting, a firework display, food and drink. The Pecket Well logo again featured prominently on the many artefacts created during this event and later.

The atmosphere of festival continued through many subsequent events, extensively recorded through photographs and wall displays. http://pecket. org/store-room/

Converting the old building into an accessible residential venue for adult basic education was a major focus of fund-raising and volunteer effort. Access activities were also incorporated into workshop learning. One photograph shows Joe Flanagan and Rena Watson 'field-testing' the newly installed lift, which was designed specially to accommodate Rena's wheelchair. Doorways and bedrooms had to be checked to make sure they were wide enough, tactile door signs were designed for people with visual impairments.

Fund-raising

Many strategies were used to raise funds for the college, including sponsorship for the stones of the Pecket Well building for which a paper pledge was designed with a photograph of an actual stone. http://pecket.org/ journey-sticks/publicising-pecket-2/

One volunteer, who later became a paid worker, remembers fund-raising ideas like the sponsored T-shirt. 'You stuck your name on it to sponsor the college. This was to get the ball rolling – one of the first things. If you signed it and wrote a comment on it, it was a pound towards a brick of the college'. The T-shirt travelled to Scotland where the wearer 'got everybody to sign it, half a crown here, ten bob there, five pound on the back'.

Writing letters directly appealing to funders was another strategy for which there is ample evidence in the archive (see Figure 12.2).

The poster incident:
http://pecket.org/journey-sticks/biscit-poster/

A conflict with the established education service was embodied in a poster for a fund-raising event where one of the words was spelt wrongly. The tutor refused to take responsibility for this saying 'if they want me to correct it they know they can come and ask me and I'll do it, but they haven't done and I haven't got authority over them'. This led to the students' committee being banned from meeting in the adult education premises without a tutor and became an iconic moment for the group. Recreated on the website, it was a shared point of reference for why and how Pecket developed as an alternative to existing provision and why owning the college building was such a key aspect of the project.

Final draft

Dear Paul Getti
It was putting the Poems
together for your trust that
helped me to find my own Voice
to talk with. It helped to
give me the confidence to put
in for an award to writers from
the yorkshire Arts Association. I
am proud to say that I was
successful. I hed one in Forty
chances to go forward! So I
am still Writing Poetry and
looking forward to fetching out
my own book of Poems.
The Pecket Well college will be
one of the anvils that will fore
the chain of success to those that
faltered with reading and writing and
therefore left their words unbnded.
If this is so, surely

Pecket Well cllege is the foundry that
We can smithey together on by fetching
oun own Passion as heat, our own tears
to temper the steel. My admiration for
all that try to Succeed with the Written

Word goes with my own recommendation
Forward to link the Chains to unite not
in desparation but in a common Knowledge
of growth. And then I can Surely sey

I am proud of being a basic
education student

yours sincerely
Peter Goode

Figure 12.2 *Letter to Paul Getty*

Multimodal publishing

http://pecket.org/wp-content/uploads/2013/07/Not-Written-Off-5.pdf

There are many, many examples in the archive of the multimodal publications produced by Pecket Well. *Not Written off* was a compilation of students' writing and images which was very typical of informal publications from community-based groups of the time. Photographs, collages and line drawings were all included interspersed with handwritten and typed texts. *Sharing Dreams* (see

Figure 12.1), the report of a course run at the college, was a more glossy illustrated publication which also had a carefully designed and arresting cover incorporating a group picture of members of the course along with an embellished version of the college logo.

Management structures and procedures

http://pecket.org/journey-sticks/our-management-wheel/

Enabling college members to have a say in the management and financial decision-making of the college was a key part of the democratic approach and as described earlier, a great deal of effort went into finding accessible ways of presenting the issues and materials involved in this.

Included on the website is a sample of training reports and records of meetings that show the hard work put into ensuring that all directors understood their roles and the issues they had to decide upon.

The annual reports of the college – including the accounts – were also carefully designed as accessible multimodal documents that were shared and read out loud at the AGM http://pecket.org/wp-content/uploads/2012/10/annual-report-1993-94.pdf

The rise and fall of Pecket –
wider political environment and change

For those individuals drawn into Pecket Well, their initial motivations and autobiographical writing expanded over time into a more collective project of documenting the experience of Pecket itself, the learning processes that were developed among people there and that went into organizing the college – management, development, funding raising, publicity and outreach. The physical building acquired by the college took on immense significance in this sense of collectivity. The publications resulting from this strong collective identity (for example, Pecket Well College, 1987) resonate with what has been called the 'testimonio form' (Yudice, 1991; Gutierrez, 2008). The collective touched many lives and members self-consciously saw themselves as part of a bigger cultural movement of emancipatory literacy. Making the processes of management, decision-making, writing and publication transparent was integral to Pecket Well 's inclusive and emancipatory aims which also aspired to produce a solidarity that could make individuals feel part of a bigger group or change project.

It is part of my argument in this chapter (not necessarily shared by members themselves) that the surrounding socio-political context within which Pecket came to be had a large part to play in its rise and fall. In particular, the alliances described above, which were set up in the 1970s–1980s, were part of the conditions necessary to provide the space for the college to be constructed. These were later eclipsed by the ferocity of neoliberal politics in the 1990s to the present with its ruthless accountability culture and outcomes-driven assessment that narrowed what counts as education and resulted in complex, precarious and time-bound project funding (Apple, 2004). These conditions have made it difficult for projects like Pecket, with its closely held democratic values, to survive. On the website some of the reasons for the difficulties are explained:

> Pecket's fundraising track record is very impressive as a full list of funding obtained demonstrates. In our earlier days our peer approach, commitment to inclusion and ability to engage many 'hard to reach' individuals and groups attracted funders. However later on changes in National and International funding policies meant that many of the courses Pecket offered were not eligible for funding. Ironically the ingredients that made Pecket courses so successful were what made finding ongoing and regular funding so difficult to find:

> - Some Pecket Wellians who ran or co-ran workshops were not qualified teachers.
> - Most people coming to Pecket didn't want pressure of 'paperwork' and 'assessment' that comes with accredited courses
> - Courses were run at a pace to suit participants and didn't always fit with the timescales that funders imposed.

> Pecket fought to maintain its successful way of working – wanting to encourage people by tailoring courses to what interested them and to what was relevant to their lives. No longer able to attract resources through the European Social Fund or mainstream national funding through the Further Education Funding Council, Pecket Wellians fought hard to survive and preserve their ways of working.
> Finding funding for Pecket's approach to education was becoming harder and harder.

Pecket's uncompromising stance on independence and its insistence on keeping professional collaborators and brokers at arm's length had consequences that the group themselves perhaps did not foresee. Their refusal to become institutionalized by linking themselves into wider structures left them needing to constantly produce themselves anew, ultimately an exhausting and depleting process.

It is particularly ironic that Pecket's ways of working were redefined by funding agencies as marginal and unaccountable given that Pecket's inclusive systems and pedagogical experiments equipped it well to incorporate new digital and accessible communications technologies into learning and to respond to diversity agendas that were elsewhere seen as presenting huge institutional challenges. The advantages to members of an open, democratically organized peer education were redefined as disadvantages, as adult literacy became enclosed by new assessment regimes, curricula and funding. To a large extent, this redefinition was not targeted at community-based projects like Pecket but they were victims of a cost-benefit approach to educational and social policy and accountability systems that assume a low-trust environment. Acceptable outcomes under such regimes, do not match well with the values of volunteering and improved quality of life on which Pecket was based.

Protecting and sustaining the Pecket way for the future – the archiving project

Without enduring institutional support, projects inevitably have a limited lifespan, and need to re-invent themselves. Pecket's most recent initiative has been to create an oral and archive history of the college (see www.pecket. org; Nugent, 2013). The aim has been to document the processes of learning, organizing courses, raising funds and managing the college, based on accounts from people involved and the artefacts that survive. These artefacts include many of those mentioned earlier. The initiative lasted for two years, and I was involved throughout as a member of the steering group. In this section I will describe how multimodality and the democratic learning process entered into this phase of the project designed to preserve and hand on 'the Pecket way'.

The participatory ideals of the organization suffused the history-making process. Pecketwellians took part in training workshops in order to participate in making video material for the website and carrying out oral history interviews.

The steering group consisted of the directors of the college all of whom are also users or Pecketwellians; college trustees and three paid workers, one co-ordinating the project, one carrying out the oral history interviews and one helping to create the website containing the documentary and oral history archive.

Long discussions focused around who should be interviewed for the oral history and what documents should be archived. The categories that should be used (a key aspect of interest to socio-material theory, see Bowker & Starr, 2000) were crucial to the aims of organizing the archive material accessibly so that it could be retrieved by people with different sensory abilities and preferences. The formats and search facilities of the online technology sometimes supported, sometimes subverted these aims. Major challenges included how to make the website accessible through designing multiple modes of navigating it, how to construct the oral history account, through sequencing the sections. The inclusion of a more analytical section documenting the wider context of the college was hotly debated and great emphasis was put on including particular events, people, names, metaphors and symbols on the website. Place-based references are included to recognize and preserve the connection with everyday experiences: for example the familiar image of the 'journey stick' was used to create a time line, while pictures of features of the Pecket Well building such as 'the green door' are used as an entrance to the online site.

The oral history and archive are souvenirs, records and obstinate markers of a set of values that were not compromised are intended to be carried forward along with the practical processes crafted over twenty years of intense collaboration. Pecket Well shared many of its core values with others such as the international co-operative movement and its work can potentially inform other initiatives. However, its activities were strongly tied to its locality and to embodied experiences that are difficult to preserve and communicate. Making these visible, sharing practice and making links within and across countries is difficult. It is therefore valuable to have multimodal artefacts like the archive and website with the potential to travel – in both space and time – where people cannot.

In conclusion

The Pecket Way is an alternative social imaginary where people with disabilities have undisputed rights to contribute to the collective and to be included within it, where literacy is seen as one among many modes of expression and communication, where education adapts to people rather than the other way round and where the experiences and social relations of learning are seen as modelling a wider citizenship. The Pecket Way is to strive for social relations within educational programmes which address students as citizens, as well as learners. The expectations and procedures for sharing the power enable people to author their own lives. Such relationships are based on trust and take time to develop.

Multimodal forms of communication and the artefacts associated with them have particular powers to realize such a project. They allow for a variety of forms of expression that can link people in different ways, reaching across their experiences to pull out common meanings. They embody, stabilize and make solid ways of being and ideals that can otherwise seem intangible, hard to grasp and believe in.

As part of this embodiment, physical spaces are important for student voices to flourish and sustain – negotiating safe spaces (Peters, 2010) – providing some 'room of your own' that in this case included the rare experience of residential learning. The college building itself provided an opportunity to seriously explore the politics and materialities of access as members converted it into a residential space for learning, celebration and communication. The physical building thus took on immense significance in the sense of collectivity and vision, and when funding ran out and the building had to be sold, it was felt as a devastating symbol of the vulnerability of the Pecket Way under current conditions of adult literacy learning and funding. Hard won physical resources are costly and difficult to recover once they are lost.

Pecket's accumulated wisdom demonstrates that voice is not just about speaking or writing and finding audiences to be heard. It is also about management and decision-making practices within educational programmes and the activities of editing and publishing – that is it is about a continuing process as well as product and event. Multimodal communication – the writing hands, oral and visual records and ways of representing structures – was crucial to developing an inclusive process at the college and offers a powerful model for others to follow.

Creating the conditions whereby student agency can develop in these ways and voices can be heard is 'slow' education and this does not fit easily with 'fast' policy and instant accountability. This is one reason why it has been difficult to sustain Pecket Well College under current conditions where education is seen as human resource development and literacy is a race to the top of an international league table. The Pecket way also challenges an underlying assumption that learning can only be successful or take place in sanctioned, controlled spaces. The participatory nature of the Internet has rendered this idea obsolete, and yet governing institutions persist in ignoring these changes rather than re-thinking what teaching and learning is and can be.

Could a new Pecket Well project establish itself today under current circumstances? In that it was always a project struggling against the countervailing status quo in education in some ways, the situation is no more difficult today than it ever was. However, if Pecket Well were to be created under current conditions, there would be even less room for it as a form of educational project than there was in the 1980s, both because of discursive shifts that exclude key aspects of Pecket's activities and because of general cut backs in educational resources.

It would, therefore, need to be reframed, with a different set of alliances. For example it might link in with projects designed for people with sensory impairments and other health issues, or with the many projects now run as social enterprises that provide employment opportunities while fund-raising for particular social groups.

New technologies could offer exciting opportunities for low-cost online communication and publishing but would also require different kinds of user training and support. The demands of financial management have changed with online banking and application processes, further complicating the burden on a voluntary organization of securing limited-term project funding. Current sources of funding such as the Big Lottery 'Reaching out to Communities' programme (Big Lottery Fund, 2013) might help people buy and maintain a building today, but such grants are still time-limited, favour innovative rather than continuing work and are subject to outcome criteria that may be hard to demonstrate. Manoeuvring between the vision of the 'Pecket way' and the discursive labels of disability and funding categories would be no easier. In order to survive, it would require the same tenacious and coherent sense of purpose as well as the ability to jump through contradictory and uncomfortable hoops and an open-mind about where funding comes from.

References

Andreotti, V., & Souza, L. (2008). Translating theory into practice and walking minefields: Lessons from the project 'Through Other Eyes'. *International Journal of Development Education and Global Learning, 1*(1), 23–36.

Apple, M. W. (2004). Creating difference: Neo-liberalism, neo-conservatism and the politics of educational reform. *Educational Policy, 18*(1), 12–44.

Archer, D., & Cottingham, S. (1996). *The REFLECT Mother Manual: A New Approach to Adult Literacy*. London: ActionAid.

Barnes, D., Britton, J., Rosen, H., & The London Association for the Teaching of English (LATE). (1969). *Language, the Learner and the School*. Harmondsworth: Penguin Books.

Big Lottery Fund. (2013). *Reaching communities buildings: Guidance notes*. Retrieved from http://www.biglotteryfund.org.uk/global-content/programmes/england/reaching-communities-buildings-england. Accessed 30 September 2014.

Bowker, G. C., & Starr, S. L. (2000). *Sorting Things Out: Classification and Its Consequences*. New Baskerville: The MIT Press.

Dei, G. J. S., & Kempf, A. (Eds) (2006). *Anti-Colonialism and Education*. Rotterdam: Sense Publishers.

Drews, W., & Fieldhouse, R. (1996). Residential colleges and non-residential settlements and centres. In R. Fieldhouse et al. (Eds), *A History of Modern British Adult Education*. Leicester: NIACE.

Facer, K., Thorpe, J., & Shaw, L. (2012). Co-operative education and schools: An old idea for new times? *Power and Education, 4*, 3.

Feeley, M. (2014). *Learning Care Lessons: Literacy, Love, Care and Solidarity*. London: The Tufnell Press.

Fenwick, T., & Edwards, R. (2013). Performative ontologies: Sociomaterial approaches to researching adult education and lifelong learning. *European Journal for Research on the Education and Learning of Adults, 4*(1), 49–63.

Flanagan, J., Goode, P., & Frost, G. (1994). Forging a common language, sharing the power. In M. Hamilton, D. Barton& R. Ivanič. (Eds), *Worlds of Literacy*. Clevedon: Multilingual Matters. Chapter 19: 227.

Flood, J., Lapp, D., & Heath, S. B. (Eds) (2004). *Handbook of Research on Teaching Literacy Through the Communicative and Visual Arts: Sponsored by the International Reading Association*. New York: Routledge.

Freire, P. (1972) *Pedagogy of the Oppressed*. Harmondsworth: Penguin Books.

Frost, G., & Hoy, C. (Undated). *Opening Time: A Writing Resource Pack Written by Students in Basic Education*. Manchester: Gatehouse Books.

Gaventa, J. (2004). Towards participatory governance: Assessing the transformative possibilities. In S. Hickey & G. Mohan (Eds), Participation – From Tyranny to Transformation?: Exploring New Approaches to Participation in Development (pp. 25–41). London: Zed Books.

Gutierrez, K. D. (2008). Developing a sociocritical literacy in the third space. *Reading Research Quarterly, 43*(2), 148–164.

Hall, C., & Thomson, P. (2007). Creative partnerships? Cultural policy and inclusive arts practice in one primary school. *British Educational Research Journal, 33*(3), 315–329.

Hamilton, M. (2012). *Literacy and the Politics of Representation*. London: Routledge.

———. (2014). Moving voices: Literacy narratives in a testimonial culture. In *Routledge Handbook of New Literacy*. London & New York: Routledge.

Hamilton, M., & Hillier, Y. (2006). *Changing Faces of Adult Literacy, Language and Numeracy: A Critical History*. Stoke-on-Trent: Trentham Books.

Hamilton, M., Nugent, P., & Pollard, N. (2014). Learner voices at Pecket – past and present. Pecket Well College oral history and digital archive project. *Fine Print, 37*(1), 15–20. VALBEC Victoria: Australia.

Hibbin, R. (2014). *Paying lip-service to speaking and listening skills: Oral storytelling, arts-based education and the hegemony of literacy practices in primary school*. Unpublished Ph.D. Thesis, University of Lancaster, Lancaster.

Horton, M. (2003). *The Myles Horton Reader: Education for Social Change*. Knoxville: University of Tennessee Press.

International Cooperative Alliance. *Cooperative identity values and principles*. Retrieved from http://ica.coop/en/whats-co-op/co-operative-identity-values-principles. Accessed 5 January 2015.

Mace, J. (1979). *Working with Words: Literacy Beyond School*. London: Writers and Readers Publishing Co-operative/ Chameleon books.

———. (Ed.) (1995). *Literacy, Language, and Community Publishing: Essays in Adult Education*. Clevedon: Multilingual Matters.

McCaffery, J., Merrifield, J., & Millican, J. (2007). *Developing Adult Literacy: Approaches to Planning, Implementing, and Delivering Literacy Initiatives.* Oxford: Oxfam.

Nugent, P. (2013). Pecket Learning Community oral history and digital archive project 2011 to 2013. *Research and Practice in Adult Literacy (RaPAL) Journal.* Spring Issue 79, 18–21.

Pecket Well College. (1987). *Sharing Dreams: Pecket Well College Residential Weekend in Basic Education.* Halifax: Pecket Well College (Accessed July 2014).

Peters, S. J. (2010). The heterodoxy of student voice: Challenges to identity in the sociology of disability and education. *British Journal of Sociology of Education, 31*(5), 591–602.

Robertson, N. (2010). *The Co-operative Movement and Communities in Britain, 1914–1960: Minding Their Own Business.* Farnham: Ashgate Publishing, Ltd.

Rogers, A., & Horrocks, N. (2010). *Teaching Adults.* London: McGraw-Hill International.

Searle, C. (1986). *All Our Words.* London: Liberation.

Shrapnel Gardener, S. (Undated). *Conversations with Strangers.* London: Adult Literacy and Basic Skills Unit.

Taylor, C. (2007). *Modern Social Imaginaries.* Durham: Duke University Press.

Webster, T., Brown, A., Stewart, D., Walton, J., & Shaw, L. (2012). *The Hidden Alternative: Co-Operative Values, Past, Present and Future.* Manchester: Manchester University Press.

Woodin, T. (2005). Building culture from the bottom-up: The educational origins of the FWWCP. *History of Education, 34*(4), 345–363.

Yudice, G. (1991). Testimonio and postmodernism: Voices of the voiceless. *Testimonial Literature Part I. Latin American Perspectives, 18*(3), 15–31.

13

Beyond Essential Skills: Creating Spaces for Multimodal Text Production within Canada's 'Minimal Proficiency' Policy Regime

Suzanne Smythe

Bob wants to send an email with an attachment. The librarian takes Bob onto the Internet using Firefox and from there to Gmail. Referring to a crumpled bit of paper he hunts and pecks a username and password. Several false starts. Then he is ready to send an email. He enters the address, also on crumpled paper. The librarian helps him with the subject line, then to find Google Docs to attach a file, likely his CV. There is much back and forth between sites, negotiating new interfaces (Firefox browser, Gmail, Google Docs, back to Gmail). 15 minutes pass and email sent! Then Bob and the librarian go on to Craigslist and navigate to 'jobs'. Bob needs to show his employment caseworker he has applied for 3 jobs a day. He clicks and scrolls through 'jobs', and eventually finds something promising. He is back to his email and needs to attach his CV again. The librarian is back. The formatting of his document has been lost because the library's Open Source/Open Office is different from the word processing program the CV was created with. More formatting, re-saving, attaching, sending. Phew! Bob sighs, pulls a camera from his bag and plugs it into the library's hard drive. He navigates to his photo files confidently and vibrant street scenes animate the screen. He asks for advice: "Which one should I submit to the photo contest?"

As Marian Thacher (2011) observes, 'in digital skills as well as other literacy skills, there are the basics that help you survive, and then the more critical thinking skills that help you thrive and excel' (p. 2). This seems particularly important to remember in a time in which, as Lankshear et al. (2000) note, it is 'practically impossible in some areas to distinguish the boundaries between literacy and technology so that we now talk about "technoliteracy"' (p. 4). While digital technologies are not necessary for multimodal meaning-making, they play a central and increasing role in communicative practices. After all, people like Bob live their everyday lives in digital landscapes and already 'draw upon semiotic modes to make meaning' (Street et al., 2009, p. 195) in their engagements with government, workplaces, family and community. Making available in adult learning settings digital tools and resources so that Bob and other adults with tenuous access to digital tools can deepen and extend multimodal literacy practices is central to projects of social and educational inclusion (Tett et al., 2012; Smythe et al., forthcoming). Yet, it was much easier for the adult learning programme Bob attends on Canada's west coast to secure access to digital technologies for the purposes of online test taking of print-based literacy skills than it was for engagement in what Tett et al. (2012) call 'powerful literacies': 'The interventions and practices that attempt to enhance the autonomy and control of learners and their communities over their environment' (p. 3). It is in the nexus of these tensions in access and uses of digital technologies that the complex relationships between multimodality and governmentality in adult learning settings unfold.

Although the Government of Canada calls for the improvement of Canadians' digital literacy skills (Government of Canada, 2011, para. 7), there is no national policy to promote digital access and education (Government of Canada, 2011) and, as I argue in this chapter, efforts to define and measure digital literacy amount to the mere appending of 'digital' onto existing frameworks of essential skills training oriented to traditional print literacy. The goal of adult learning remains the acquisition of basic skills of survival among a 'problematic' population of low skilled Canadians (ABC Literacy, 2005; Langlois, 2012; Atkinson, 2013) rather than the cultivation of technoliteracies and potentially more powerful practices of critique, production, collaboration and extended practice through which people may 'thrive'.

I develop these ideas in the presentation of three policy stories of adult literacy and multimodal learning in Canada. The first story describes the intertwining of national and transnational projects to define and measure adult digital skills, and what happened when these measurement tools found their way into an adult literacy programme in Ontario. The second story illustrates the efforts of the Antigonish County Adult Learning Association (ACALA) in Nova Scotia as it worked around government policies oriented to basic skills training for entry-level, low-wage jobs, and instead mobilized the affordances of digital video production towards more powerful social and economic ends for community members. The third story, located in an urban literacy outreach programme on Canada's west coast, traces how dynamics of social exclusion were tied up with digital technologies and multimodal learning, reminding us that the incorporation of new tools and modes of learning cannot on their own transform existing patterns of social inequality. Stories two and three emerged from a multisite case study of digital technologies in adult literacy settings carried out in five communities in Canada (Smythe, 2012).

Before presenting these stories, I elaborate the concepts of multimodality and governmentality in relation to adult digital literacies, and consider the analytic affordances of these concepts for understanding the workings of 'minimum proficiency' print literacy.

Multimodality and adult digital literacies

Researchers have called attention to the pedagogic possibilities of incorporating digital production tools into education settings to support and expand new and multimodal literacies (Sheridan & Rowsell, 2010; Lankshear & Knobel, 2011; Street, 2012; Gee, 2013). In this chapter, a mode is understood 'as a regularised organised set of resources for meaning-making which might include image, gaze, gesture, movement, music, speech, writing' (Street, 2012, p. 2). Kress (2003) observed that the mixing of modes to make meaning by design, experimentation, experience and often serendipity is *creativity*: a certain way that an image accompanies voice, the particular font used to inscribe a poem published on a blog or in a book, the uses and effects of colour and sound and emotion and tone on a page, screen or stage. Multimodal meaning-making, in this sense, implies the strategic uses of particular literacies, in particular social contexts, and as Rowsell (2013) noted, 'we are constantly in the flow of multimodality from what to wear, from what and when to Tweet, what register to apply to a given situation, whether to use caps versus lower case letters; there are so many choices when we communicate' (p. 1). While multimodal meaning-making is by no means a new set of practices and nor is it limited to the uses of digital technologies, these technologies introduce new multimodal meaning-making possibilities and audiences. Glister (1997) argued that texts read and created on computers are intrinsically multimodal: image, space, text, time and sound combine and recombine in each instance of text production. Gee (2003) has similarly noted that the ubiquity of the digital, and diverse domains in which people create meanings, means that people need to be literate in a variety of semiotic domains that include but are not limited to print. For many scholars and practitioners of multimodality, the pedagogical struggle to incorporate and value multimodal production in education settings is a project of social and educational equity. Access to repertoires for multimodal learning can afford people who struggle with conventional print literacy and language-based instructional pedagogies new opportunities for text processing and production (O'Brien & Voss, 2011, p. 76) and new audiences for sharing socially meaningful texts (Bhatt, 2012). Hull and Nelson (2005) propose the potential democratizing effects of the expansion of meaning-making repertories:

> [T]he increasingly multiplex ways by which people can make meaning in the world, both productively and receptively, can potentially represent democratizing force whereby the views and values of more people than ever before can be incorporated into the ever-changing design of our world. (p. 206)

This opens us to a view of digital literacies and, more broadly, multimodal literacies as socially situated repertoires of practice, wherein, as Rowsell, observes, 'certain materials afford more meaning-making potential than others' (2013, p. 4). As I observed in previous research into digital technologies in adult basic education settings (Smythe, 2012), new technologies have always spurred new contestations over 'what counts' as literacy, and the goals of learning. With the emergence of new technologies and new repertoires of multimodal meaning-making, these contestations have intensified, particularly in relation to who has access to valued tools and materials for making, and which practices are privileged in educational settings (Warschauer, 2003; Hayes, 2010; Gee, 2011).

Siegel (2012) argues that these are questions of social justice, and should be considered in light of these 'hard times' for educators and adult learners, who are caught in what she defines as 'impossible' demands for accountability, public distrust in education and deepening income and educational inequalities. Just as the repertoires for meaning-making are expanding, adult literacy educators encounter a narrowing of concepts of literacy as equated with a minimum proficiency in print literacy (Conference Board of Canada, 2013) and with 'obtaining a job' (Ottawa Citizen, 21 May 2014, para. 10).

Moreover, digital technologies are also a means through which adults may be subject to new forms of social regulation (Chovanec & Meckelborg, 2011). Even when there are no screens present in the actual learning setting, rules and practices surrounding eligibility for literacy programmes, programme fees, valued learning outcomes and reporting requirements are decided upon and circulated through digital technologies with implications for those who have access to education programmes and the kinds of learning people can do there (Smythe, 2012). It is in this very terrain of creativity, voice, production, democratization and regulation that the affordances of multimodal learning conflict with the 'power code' (Siegel, 2012, p. 674) of minimum proficiency print literacy, and here too multimodality is brought into conversation with governmentality.

Governmentality, biopower and statistics

Foucault used the term governmentality to describe new forms of governance employed by nation states from the eighteenth century onward to manage large, free-moving, more urban populations (Foucault, 1991). No longer feasible to display state power and control through public displays of punishment (Foucault, 1997, pp. 239–243) or the brute defence of territorial borders, governmentality is the expression of state power through more subtle regulatory policies and disciplinary practices. As Foucault explained: 'Basically, power is less a confrontation between two adversaries or the linking of the one to the other than a question of government' (Foucault, 1997, p. 284). But what kinds of government? Foucault argued that the key to successfully managing populations is for populations themselves to become invested in their own discipline and regulation (Foucault, 1997). This he referred to as self-regulation or 'technologies of the self'. Indeed, Foucault was interested to articulate 'a history of the different modes in our culture through which humans are made subjects' (1997, p. 284), arguing that in the seventeenth and early eighteenth centuries, disciplinary techniques such as 'exercise and drill, systems of surveillance, hierarchies, inspections, bookkeeping, and reports' (1997, p. 242) were directed upon the individual to various governance ends, such as greater productivity, efficiency, conformity and so on.

In the second half of the eighteenth century, a new set of 'biopower' techniques emerged oriented to managing humans not as individuals but as populations. Here emerged 'the birth rate, the mortality rate, longevity' (1997, p. 243) and indeed, statistics. This, Foucault argued, was biopolitics, the construction of populations as 'political problems' (1997, p. 244) wherein the goal was 'ensuring man-as-species was not only disciplined, but regularized' (1997, p. 247). It is here that statistics and number have come to play a central role in normalization activities; creating, measuring and calculating 'normal' and 'normal distributions' so that the problems are known and the risks managed (Ball, 2012, p. 48). As Ball argues, schools are 'a cluster of such activities' (2012, p. 59) and so too, I argue in this chapter, is the Organization of Economic Cooperation and Development (OECD). As I elaborate below, this supranational policy organization has invested billions of dollars in elaborate and large-scale projects of mass testing of children (e.g. PISA) and of adults, the most recent being the Program of International Assessment of Adult Competencies (PIAAC) (OECD, 2009) which measures, rates and ranks populations according to not only their literacy skills but also their cognitive and non-cognitive traits, including physical and mental health such as moods, feelings, body weight and disease (OECD, 2013b). This construction of populations as categories of risk is an effect of biopower: 'the normal curve [that] had within it deep assumptions of unity by which individuals could be compared on the same conceptual space to the entire population' (Foucault, 2004a, p. 252, in Ball, 2012, p. 60). Indeed, large-scale literacy assessments increasingly communicate their results and interpretations to individuals as well as to governing institutions, with the goal to explain to individuals where they may rank in relation to other groups in the population, both national and global, and why they should invest in their own literacy education. Here, the state 'render[s] individuals "responsible" [for their literacy skills] without at the same time being responsible for individuals' (Lemke, 2001, p. 201). This 'responsibilising of the self' (Peters, 2001, p. 58), *responsibilization*, is seen as one of the more powerful 'technologies of the self' in the neoliberal era.

These large-scale literacy assessments also regulate access to multimodal learning and expression by privileging print literacy outcomes in accountability measures linked to adult literacy programme funding. One effect is that adults may have little access to digital technologies for learning in adult literacy programmes unless these are used to complete online standardized assessments. These ideas are developed below in the presentation of the three policy stories. To recall, the first is a story of the workings of the minimal proficiency literacy regime as an illustration of the governmentality technologies of biopower and responsibilization at work in national and supranational adult literacy measurement projects. I then offer two stories that illustrate how adult literacy programmes negotiate minimum proficiency print literacy regimes to make spaces for powerful literacies (including digital and multimodal literacies) in adult learning programmes.

A minimum proficiency policy story: The Digital Skills Framework

Scholars have engaged in substantial critique of the discursive techniques, measurement strategies and social consequences of international adult literacy surveys and Canada's Essential Skills framework (see e.g. Hamilton & Barton, 2000; Hamilton, 2001, 2009; St. Clair, 2012; Pinsent-Johnson, 2011; Atkinson, 2013; Hayes, 2013; Smythe et al., forthcoming). I re-trace this terrain to the extent necessary to illustrate how these assessments and frameworks have shaped the development of a national 'Digital Skills Framework'. In 2005, the International Adult Literacy Skills Survey (IALSS) results were published as categories of adults in seven countries who fell into four levels of literacy proficiency (Level One–Level Four/Five) across four domains of literacy proficiency named as prose literacy, document literacy, problem-solving and numeracy. In spite of the different practices measured in each domain, policy products from IALSS commonly collapsed categories Level One and Two as those people who 'typically have not yet mastered the minimum foundation of literacy needed to attain higher levels of performance' (HRDSC, 2005, p. 14). As Hamilton (2001) noted, 'It is important to understand that this distribution is created by the statistical procedures of the IALSS and may bear no relation to the distribution of everyday tasks people perform in their lives'(p. 184). And yet, the IALSS data were re-contextualized by governments, funders, literacy groups and the media to describe individuals who constituted a dangerous population: 'Four out of ten Canadian adults have literacy skills too low to be fully competent in most jobs in our modern economy' (Conference Board of Canada, 2013, para. 2). This minimum proficiency discourse has led to recommendations that literacy programmes focus on the 'nearly there', for example 'upper Level Twos'(Conference Board of Canada, 2013, para. 7), and for literacy organizations to argue that investing in literacy skills for 'upper level twos and threes' can result in savings to the country's employment insurance programmes (Murray & Shillington, 2012). This exemplifies the workings of biopower; how people are worked into categories to define who is 'considered worthy of investment' (Ball, 2012), in this case, a category of adults deemed upper level twos or 'marginally literate', with consequences for education provision for adults who are deemed to fall into 'Level One'. This minimal proficiency discourse has influenced the ways in which digital skills have been incorporated into Canada's Literacy and Essential Skills (LES) rubric.

Canada's Literacy and Essential Skills framework is closely linked to IALSS; developed in 1994 to describe core skills necessary for all kinds of work, it has evolved into a curricular and assessment framework to gauge people's readiness and suitability for certain kinds of jobs. Following the logic of IALSS, the LES framework identifies nine skills; the first four are considered literacy skills of reading, writing, document use and numeracy. Computer use, thinking, oral communication, working with others and continuous learning are configured as essential skills. Of interest, 'computer use' is listed as a discrete skill, which can be combined with one or more of the other skills. In 2011, Canada's Office of Literacy and Skills commissioned psychologists Chinien and Boutin (2011) to review the LES framework in light of the challenge new digital technologies pose to these constructs of 'computer use'. These authors acknowledged that conceptualizing 'computer use' as distinct from other skills is antiquated, requiring an 'expand[ed] definition of what it means to be literate' (2011, p. 27). With the goal to gain a more 'precise understanding of what digital skills are' (Boutin & Chinien, 2013, p. 1), the authors carried out a review of literature and interviews with fifteen informants 'from various sectors of the Canadian economy' (Boutin & Chinien, 2013, p. 1), which included employers but not unions or individual workers or adult learners.

The resulting *Digital Skills Framework: Essential Digital Skills for the Canadian Workplace* still draws heavily upon the IALSS and Essential Skills apparatus, and encodes a minimum proficiency literacy ideology to argue for a hierarchy of increasingly complex cognitive-processing skills from the basic to the 'more precise' skills of digital information processing. The semiotics of the framework design inscribes this hierarchy; the *Foundation Skills* of reading, writing, oral communication, document use and numeracy are placed across the bottom of the diagram in blue as 'gateway basic literacy and numeracy' for which '... there is often or always a minimum proficiency level required before someone can engage with digital technology and demonstrate or develop the more precise digital information processing skills' (Chinien & Boutin, 2011, p. 30). This establishes the rationale for positioning *Transversal Skills* (working with others, thinking, problem solving and continuous learning) as higher order cognitive skills. At the very top is a list of the 'more precise' *Digital Information Processing Skills* (a proposed new term for 'computer use') configured as cognitive skills, including 'select information', 'create information', 'apply information' and 'access information'.

In this elaborate casting, 'digital' is appended to the traditional print-based Literacy and Essential skills apparatus. A follow-up project funded by OLES is to develop an online cognitive training programme for 'low skilled adults' to prepare them for participation in higher order digital information processing skills. As the authors describe, '[t]hese engaging materials will enable adults to enhance their analytical cognitive control so that they can more effectively acquire, and more efficiently deploy, essential digital skills' (p. 3). It seems adults in adult literacy instruction settings are meant to prepare for, rather than authentically use, digital literacies.

Indeed, there are parallels between the Digital Skills Framework and the OECD's development and publication in 2013 of PIAAC's Survey of Adult Skills (SAS) (OECD, 2013c), which measured a new skill domain called problem solving in technology-rich environments (PS-TRE). This is not digital literacy, but rather the cognitive psychology construct of 'problem solving' using computers (OECD, 2009, p. 6). Like Boutin and Chinien's Digital Skills Framework, proficiency in foundation (print-based) literacy and numeracy is seen as a precondition for success in undertaking more complex problem-solving tasks. According to the OECD, the PIAAC results suggest '[] a certain level of proficiency in literacy and numeracy appears to be a pre-condition for success in undertaking more complex problem-solving tasks' (OECD, 2013d, p. 51). Moreover, the creators of PIAAC declare that 'literacy does not involve the production of texts (writing)' (2013b, p. 3).

A commercialized by-product of the PIAAC project is the Education and Skills Online Assessment (ESOA), also known as the 'online PIAAC', designed as a self-administered skills assessment of 'cognitive and non-cognitive' (OECD, 2013b, para. 3) skills. In an enactment of biopower and the governmentality technology of responsibilization, the OECD (2013b) proposes that results of the ESOA 'can be used for adults of any age who want to demonstrate their workforce-readiness skills and benchmark themselves with adults of similar background in their country or internationally' (p. 1). The assumption is that adults are responsible for maintaining their skill levels in relation to other populations, and should be spurred to invest in their own education to conform to the norms of 'similar adults' across the world. This is in keeping with the concerns for global competition and productivity underpinning PIAAC logic. However, it is not only the cognitive skills tests results that are of interest to PIAAC. ESOA also includes a range of 'non-cognitive' questions about health, emotions and social relationships; 'results' are presented in tabular form to 'help organizations and individuals to think about their occupational choices' (OECD, 2013b, p. 2) (and here again, the assumption is that people's jobs are a function of their personal choice and responsibility).

In a survey carried out among fifteen literacy programmes that piloted ESOA to measure learning gains of adult students (AlphaPlus, 2013), practitioners reported that survey questions did not seem to relate to people's actual literacy learning needs. They noted that the repetitive questioning (a function of the IRT validation methodology) was confusing and distracting: 'The same item would pop up a few times juxtaposed against a different second choice each time, I found myself trying to figure out the tricks the test was playing rather than answer the questions honestly' (AlphaPlus, 2013, p. 5). Others noted that the test likely measured fluency with the test taking tool rather than actual literacy knowledge, as the online interfaces were complex and the test was exhausting at over two hours, with no indicators of progress through the test (AlphaPlus, 2013, pp. 6–7); as one respondent commented, 'It feels like it goes on and on forever' (p. 6). Some commented on the role of this new test among existing testing and reporting requirements. For example:

I'm concerned about the number of assessments at intake and exit. When a new person comes in, we currently have to do a standard assessment (usually CAMERA), some specific goal related assessments, and now a

Learner Gains assessment that can take several hours. The exit process is even worse. We already have to do an exit milestone, plus the culminating task [from OALCF] that can take up to 3 hours. When this 2-hour learner gains assessment is added to all of that, it is going to be incredibly difficult getting all of these assessments completed. (AlphaPlus, 2013, p. 6)

Perhaps of most concern to respondents, however, were the 'surprising' (p. 5) questions in the last section of the test related to health and well-being that PIAAC claims will create convincing links between skills levels and the health of the population. One educator noted: 'The questions at the end are very odd and some of the students weren't thrilled to be answering them. One question asked a student for his weight. They were too personal and seemed odd' (p. 5). Another stated, 'I don't understand the need for the wildly inappropriate personal questions at the end of the assessment. I think many people would be very uncomfortable answering them. I know I was' (p. 6).

While the future of ESOA in Canada is still uncertain, the inclusion of questions about moods, body weight, relationships and health on a 'learning gains' test may be thought of as part of a broader 'biopolitical regime of testing' (Allen, 2012, p. 647) concerned with harnessing the complexity of education and learning in the life course through the collection of personal data among populations already likely to be under forms of surveillance (Atkinson, 2013). The effect of such a testing regime, according to Lemke, is to 'shift responsibility for social risks such as illness, unemployment, poverty, and for life in society into the domain for which the individual is responsible and transforming it into a problem of "self-care"' (Lemke, 2001, p. 201).

Indeed, problems of income, poverty, employment and economic productivity have been attributed to a deficiency in literacy skills among people lacking 'analytical cognitive control' (Chinien & Boutin, 2011, p. 3). This obscures people's actual digital practices and learning experiences, such as those in which Bob is engaging in the opening vignette. What might we learn about multimodality and governmentality when these minimum proficiency regimes are materialized in local literacy settings?

Story Two: Powerful ways with digital media: A Nova Scotia experience

The Antigonish County Adult Learning Association is located in a semi-rural traditional farming and fishing community on the east coast of Canada, offering academic upgrading, secondary school completion, employment preparation and supported work placement. The Executive Director of ACALA saw the potential for video-making to provide adults in the community, many of whom were current and former adult learners at ACALA, an opportunity to learn skills in video-making and production, while raising awareness among more affluent community members, policy makers and local government about the vital issue of housing affordability at the root of many other socio-economic challenges in the community. Because the provincial and federal funding criteria would not allow for 'capital investment' in digital devices needed for video production, nor for training and mentorship from film-makers, ACALA applied to a private non-profit agency to hire local professional film-makers to train adult learners in the production of digital video. But they still required provincial government funding to support the students during this employment training. To qualify for these funds, ACALA needed to demonstrate that within 3–12 months of participation in video-making workshops, adult learners (called 'clients' by the provincial government) were 'attached to the labour force, had new levels of certification, and/or increased average hourly earnings'.

ACALA thus found itself caught between the narrow goals of government-funded training oriented to place adults in often poorly paid and unstable entry-level jobs (often in competition with university graduates in this high-unemployment region) and the slower-paced, hands-on learning of multimodal text production that helped ACALA students not only survive but also 'thrive and excel' (Thacher, 2011, p. 2). Within a few months of their training, some students were making their own videos to advertise their hair styling and other small businesses, and were in demand to help others do the same. One student was hired to run digital storytelling workshops for a local community group wishing to raise awareness of mental health. With these promising outcomes, ACALA decided to pursue digital production as a means of learning new literacies, supporting self-employment in the community, and as a platform for raising awareness of social issues. But to do this, they needed to reduce their reliance on government funding and narrow regimes of 'what counted' as literacy learning. They decided to launch a social enterprise ACALATV, which would, among other activities, bid for contracts with the community television network *Eastlink* to create one hour of content for local audiences each week entitled 'ACALATV presents'. This secured an all-important and ongoing authentic audience for video production work, an opportunity to recover costs for the development of this content and for hands-on training in job skills that could lead to the creation of new jobs in the community. ACALA also joined with other community partners to secure additional private funding to make a series of videos about housing in Antigonish. The first video entitled *Affordable Antigonish* premiered at the Antigonish Film Festival. The second, *Looking for Change* premiered in early 2013.

ACALATV's programme manager Philip Girvan (2012) wrote in the ACALA newsletter that adult learners and film-makers alike engaged in complex multimodal learning practices to produce videos to known audiences, including collaboration, problem-solving, storyline development, communication skills (interviewing, negotiation), photography, sound recording and filming, planning, logistics and multimodal text editing. While some members of the team were clearly more experienced than others, it was hard to pick out a basic skill from a 'higher order' one (as is the practice in the cognitive-processing model of literacy testing), as all kinds of diverse practices were necessary for completion of the final product. Significantly, people described their work as video-making or film-making, not literacy learning. Students in the high school completion programme were employed as apprentices to work on Affordable Antigonish and *Looking for Change*, drawing upon their own difficulties finding affordable housing, as well as their social networks to set up and carry out interviews for the film that represented the diverse housing needs of the community. In a local newspaper article reporting on the public debut of *Looking for Change*, Shabala, one of the apprentices, is quoted as a member of the production team who contributed technological skills (setting up camera shoots and locations) as well as experiential knowledge of housing insecurity in her community (The Casket, 2013). Her positioning in the project as a knowledgeable member of her community authoring productions of social value is distinct in many ways from the casting we have reviewed in the first story, wherein people are worked into 'categories' of those deemed not yet able to engage with digital technologies.

Story Three: Dynamics of digital access, use and social distance on Canada's West Coast

Jake has spent 4.5 years teaching adults computers in a variety of community-based programmes on the West Coast of British Columbia, Canada. His experiences offer a lens into the relationships between digital technology and literacy among very marginalized and low-income adults who strive to learn amidst many competing struggles for housing, health, food and safety. From Jake's perspective, access to computers and to high-speed Internet is important in a democracy that is increasingly moving 'online'. Many government forms and applications for subsidies or financial support are now available only online, so Internet and computer access is important to ensure everyone is able to find and apply for these resources. Indeed, people engage in these digital tools and texts regardless of their educational levels if they can get access to them; they have little choice, and Jake insists that engagement with digital tools pulls along traditional print literacy.

Much of the invisible work of literacy workers such as Jake is to help people access government sites to apply for social assistance, employment insurance, childcare benefits and so on. Indeed, the usual practice is for government agencies to give their 'clients' a file number and instruct them to go apply for resources and programmes on their own (or visit a library or literacy programme for help). Government sites are complex to navigate, with high stake consequences in the event of an error (such as being refused benefits).

In the drop-in centre in which Jake works, adults get help with these forms or choose to use the computers for a variety of tasks from Facebook posts to checking emails; some may also decide to work with a tutor on other literacy projects, or develop skills for further academic study. Jake also takes laptops into local parks, shelters and housing projects to reach out to people who may not come to a Learning Centre. His goal is to introduce adults to computers, keeping in mind that many people are very curious about them, but also very fearful of making mistakes, or wary that it will be 'too hard' and they won't be able to manage. Sometimes people expect to fail when they learn something new, Jake explains, a result of negative learning experiences in their past.

Jake starts his computer tutorials with the question, 'What do you want to be able to do?' Almost everyone wants an email or Facebook account and to surf the Internet. In a short time, one man with a new Facebook account found his brother, whom he had not seen in eighteen years. Another young man continued to expand his computer-based learning. Jake learned that this man had his Grade 10, and he is now completing his secondary school graduation. Jake has also found that sometimes when people say, 'I want to learn computers' what they also really want is to improve their reading and writing. For example, when an adult types in a URL or a Facebook message, they will often comment that they would like to work on their spelling, or type faster. Here, Jake connects them to other literacy learning opportunities: a tutor, a reading club, perhaps an ABE class and in this way digital literacies intersect with print literacies and one pulls along the other. Importantly, however, learners are invited to follow their own learning interests, not to compete or compare themselves with the skills of other people a world away.

Jake maintains that linking digital instruction to the technologies that adults have access to outside of the drop-in classes is central to learner-centred practice. In this way, he is wary of taking up the newest digital tools for use in formal learning settings, when students don't have access to these in their everyday lives. For example, it may be fun to have a class set of iPads, so people can play with applications, but how does this support learning when the instructor collects the iPads at the end of the class and the learners go home empty handed? In this way, 'first tier' digital tools can support literacy learning in very creative ways in some settings. But they can also widen the social distance between instructors and learners: 'I have this and you don't', as well as create relations of dependency whereby the tutors are in control of the digital means of production.

Similarly, Jake suggests that technologies work best in adult learning when they start from where learners are in their interests and confidence, rather than from where a test result says they should start. He suggests a process wherein students master the many different tools embedded in a computer at their own pace: word processing, using a printer, attaching files, finding images and music and so on, building confidence, control and learner engagement, so that when they come to create digital stories (if they choose to) or other multimodal content, they are able to participate more actively in the process.

Here, Jake comes full circle in the relationship between digital technologies and literacy: 'What do people need the tools for? Are digital technologies for learning a means to an end, or an end in themselves?'

Discussion: Digital access, minimum proficiency and ways forward

These stories draw attention to the conditions for multimodal text production, such as to whom and how tools for multimodal production and consumption are distributed, the role of discourses and technologies of biopower in the production of these institutional practices and the strategies that practitioners and learners adopt to create spaces for multimodal productions. The second and third story illustrate just how hard groups have to work to overcome policy and accountability requirements to create learning conditions in which people can thrive (Thacher, 2011). In this way, 'to start from where learners are at', as Jake advocates, is a radical educational practice, rooted in the recognition that learning is situated and always already involving problem-solving, critical thinking and attention to audiences and modes of production: Which email programme is better to use? What subject line will work best writing to a brother I haven't seen in a long time? How do I protect my privacy? How can I tell the stories of affordable housing so that people will listen, but also protect the dignity of my neighbours?

A second issue raised in these stories is sustainability and accessibility of digital resources for learning. Drawing upon Reder (2009), one of the arguments of PIAAC is that literacy skills needed in work and everyday life are changing in the context of widespread uses of ICT (information and communication technologies), and that frequency of ICT use at home and work, drives proficiency, just as proficiency drives use. The case is for equitable access to lifelong learning to promote levels of proficiency, and so increase skills and income (OECD, 2013a, p. 13). Who could argue with that?

But the construct of 'minimum proficiency' in both the Essential Digital Skills Framework and PIAAC tools create a large category of people who are said not to be able to engage in or benefit from digital learning until they achieve some kind of minimum level in print-based reading or 'cognitive control'. However, the experiences of adult learners and educators in Nova Scotia and British Columbia suggest that the actualities of literacy learning are far more complex and indeed print and digital modes of learning intersect and pull each other along. Nevertheless, a powerful consequence of the minimum proficiency regime is to create categories of people 'deemed worthy (or not) of investment' (Ball, 2012, p. 109), and this is an effect that should be countered and challenged at every turn.

References

ABC Literacy (2005, November). *One in four Canadians say low adult literacy a problem*. Retrieved from http://abclifeliteracy.ca/one-four-canadians-say-low-adult-literacy-major-problem-ipsos-reid-survey-abc-canada

Allen, A. (2012). Cultivating the myopic learner: The shared project of high-stakes and low-stakes assessment. *British Journal of Sociology of Education, 33*(5), 641–659.

AlphaPlus (2013, October). *Voices speak to the data: Feedback from participants in the PIAAC online field-trial*. Retrieved from http://alphaplus.ca/en/web-tools/online-publications-a-reportsgroup1/voices-speak-to-the-data/cat_view/77-voices-speak-to-the-data-feedback-from-participants-in-the-piaac-on-line-field-trial.html

Atkinson, T. (2013). *Negotiating responsibilization: Power at the threshold of capable literate conduct in Ontario*. Unpublished Ph.D. thesis. Ontario Institute for Studies in Education: University of Toronto.

Ball, S. (2012). *Foucault, Power and Education*. Routledge: Ottawa.

Bhatt, I. (2012). Digital literacy practices and their layered multiplicity. *Educational Media International, 49*(4), 289–301. doi:10.1080/09523987.2012.741199

Boutin, F. & Chinien, C. (2013, 27–29 October). *Cognitive skills training to bridge the cognitive skills divide in digital technology*. Presentation at the 2013 Quebec Centre for Literacy Summer Institute, Montreal. Retrieved from http://www.centreforliteracy.qc.ca/sites/default/files/WDM_Cogskills_FI2013_en.pdf

The Casket (2013, 16 April). *Second film in ACALA series debuts*. Retrieved from http://www.thecasket.ca/archives/27755

Chinien, C., & Boutin, F. (2011). *Defining Essential Digital Skills in the Canadian Workplace: Final Report.* Ottawa: HRSDC.

Chovanec, D., & Meckelborg, A. (2011). *Social Networking Sites and Adult Literacy Learning: Raising the Issues.* Toronto: AlphaPlus.

Conference Board of Canada (2013). *Adult Literacy Rates: Low Level Skills.* Retrieved 2 March 2014 from http://www.conferenceboard.ca/hcp/details/education/adult-literacy-rate-low-skills.aspx

Foucault, M. (1991). Questions of method. In G. Burchell, C. Gordon & P. Miller (Eds), *The Foucault Effect: Studies in Governmentality* (pp. 73–86). Hemel Hempstead: Harvester Wheatsheaf.

———. (1997). *Michel Foucault: 'Society Must Be Defended'.* New York: Picador.

Gee, J.P. (2003). *What video games have to teach us about learning and literacy.* New York: Palgrave Macmillan.

Gee, J. P. (2011, May 23). Digital natives, digital brains? [online newspaper article]. *Huffington Post.* Retrieved from http://www.huffingtonpost.com/james-gee/digital-natives-digital-b_b_865263.html

———. (2013). *The Anti-Education Era: Creating Smarter Students Through Digital Learning.* Hampshire: Palgrave Macmillan.

Girvan, P. (2012). ACALA TV. *Literacy Nova Scotia News.* Retrieved 18 July 2013 from http://www.ns.literacy.ca/printnews/Fall2012.pdf

Glister, P. (1997). *Digital Literacy.* New York: John Wiley & Sons, Inc.

Government of Canada (2011). *Building Digital Skills for Tomorrow.* Retrieved from http://www.ic.gc.ca/eic/site/028.nsf/eng/00041.html

Hamilton, M. (2001). Privileged literacies: Policy, institutional processes and the life of IALS. *Language and Education, 15*(2–3), 178–196.

———. (2009). Putting words in their mouths: The alignment of identities with system goals through the use of Individual Learning Plans. *British Educational Research Journal, 35*(2), 221–242.

Hamilton, M., & Barton, D. (2000). The International Adult Literacy Survey: What does it really measure? *International Review of Education/Internationale Zeitschrift Für Erziehungswissenschaft, 46*(5), 377–389.

Hayes, B. (2013). *Adult Literacy in Canada: Where Have We Been? Where Should We Be Going?* Retrieved from http://sarn.ca/?p=1159

Hayes, E. (2010). Reconceptualizing adult basic education and the digital divide. In A. Belzer (Ed.), *Toward Defining and Improving Quality in Adult Basic Education: Issues and Challenges* (pp. 203–220). Hillsdale: Laurence Erlbaum Press.

Hull, G. A., & Nelson, M. (2005). Locating the semiotic power of multimodality. *Written Communication, 22*(2), 224–261. doi:10.1177/0741088304274170

Human Resources and Social Development Canada (HRSDC) (2005). *Building on Our Competencies: Canadian Results of the International Adult Literacy Skills Survey.* Ottawa: Government of Canada.

Kress, G. (2003). *Literacy in the new media age.* London: Routledge.

Lankshear, C., Snyder, I. and Green, B. (2000). *Teachers and technoliteracy: Managing literacy, technology and learning in schools.* Sydney, Australia: Allen & Unwin.

Langlois, M.-C. (2012, September). *HillNotes: Literacy in Canada.* Retrieved from http://www.parl.gc.ca/Content/LOP/ResearchPublications/2012-46-e.htm

Lankshear, C., & Knobel, M. (2011). *New Literacies: Changing Knowledge and Classroom Learning* (3rd edition). Buckingham: Open University Press.

Lemke, T. (2001). The birth of bio- politics': Michel Foucault's lecture at the Collège de France on neo-liberal governmentality. *Economics & Society, 30*(2), 190–207.

Murray, T.S., & Shillington, R. (2012, July). *Investing in Upskilling: Gains for Individuals, Employers and Governments in Focus-Benefit Receipt Payments.* Ottawa: Canadian Literacy and Learning Network (CLLN).

O'Brien, D., & Voss, S. (2011). Reading multimodally: What is afforded? *Journal of Adolescent & Adult Literacy, 55*(1), 75–78. doi:10.1598/JAAL.55.1.9

OECD (2009). *PIAAC problem-solving in technology-rich environments: A conceptual framework.* OECD Education Working Paper No. 36. Retrieved from http://search.oecd.org/officialdocuments/displaydocumentpdf/?doclangua ge=en&cote=edu/wkp(2009)15

———.(2013a). *Skilled for life? Key findings of the Survey of Adult Skills.* Retrieved 8 March 2013 from http://www.oecd.org/site/piaac/ SkillsOutlook_2013_ebook.pdf

———.(2013b). *Education Skills Online Assessment (ESOA).* Retrieved from http://www.oecd.org/site/piaac/ENG_Brochure%20Education%20and%20 Skills%20Online%20SAS_Feb%2014.pdf

———. (2013c). *OECD skills surveys: Literacy test items.* Retrieved 9 March 2013 from http://www.oecd.org/site/piaac/Sample%20Items_all_rev.pdf

———. (2013d). *Skills Needed in the 21st Century: First Results from the Survey of Adult Skills.* Paris: OECD.

Ottawa Citizen (2014, May 21). *Literacy organizations say federal government abandoning them.* Retrieved from http://ottawacitizen.com/news/local-news/ literacy-organizations-say-federal-government-abandoning-them

Peters, M. (2001). Education, enterprise culture and the entrepreneurial self: A Foucauldian perspective. *Journal of Educational Enquiry, 2*(2), 58–71.

Pinsent-Johnson, C. (2011). Essentializing the experiences and expertise of adult literacy educators in Canada. In *Proceedings of the Joint Conference of the Adult Education Research Conference (AERC) and the Canadian Association for the Study of Adult Education (CASAE/ACEEA)*(pp. 529–535). Toronto: CASAE.

Reder, S. (2009). The development of literacy and numeracy in adult life. In S. Reder & J. Bynner (Eds), *Tracking Adult Literacy and Numeracy: Findings from Longitudinal Research* (pp. 59–84). New York & London: Routledge.

Rowsell, J. (2013). *Working with Multimodality: Learning and Innovation in the Digital Age.* London: Routledge.

Sheridan, M., & Rowsell, J. (2010). *Design Literacies: Learning and Innovation in the Digital Age.* London: Routledge.

Siegel, M. (2012). New times for multimodality? Confronting the accountability culture. *Journal of Adolescent & Adult Literacy, 55*(8), 671–681. doi:10.1002/ JAAL.00082

———. (2012). *Incorporating Digital Technologies in Adult Basic Education Settings.* Toronto: AlphaPlus.

Smythe, S., Toohey, K., & Dagenais, D. (Forthcoming). Production pedagogies and education policy. *Educational Policy.* doi 10.1177/0895904814550078.

St. Clair, R. (2012). The limits of levels: Understanding the International Adult Literacy Surveys (IALS). *International Review of Education, 58*(6), 759–776.

Street, B. (2012). *Literacy and Multimodality: STIS Lecture: Inter-Disciplinary Seminars O Laboratório SEMIOTEC, da FALE/UFM.* Belo Horizonte: Faculdade de Letras.

Street, B., Pahl, K., & Rowsell, J. (2009). Multimodality and new literacy practices. In K. Hewitt (Ed.), *Handbook of Multimodal Analysis* (pp. 191–200). London: Routledge.

Tett, L.,Hamilton, M., & Crowther, J. (Eds) (2012). *More Powerful Literacies.* Leicester: NIACE.

Thacher, M. (2011, May 27). *Classes of digital natives* [Weblog entry]. Retrieved from http://marianthacher.blogspot.com/

Warschauer, M. (2003). *Technology and Social Inclusion: Rethinking the Digital Divide.* London: MIT Press.

Afterword

In the introduction to this book, we articulated the opening up of possibilities emerging through multimodal forms of communication and equally, our ongoing concerns surrounding technologies of governance. We reached out to scholars working in various international contexts, inviting them to consider these significant issues across domains and teaching and learning situations, and to suggest the implications for educators, learners and communities.

Each of the contributions, in its own way, suggests the potentiality of multimodality for expanding people's communication repertoires and identity options and for helping literacy to *do* more: for instance, in Chapter 1, Kalantzis and Cope argue that multimodality as conceptualized through multi-literacies provides opportunities for changed practices of meaning-making which could support those engaged in educational endeavours as they work to change social practices; next, Murphy re-imagines (multimodal) literacy assessment in-line with the responsible exercise of freedom; Luttrell and Fontaine re-centre the role of care in young people's multimodal literacies in collaborative, agentive ways; Rose offers a literacy program based in multimodality to improve the literacy outcomes of Aboriginal learners in ways that refuse to pathologize them; and Hibbert provides a cloud-based literacy curriculum that indexes the affordances of multimodality in new times. Visible in these instances is how the present era can hold spaces for multimodal communication options which may produce shifts in the participatory culture envisioned by Cope and Kalantzis (2000) over a decade ago. Indeed new research continues to emerge documenting participatory communication and culture, such as Brough's (2014) documentation of 'new forms of youth civic engagement and public participation, invigorated by digital technologies, practices and cultures' (n.p.).

At the same time, the content and very existence of this book gestures with some urgency towards new forms of governance and governmentality that constrain communication and identity options. Flewitt and Roberts-Holmes, for example demonstrate the regulatory gaze inflicted on young children through a large-scale phonics assessment; Stooke details how the early childhood educators' gaze is itself directed even within multimodal forms of assessment; and in an adult education context, Smythe highlights the exclusion of an entire group of adult learners from participating in the very literacies that might allow them to be part of a participatory culture. Our era is one where the production of literacy learning opportunities, literacy practices and literate subjectivities are produced through complex systems of governance that can be at once powerful and hard to track.

Our entree for conceptualizing issues of power in this book came from a reading of Foucault's governmentality which offers a way of thinking through how multimodality can be produced by and enlisted in governance; for instance governmentality offers a way of seeing how various technologies (e.g. standardized assessments) and inscription devices (e.g. assessment data) can be implemented to amass knowledge of people (e.g. students) which in turn can be used to track them in, for example a system (e.g. schools) with the ultimate goal of guiding their conduct (e.g. literacy practices and achievement) (Rose, 1999). Such guidance is not overt as it can be internalized such that people regulate their own behaviour, taking on the form of a 'calculable subject' (Fenwick & Edwards, 2010, p. 115). Governmentality here is slippery, as it can be manifest as a form of care where overt control is passed over in favour of this more liberal self-governance which is exercised in the promotion of the well-being of, to use Foucault's metaphor of the shepherd, the flock (Foucault, 1981).

In taking governmentality as our starting point, we were aware that it would not be the complete nor sometimes even the most useful theoretical frame for describing and/or analysing the complex and varied stories of multimodality that would come with this book. We were well-cognizant of and sensitive to, for instance, the critiques of governmentality as overly deterministic and absolute. In particular, we were concerned about two implications of governmentality: first, 'there are no subjects nor processes of subjectification outside governmental production' and second, 'resistance, and thus agency' could only be 'understood as the coexistence of competing regimes of subjectification that act upon subjects in diverse directions, and not as the possibility of engendering critical forms of subjectivity... that may escape present constellations of power relations' (Savransky, 2013, p. 97). We hoped to learn the myriad ways in which governmentality and governance could be theorized and conceptualized, and how issues of power and multimodality are playing out across domains and contexts.

Captured within the pages of this book are diverse and emerging theories and methodologies for conceptualizing and apprehending issues of power, including the power of multimodality. We see these theories and methodologies as complementary to one another and as forwarding our ability to identify and analyse what enables multimodal possibilities and how contemporary forms of communication such as big data might themselves be complicit in constraining communication options. Heydon's chapter, for instance demonstrates the power of number, in the form of numbers of children, and its implication of opening up or closing down learners' expressions and the ability of educators to hear. It argues not for the theoretical Foucauldian prison, but rather for a combination of governmentality and actor-network theory to reckon with the complex and mutable movements of networked power and its effects on multimodal opportunities. Murphy's chapter also takes issue with and makes use of governmentality, arguing for redefined notions of (ethical) agency. Her contribution taps into the understanding that leading a meaningful life with purpose is fundamental to the human condition. What counts, however, is too often defined by measures that align with externally identified objectives that fail to index the things that educators, learners and communities may care deeply about, or see the purpose in. She argues that multimodality can contribute to the development of agency, in part because of its affordances for diverse representation and communication. The chapters challenge punitive forms of accountability and stress the importance of supporting what is grassroots. Hamilton's chapter provides a rich case in point.

We recognize too, through the contributions, an emergent call for what we might think of as *critical multimodality* – an engagement with multimodality that is vigilant about how it is (or is not produced) and what in turn it produces. Albers, Harste and Vasquez argue that critical multimodality contributes to more complex literacy practices, practices that promise a move away from docility, and help educators think divergently and differently about learners. In their work, art was one way for teachers to participate in engagements that promote critical awareness of the relations of power. Hibbert imagines ways in which participating in multimodal communication opens up rich and divergent ways for educators to see their students anew. She is hopeful that participation in new and emerging forms of communication will destabilize cemented ways of understanding teaching and learning interactions and allow both teachers and students to work together in more meaningful ways. Luttrell and Fontaine argue that the multimodal space opens up new ways of participating, but remind readers that reflective, critical framing is needed to disrupt, complicate and speak back to normative discourses forwarded by a neoliberal agenda. Similarly, Flewitt and Roberts-Holmes emphasize the need for critical approaches to multimodality to afford liberatory pedagogical spaces that resist sliding into narrowly defined performativities, and Boistrup flags the opportunities for meaningful engagement with students that cannot arise unless educators adopt a critical sensitivity to the kinds of multimodal communication they are having with students within assessment encounters.

The compilation of this book has been instructive. We remain mindful of Foucault's appreciation that power is not possessed, but *exercised* within a constant struggle that includes both victories and defeats. Understanding how power circulates, and how our own participation within institutional practices shapes us and our communication, is helpful to raise the critical awareness that so many of the contributors have advocated for. We posited many questions in the introduction, questions that centred on agency and literacy, our hope is that this book will be read as an invitation for further questioning and response.

References

Brough, M. (2014). *Participatory Public Culture and Youth Citizenship in the Digital Age. The Medellin Model.* Los Angeles: University of Southern California, UMI Dissertation Publishing.

Cope, B., & Kalantzis, M. (Eds) (2000). *Multiliteracies: Literacy Learning and the Design of Social Futures.* New York: Routledge.

Fenwick, T., & Edwards, R. (2010). *Actor-Network Theory in Education.* London: Routledge.

Foucault, M. (1981). Omnes et singulatim: Towards a criticism of 'political reason'. In S. McMurrin (Ed.), *The Tanner Lectures on Human Values Volume 2* (pp. 223–254). Salt Lake City: University of Utah Press.

Rose, N. (1999). *Powers of Freedom: Reframing Political Thought.* Cambridge: Cambridge University Press.

Savransky, M. (2013). Of recalcitrant subjects. *Culture, Theory and Critique, 55*(1), 96–113.

Index

Note: The letters 'f' and 'n' following locators refer to figures and notes